Innovations in Governance and Public Administration

Replicating What Works

Department of Economic and Social Affairs

United Nations
New York, 2006

DESA Mission Statement

The Department of Economic and Social Affairs of the United Nations Secretariat is a vital interface between global policies in the economic, social and environmental spheres and national action. The Department works in three main interlinked areas: (i) it generates, compiles and analyses a wide range of economic, social and environmental data and information on which Member States of the United Nations draw to review common problems and to take stock of policy options; (ii) it facilitates the negotiations of Member States in many intergovernmental bodies on joint courses of action to address ongoing or emerging global challenges; and (iii) it advises interested governments on the ways and means of translating policy frameworks developed in United Nations conferences and summits into programmes at the country level and, through technical assistance, helps build national capacities.

Notes

ST/ESA/PAD/SER.E/72
United Nations publication
Sales No. E.06.II.H.1
ISBN 92-1-123158-2
Copyright © United Nations, June 2006
All rights reserved
Printed by the United Nations, New York

Foreword

As shown by the United Nations Public Service Awards and a number of other award programmes in various regions of the world, there is great capacity in all corners of the globe to reinvent government and to launch innovative practices in governance. Disseminating information about innovations in government, and most importantly, transforming this information into knowledge so that it may benefit countries looking for effective solutions to governance problems, is a challenge that the United Nations has taken up very seriously. Although there are no "one-size-fits-all" solutions to complex issues, sharing successful experiences offers an opportunity for innovation in governance and public administration. We strongly believe that sharing information and transferring knowledge on innovations are important tools for stimulating and inspiring governments in their reform efforts toward more inclusive development. In fact, learning from other countries' experiences in reinventing government can save time, inspire new reforms, and in some cases help countries to leapfrog stages of development. Moreover, focusing on best practices rather than on failures is a way to provide positive incentives for reform efforts and encourage a constructive outlook on development. It affords the opportunity to shift our attention from *what* the State should do to *how* it should do it, i.e., how it should solve the many challenges it is presented with on a daily basis.

In light of the above, the United Nations General Assembly reiterated, in resolution 57/277, that particular emphasis should be given to the exchange of experiences related to the role of public administration in the implementation of internationally agreed goals, including those contained in the Millennium Declaration. In resolution 50/225, it also underlined the importance of enhancing international cooperation in the field of public administration, including South-South and interregional cooperation. Accordingly, the United Nations Department of Economic and Social Affairs (UNDESA) is dedicated to promoting the exchange of ideas and experiences of innovations in governance and public administration in order to contribute to social and economic development.

One of the most important vehicles for sharing information and knowledge on innovation in government is the United Nations Global Online Network in Public Administration (*http://www.unpan.org*) established by UNDESA, through its Division for Public Administration and Development Management (DPADM). UNPAN links e-networks and regional centers working in the area of governance and public administration worldwide and provides information and useful resources on a number of governance issues. In terms of advocacy, the United Nations General Assembly proclaimed June 23 as "Public Service Day" to celebrate innovation, creativity and initiative of civil servants by granting UN Public Service Awards to government organizations that have excelled in reinventing themselves. This occasion offers the opportunity to share information about innovations in government from all regions of the world through live web-cast and the UNPAN. UNDESA also supports the establishment of Networks of Innovators in Governance at the international and regional levels, including in the Mediterranean area, since knowledge networks have the capacity to pool knowledge resources together. As part of the United Nations' effort to promote excellence in government, DPADM also provides support to the Global Forum on Reinventing Government, which has become the major international gathering of policy-makers and experts in the area of governance and serves as a worldwide laboratory for new ideas and policy development. In terms of capacity-building at the national and regional levels, DPADM has established a number of technical assistance programmes aimed at promoting good governance. For example, the Programme for Innovation in Public Administration in the Mediterranean Region (InnovMed) is one of the flagship activities of DPADM; its main objective is to contribute to the improvement of governance systems in Northern Africa, the Middle East and Western Balkans by sharing information on best practices and by supporting the transfer and adaptation of innovations. In particular, the InnovMed Programme aims at reinforcing the capacity of national governments, in terms of institutions, human resources, technological adequacy and financial management, to better cope with emerging national, regional and international challenges, as well as to respond more effectively to citizens' demands and needs.

This publication is one of the analytical products of the InnovMed Programme and it is intended for policy-makers and practitioners, as well as scholars and researchers of innovation in governance and the public at large. Its aim is to provide interested Governments with both conceptual and policy tools to select and adapt innovations.

The contributions contained in this publication were prepared for the International Experts Meeting on "Approaches and Methodologies for the Assessment and Transfer of Best Practices in Governance and Public Administration," organized by DPADM in June 2005 in Tunis. This book focuses on four main themes: challenges and perspectives of best practices and innovations in governance; transferability of innovations; capacity to absorb and implement innovations, and approaches and methodologies for the adaptation of innovations. Since good governance is not a "one-time" exercise, but a continuous process of refinement, re-assessment of strategies and practices as well as incremental institutional development, I hope that this publication will contribute to supporting and improving democratic governance by providing key ideas and useful tools for the transfer of innovations in governance and public administration.

Guido Bertucci, Director
Division for Public Administration and Development Management
Department of Economic and Social Affairs
United Nations

Acknowledgements

This publication was prepared under the overall responsibility of Guido Bertucci, Director of the Division for Public Administration and Development Management (DPADM) of the United Nations Department of Economic and Social Affairs (UNDESA) and John-Mary Kauzya, Chief of the Governance and Public Administration Branch, DPADM. Adriana Alberti was the principal coordinator of this publication and co-author of the first chapter. She was also the editor together with Vilhelm Klareskov. Meredith Rowen and Sarah Waheed Sher provided useful comments to the final draft of the publication. Special thanks also go to D & P Editorial Services, the typesetter of this book, and to one of the principals, Joanna V. Pomeranz, who designed the book. Administrative support was provided by Corazon Cabigao.

The publication is based on the papers and findings of the International Experts Meeting on "Approaches and Methodologies for the Assessment and Transfer of Best Practices in Governance and Public Administration" which was organized by UNDESA, through its Division for Public Administration and Development Management. The Meeting took place in Tunis, Tunisia on 13–14 June 2005. Its overall objective was to explore, discuss and agree on approaches and methodologies that are appropriate for the transfer of innovations in governance and public administration within, and across, countries and regions. More specifically, the Meeting aimed to: (a) enhance the knowledge and understanding of the concept, potential and adaptation of successful practices and innovations in public administration and (b) provide the opportunity for an exchange of views on how the United Nations, together with other relevant partners, can more effectively assist governments in the area of sharing and replicating best practices.

More than 25 international experts from over 20 countries took part in this event. Participants included academics, practitioners, and representatives of sub-regional, regional and international institutions. The experts came from Albania, Brazil, Canada, Croatia, Egypt, Italy, Jordan, Malaysia, Mexico, Morocco, National Palestinian Authority, Philippines, South Africa, Spain, Syrian Arab Republic, Tunisia, Turkey and the United States of America.

The Meeting was organized within the framework of the UNDESA Programme for Innovation in Public Administration in the Mediterranean

Region, which is implemented in collaboration with Formez–Training and Research Centre through the Centre for Administrative Innovation in the Mediterranean Region—C.A.I.MED. The Programme is made possible thanks to the generous support of the Government of Italy through Funds in Trust to the United Nations Department of Economic and Social Affairs.

We wish to thank the people and institutions that contributed to and took part in the International Experts Meeting, including: Ladipo Adamolekun, Federal University of Technology, Nigeria; Zuhair Al-Kayed, Higher Population Council, Jordan; Ante Barišić, Croatian Association for Public Administration; Khalid Ben Osmane, *Ecole National de l'Administration* (ENA), Morocco; Giovanni Bisogni, *Fondazione per la Ricerca sulla Migrazione e sulla Integrazione delle Tecnologie* (FORMIT); Carlos Conde Martínez, European Public Administration Network (EPAN) and University of Granada, Spain; Juan Carlos Cortázar, Inter-American Development Bank (IADB); Marta Ferreira Santos Farah, *Fundação Getulio Vargas*, Brazil; Martin Forst, Organisation for Economic Co-operation and Development (OECD); Joseph Galimberti, Institute of Public Administration of Canada (IPAC); Korel Göymen, Sabanci University and Istanbul Policy Centre, Turkey; Ghazi Ghrarairi, *Faculté de Droit et de Sciences Politiques de Tunis*, Tunisia; Tonatiuh Guillén López, *El Colegio de la Frontera Norte*, Mexico; Najwa Kassab Hassan, Damascus University of the Syrian Arab Republic; Peter Kiuluku, Eastern and Southern African Management Institute (ESAMI); Donald Klingner, University of Colorado and American Society for Public Administration (ASPA); Ragaa Makharita, International Senior Consultant for UNDESA, United Nations Development Programme (UNDP) and other organizations; Gillian Mason, Commonwealth Association for Public Administration and Management (CAPAM), Canada; Imraan Patel, Centre for Public Service Innovation (CPSI), South Africa; Austere Panadero, Gawad Galing Pook Foundation, Philippines; Giuseppe Pennella, Alberto Corbino and Angela Scotto, Centre for Administrative Innovation in the Mediterranean Region (C.A.I.MED), Italy; Gowher Rizvi, Ash Institute for Democratic Governance and Innovation, Harvard University; Fatma Sayed, European University Institute (EUI); Lakhbir Singh Chahl, Regional Network for Local Authorities for the Management of Human Settlements in Asia and the Pacific (CityNet); Usama Shahwan, Bethlehem University Beit-Jala, National Palestinian Authority; Zana Vokopola, Urban Research Institute, Albania; and Nicholas You and Vincent Kitio, United Nations Human Settlements Programme (UN-HABITAT).

DPADM was represented by Guido Bertucci, Director; John-Mary Kauzya, Chief, Governance and Public Administration Branch; Adriana Alberti, Chief Technical Adviser, Programme for Innovation in Public Administration in the Mediterranean Region; and Bechir Bouzid, Governance Specialist, who provided invaluable support in the organization of the above mentioned Experts Meeting.

Executive Summary

In *Chapter 1,* Adriana Alberti and Guido Bertucci provide an overview of the publication, which envisages a new agenda for innovation in governance and public administration. The authors believe that international development efforts can significantly benefit from knowledge-sharing, particularly in the case of innovations and good practices.

The authors argue that although innovations in government are circumscribed in scope, they have the potential to trigger a bigger process of transformation of the State. By providing governments with a menu of innovations and tools to adapt to their own context, the international community can play a critical role in promoting good governance and the creation of new democratic spaces. This publication therefore looks at the process, capacities, and environment required for the successful transfer, adaptation, and implementation of innovations in governance and public administration.

In light of the above, the chapter begins by debating why governments should innovate. It then introduces different definitions of the concepts of innovation and best practices and examines the process of innovation. It notes that the sustainability and effectiveness of new practices depends on many intangible factors, such as partnerships and community involvement. Innovations must similarly be institutionalized to ensure that they will not fade away with a change in leadership. At the same time, the environment in which innovation takes place also requires attention. Moreover, the capacity of an organization to adapt, implement, and institutionalize innovations that have been successful in other quarters is a critical aspect of the process that is often overlooked. If the recipient has insufficient capabilities, there is a risk that the innovation will slip through the cracks of the organization. Above all, different circumstances require different solutions, and in the case of innovations there is no "one size fit all" solution. The chapter further analyses the transferability of innovations and best practices by highlighting many award programmes that enhance the visibility of innovative processes and offer collective knowledge based on thousands of cases. Finally, the authors summarize the different approaches and methodologies that have proven successful in the transfer and dissemination of innovations and best practices.

Part One, "Innovation in Governance: Perspectives, Challenges and Potential," focuses on ideas and approaches to innovation and best practices. The authors agree that the term "best practice" is problematic in relation to governance and public administration since it presupposes that a practice has been actually benchmarked against all other similar practices at the national and international levels. It also implies that there is one best way to do things when reality is that there are many ways of implementing innovative ideas. Terms such as "smart options," "good practices" or "successful practices" are better suited for the field of governance. Yet, because there is no consensus on what term could replace "best practices," we will continue using it for ease of reference. Part One also provides guidelines for better understanding and conducting research in the field through the use of analytical tools such as a narrative approach. In addition, it discusses the abandonment of previous approaches to best practices, which often saw the process of replication as based on universal blueprints waiting to be implemented.

In *Chapter 2*, Imraan Patel sets out to improve the understanding of innovations and best practices by highlighting that focus should be on the organizational context rather than on single innovations. To that end, Patel introduces two conceptual models for innovative processes within the public sector. He then reviews the concepts of best practices, innovation and improvement and determines whether these are helpful. Patel argues that despite the importance of conceptual clarity when undertaking academic studies on innovation adopting various definitions of innovation may sometimes have advantages in other environments. A variable definition shifts the focus to the conditions of learning from the experiences of others, and Patel therefore emphasizes the importance of knowledge-sharing and replication. Finally, by analyzing selected issues associated with the transfer of improvements and innovations Patel offers suggestions for developing methodologies and tools to facilitate this process.

In *Chapter 3*, Juan Carlos Cortázar proposes a concept of public management practices that makes it possible to learn from them. He maintains that what should be transferred about best practices are the lessons, i.e., practical arguments to enable public managers to adapt a practice and make it work in a way that is suitable for its own environment. In order to produce and present empirical evidence of such practices, the author suggests the adoption of a narrative approach, which enables researchers to deal with highly complex experiences in a systematic manner. Such a research agenda includes the fundamental step of narrowly defining the subject by identifying directly related events to the management practice under study as well as establishing how identified events affected each other. This methodology makes a valuable contribution to understanding the development and operation of public management practices, as well as to producing lessons about best practices that can be applied rigorously in other contexts. It has been used by the Inter-American Development Bank's Social Development Institute to study social management practices in recent years.

In *Chapter 4*, Donald E. Klingner establishes the importance of innovation to governance in general and development administration and implementation in particular. The author notes that in response to the discredited traditional approach to development administration, alternative approaches have emerged that attempt to offset previous flaws of ethnocentrism and ignorance as well as promoting understanding instead of focusing exclusively on evaluation and recommendation. The author establishes the importance of innovation to governance in general and development administration and implementation in particular and critiques the utility of best practices in development administration accordingly.

Part Two, "Transferability and Adaptation of Best Practices and Innovations" provides a host of examples of innovation transfers and dissemination. From the transfer of institutions and policies to the experiences of local and national awards programmes, the present chapters provide insights into how innovations and best practices move successfully from a host to a recipient. The chapters based on awards programmes serve to emphasize the importance of documentation in the innovation process. Without proper accounting for these processes, innovations and best practices will continue to be a black box without any determinants or principles for success. In this vein, one indicator is whether an innovation or best practice targets a perceived challenge, i.e., serves a specific need in the community.

In *Chapter 5*, Ladipo Adamolekun reviews the experience of transferring two governance institutions on a worldwide scale—the ombudsman institution and independent commissions against corruption. He provides an overview of the diffusion of these two institutions and then draws attention to the factors that have made the transfer possible, including a distinction between formal institutional transfers and their effective functioning in different countries. Adamolekun emphasizes that there is an important distinction to be made between an impressive transferability record of the governance institutions considered here in terms of diffusion on the one hand and the actual functioning of the institutions in the countries that have adopted them on the other. He further argues that the factors for "success" in diffusion are different in significant respects from the factors for ensuring effective functioning of the governance institutions in the different countries concerned.

In *Chapter 6*, Carlos Conde Martínez notes that the significant number of replication of policies as well as the intense policy cooperation between industrialized countries indicates that there is great interest in the concept of transfer, its mechanisms and the conditions for its success. Conde underlines that the knowledge factor in transfers is critical to successful adaptation. He argues that transfers can fail for three reasons: they are uninformed, incomplete or inappropriate. That is to say, information about the innovation or policy is inadequate; crucial elements of the policy have not been introduced; or differences in economic, social, political and ideological contexts are not taken seriously into account. The author sets out to discuss competing agendas for successful transfer that focus, on one side, on generalized principles and, on the other side, on specific variables. To that end, Conde Martínez first discusses three different concepts of policy transfers, and outlines the key factors to effective policy transfers, including policy convergence and institutionalization, local variety and policy content, as well as political factors. The author also identifies selected variables, such as constraints of transfer and internationalization.

In *Chapter 7*, Marta Ferreira Santos Farah makes a contribution to the discussion of innovation and dissemination in government and the public sector using examples from "The Public Management and Citizenship Program," which promotes innovation in sub-national governments in Brazil. On a backdrop of government and public sector innovation trends in Brazil recent decades, Farah examines why innovations are disseminated and asserts that the mere existence of similar problems in other jurisdictions is not sufficient to prompt the transfer of innovations. A problem has to be perceived as a social and political issue before innovations will be adopted. Similarly, convergence between policy agendas of local governments and innovations improves the chances of successful transfer.

In *Chapter 8*, Joseph Galimberti discusses best practices and innovation drawing on some of the experiences of the Institute of Public Administration of Canada (IPAC). The chapter describes the successful adaptation of Canadian best practices by other jurisdictions in Lithuania and China, and suggests how the success of these transfers can best be measured. The author emphasizes that the methodology for transferring best practices was based on a practitioner-to-practitioner relationship in which the mentor jurisdiction removed flaws in current practices and advised on expected difficulties in the implementation stages. The chapter also uses material from the IPAC Award for Innovative Management, established in 1990, to provide insights on innovation and relate some successful adaptations of Canadian innovations to other jurisdictions. Galimberti argues that the single most important factor in disseminating innovation is recognition to which end awards programmes play a significant role (see also Part 3). The chapter concludes that the idea behind a specific innovation is more important than the innovation itself and calls for the establishment of a knowledge network of innovation to facilitate the successful transfer of new ideas.

In *Chapter 9*, Tonatiuh Guillén López analyses the capacities needed to adapt best practices in governance based on the experience of the Mexico's Government and Local Management Award (GLMA). Interestingly, innovation at the local level is determined neither by political affiliation, population or geographical location of the local government, nor is the amount of resources a determinant of innovation. The author identifies the local need and simultaneous apprehension of that need by leading institutional and social actors as prerequisites for successful innovation. The GLMA programmes analysed furthermore reveal the key role played by the municipal president for successful innovation in terms of leadership. Finally, the chapter highlights the problem of documentation that primarily happens on an informal and oral basis, which despite GLMAs efforts still is a major impediment in the diffusion, transfer and replication of best practices.

Part Three, "Approaches to Transferring and Adapting Best Practices and Innovations," looks at how best practices and innovations are effectively disseminated. By outlining three different approaches to transferring best practices and innovations, the chapters highlight, for example, how peer-to-peer transfers can act as a flexible and powerful tool to better match expertise and experience of host and recipient—and that including the media as an integral player may help raise awareness and mobilize political support. Another important conclusion is that it is not adequate to focus solely on the innovation in order to achieve successful transfer, but that due attention should also be given to the process that made an innovation possible.

In *Chapter 10*, Vincent Kitio and Nicholas You provide an outline of how UN Habitat works with best practices. From the original call for best practices in 1996 to the establishment of the Best Practices and Local Leadership Programme (BLP)—a global network of public, private and civil society organizations devoted to the sharing and exchange of lessons learned from experience—UN Habitat has promoted best practices as a means of identifying solutions to some of the most pressing social, economic and environmental problems facing an urbanizing world. In the chapter, Kitio and You explain the UN Habitat process of identifying, documenting and assessing best practices while emphasizing the use of a standardized reporting format. The authors focus on the importance of the BLP knowledge management framework for best practices. The strength of the framework lies in the involvement of a global network, which enables BLP to compare lessons learned across the board. Adopted and customized by several governments, institutions and organizations, one tangible impact of the framework has been its ability to mobilize the media as well as use best practices to inform the political process.

In *Chapter 11*, Lakhbir Sing Chahl shares lessons learned from a series of pilot transfers in Asia involving best practices in improving the living environment. The author shows the value of peer-to-peer learning and identifies four principal steps in the transfer process while calling attention to the role of the intermediary as catalyst, broker, facilitator and evaluator. Besides outlining the key actors to be given consideration in an innovation transfer, Sing Chahl also identifies political, administrative and socio-economic, environmental, and cultural indicators for the effective transfer of practices. Through examples of some of the transfers, the chapter provides both information and worksheets that can be used in the transfer process. Finally, it suggests how to overcome obstacles and challenges, and how to select projects and partners for transferring best practices.

In *Chapter 12*, Austere Panadero examines replication strategies for local governance as applied and experienced by the Gawad Galing Pook Foundation in the Philippines. The author explains how the Foundation focuses on information transfer in order to enhance learning transferability and nationally driven transfers. This involves cooperation between government departments and peer-to-peer coaching as a capacity-development methodology to replicate exemplary practices in local governance. Panadero extrapolates what elements make a practice transferable, emphasizing that a practice becomes more replicable if there is evidence of its success. The author also highlights the critical factors needed for any replication process, such as willingness and commitment on behalf of both the host and the recipient.

Contents

Boxes

Figures

Tables

Chapter 1

Replicating Innovations in Governance
An Overview

Adriana Alberti and Guido Bertucci

Innovations in Governance: Perspectives and Challenges

This chapter provides an overview of innovations in governance and underscores the positive impact of knowledge-sharing in development efforts. It analyses tools and approaches to use and adapt innovations in governance. Accordingly, it explores conceptual issues related to best practices and innovations in governance; examines what makes an innovation transferable; analyses what capacities are needed for governments to absorb an innovation; and finally, looks at some methodologies and approaches for transferring/adapting innovations and best practices in governance.[1]

Why Should Governments Innovate?

In the last half of the twentieth century and even more so at the beginning of the new millennium, governments have been under pressure to respond to the demands of their citizens and to the increasing complexity and change in their global environments. On the one hand, governments need to tackle a number of complex social and economic issues, including poverty, spread of diseases (particularly severe in the case of HIV/AIDS), unemployment, poor education systems and environmental degradation. On the other hand, they need to readjust their policies and skills to effectively integrate into the world economy. Managing the public sector in today's environment of constant change has become a demanding challenge for policy makers, service delivery managers and civil servants—a challenge that is especially daunting for those in developing countries and countries with economies in transition.

Overall, Governments are faced with three main domestic challenges. First, they need to operate and provide more far-reaching and higher quality services with reduced resources and limited operational capacities. That is to say, governments need to use their resources and build capacities not only more effectively, but also more creatively by, for example, enlisting the support of the private sector and civil society in service delivery. Second, they need to make public institutions more accountable, responsive and effective by promoting a more citizen-oriented public administration. Third, and most importantly, they need to respond more adequately to the demands from citizens for greater participation. Although government is still central to society, it is now widely recognized that governance is not the sole prerogative of governments, but that civil society and the private sector also have an important role to play in this sphere. Citizens no longer perceive themselves as passive "consumers" of government services, but as part of the solution to deal more effectively with emerging issues.[2] Deepening democracy in order to provide opportunities not only for improved representation, but also more active participation and engagement in public affairs requires innovative institutional mechanisms, processes and policies.

While the challenges are many, so are the opportunities for innovation in the public sector. In fact, it has been gradually recognized that the State and public administration have a crucial role to play in meeting these challenges. The myth that markets and the private sector alone can accelerate development, spearhead growth, eliminate inequalities and make life better for all has been replaced by bitter disappointment. People are therefore looking back at government and at public administration as a catalytic force. Public administration, however, cannot remain its old self. In fact, several countries around the world are attempting to revitalize their public administration, make it more proactive, efficient, accountable, and especially more service-oriented. To accomplish this transformation, governments are introducing innovations in their organizational structure, practices, capacities, and how they mobilize, deploy and utilize the human, material, information, technological and financial resources for service delivery to remote, disadvantaged and challenged people.

Experience has shown that introducing innovations in governance has a number of positive results. First, it can help maximize the utilization of resources and capacities to create public value as well as encourage a more open/participatory culture in government, therefore improving good governance in general. Second, by improving the image and services of the public sector it can help governments regain people's trust and restore legitimacy. Third, innovation in governance can boost the pride of civil servants working in the public sector, as well as encourage a culture of continuous improvement. Innovations can have an inspirational capacity which builds a sense of the possible among public officials. Fourth, although innovations are limited governance interventions or micro-level initiatives, they can produce a domino effect in that a successful innovation in one sector can open the door to innovations in other areas. Each innovation can create the opportunity for a series of innovations leading to a favorable environment for positive change. Innovations can lead to building a new block of an institution, and change the relationship between levels of government and within government departments. The chapter by Lopez shows that innovations are strongly contributing to the democratization of institutions and processes. Thus, although an innovation *per se* is a small process, it can trigger a bigger process of transformation of the State.

Accordingly, innovations can contribute to the promotion of good government and to the creation of new democratic spaces. This is certainly true for countries that are slowly building democratic institutions. It is also true for advanced democracies since good government is a key factor in strengthening democratic governance. It is well known that even in mature democracies, State institutions are not always well equipped to face complex emerging challenges. In fact, although the basic values behind any constitutional democracy are universal and well accepted by many countries around the world, how well institutions work and adequately reflect those values is an open-ended process. In recently established democracies, making government work is even more critical to the survival of democratic governance. It is well-known that although several countries have adopted democratic systems in the past decades, governments have not functioned as expected. In various regions of the world there seems to be a growing disconnection between formally designed democratic systems and their actual operation; between substance and rhetoric. This is strongly evidenced by the mounting dissatisfaction of citizens and civil society organizations towards how democracies function. In some relatively new democracies, such as the case of Latin American countries, citizens have gone as far as to question democracy itself as the best governance arrangement. The fact that many people tend to fuse two very different concepts, i.e., democracy as a political regime and public administration (how government works), can lend itself to dangerous political alternative outcomes.

As can be easily inferred, innovations in governance and public administration should not be regarded as a fashion or trend. Governments that have dealt effectively with increasingly complex national, regional and international challenges have introduced innovative ideas and practices in governance and public administration systems and processes. It is also very important to bear in mind that innovation is not an end in itself, but a means to improve public administration in order to enhance the quality of life of all citizens. In addition, innovations should be seen as complementary mechanisms to reinforcing democratic governance but not as a substitute for existing institutions, including Parliament, public administration, etc. Furthermore, each organization in the public sector should decide how much innovation it needs and how to balance stability and continuity on the one hand, and innovation on the other. Not everything in the public sector can be about innovation. Finally, it should be mentioned that innovations are not a "special benefit" of countries with developed administrative systems. As shown by the increasing number of applications submitted to the United Nations Public Service Awards, successful practices are initiated both in developed and developing countries and have been transferred from the latter to developed countries (e.g., the integrated public services system launched by the State of Bahia in Brazil was adopted by Portugal, Mozambique and South Africa). In sum, innovation in governance and revitalization of public administration is today an imperative for governments that wish to effectively deal with emerging national, regional and international challenges and to strengthen democratic governance.

Definitions of Best Practices and Innovations

Documenting and sharing innovations in public administration is a very important tool in fostering innovation in government and promoting development. Despite the wealth of good examples around the world, the challenge is to distinguish between cases that are indeed best practices in governance and cases that do not fall under this category. In other words, what is presented as an innovative practice is not always a successful long-term experience that can be disseminated to other countries. To assist Member States who are interested in replicating innovations, it is necessary to define what is meant by innovation and by "best practice."[3] Based on the "Report of the Preparatory Committee for the United Nations Conference on Human Settlements," presented to the General Assembly, "best practices": (1) Have a demonstrable and tangible impact on improving people's quality of life; (2) Are the result of effective partnerships between the public, private and civil society sectors; and (3) Are socially, economically and environmentally sustainable (UN, 1995, A/50/37). The General Assembly, based on the UN-Habitat Agenda, further recommends that best practices be used as one of the two key instruments for assessing progress in achieving its twin goals of shelter for all and sustainable urbanization (A/RES/S-25/2).

The concept of best or successful practices is widely used to distinguish exemplary or improved performance in organizations. There is wide consensus that the term "best practice" is problematic in relation to governance and public administration since it presupposes that a practice has been actually benchmarked against all other similar practices at the national and international levels. It also implies that there is one best way to do things whereas in reality there are many ways of implementing innovative ideas. Terms such as "smart options," "good practices" or "successful practices" are better suited for the field of governance.

A best/successful practice can be defined as an activity or procedure that has produced outstanding results and can be adapted to improve effectiveness and efficiency in another situation. For UNAIDS, focusing on "best practice" means accumulating and applying knowledge about what works and what does not work in different situations and contexts. It is both lessons learned and the continuing process of learning, feedback, reflection and analysis. The focus of analysis is on "success stories" in order to discover the chain of practices; the ways of doing things that achieve results. The conceptual distinction between innovations and "best/successful practices" is, however, contested. Some believe that if innovations are sustainable, they become successful practices. From this perspective, the difference between the two concepts lies in the time frame. Others instead maintain that one of the defining criteria of an innovation is sustainability. The difference between an innovation and a successful practice could also lie in the element of novelty that is part of the latter concept but not always the former. It is also interesting to note, that since the field of innovation in governance is not as well-developed as that of innovations in the private sector, there are different definitions of what an innovation in governance and public administration is. For example, one of the criteria to select winners for the United Nations Public Service Awards is "the introduction of a new concept," i.e., government introduces a unique idea, distinctively new approach to problem solution or unique policy or implementation design, in the context of a given country or region, for transparency, accountability and responsiveness of public service.[4] The American Government Awards program's selection of innovations in the United States uses four criteria as illustrated by Table 1.1.

Table 1.1 Criteria of the American Government Awards

Novelty	A leap of creativity
Effectiveness	Tangible results
Significance	Addresses a problem of public concern
Transferability	Replicability and scalability

Source: American Government Awards

The Impumelelo Innovations Awards Trust in South Africa,[5] which rewards exceptional projects involving partnerships with the public sector that enhance the quality of life of poor communities in innovative ways, uses the following evaluation criteria to define an innovation (see Table 1.2).

Table 1.2 Impumelelo Evaluation Criteria for Innovation

Innovativeness	The extent to which initiative, creativity and new procedures have been developed to address major poverty related issues.
Government Involvement	Involvement of Government and partnerships.
Effectiveness	The extent to which the project has achieved or is on its way to achieving its stated objectives and other socially desirable outcomes.
Poverty Impact	The demonstrable effect of the project in improving the quality of life of poor communities and individuals.
Sustainability	The viability and sound functioning of the project within the constraints such as funding, staffing and so forth.
Replicability	The value of the project in teaching others new ideas and good practices for poverty reduction programmes.

Source: Impumelelo Innovations Award Trust (*http://www.impumelelo.org.za*)

Winners of the American Society for Public Administration Public Service Awards are selected among those who have, on a sustained basis, done some or all of the following:

- Made a profound difference in improving service to the public;
- Been willing to take risks to achieve change;
- Fostered a more democratic society;
- Served as a champion of social equity;
- Changed the way a governmental organization operates so that it better achieves its goals;
- Achieved substantial savings in government operations; and
- Developed a cadre of other government leaders.

In general terms, innovation in governance is a creative idea which is successfully implemented to solve a pressing public problem. It is the act of conceiving and implementing a new way of achieving a result and/or performing work. An innovation may involve the incorporation of new elements, a new combination of existing elements or a significant change or departure from the traditional way of doing things. It refers to new products, new policies and programs, new approaches, and new processes. Public sector management innovation may also be defined as the development of new policy designs and new standard operating procedures by public organizations to address public policy problems. Thus, an innovation in public administration is an effective, creative and unique answer to new problems or a new answer to old problems. Furthermore, an innovation is not a closed and complete solution, but an open solution, transformed by those who adopt it. There are different types of innovations in public administration, including:

- *Institutional innovations*, which focus on the renewal of established institutions and/or the creation of new institutions;
- *Organizational innovation*, including the introduction of new working procedures or management techniques in public administration;
- *Process innovation*, which focuses on the improvement of the quality of public service delivery; and
- *Conceptual innovation*, which focuses on the introduction of new forms of governance (e.g., interactive policy-making, engaged governance, people's budget reforms, horizontal networks).

The areas of innovation are also varied, including human resources development and management, public service delivery, Information and Communication Technologies (ICT) applications in government operations, decentralization, etc. For example, the Institute for Public Administration of Canada (IPAC) Awards for Innovative Management, established in 1990, have been awarded for one-stop shops, online business registrations (eight ministries, one form); horizontal innovation (team focus on planning, zoning, and law enforcement as well as horizontal planning) and inter-sectoral cooperation for youth problems.

Innovation for Achieving a Better Life for All

A number of innovative and successful solutions are being applied to governance and public administration challenges. Examining innovative cases of government services selected by the United Nations Public Service Awards and other internationally renowned awards, a number of key principles and strategies for innovation in governance emerge as prominent:[6]

- Integrating services;
- Decentralizing service delivery;
- Utilizing partnerships;
- Engaging citizens; and
- Taking advantage of Information and Communication Technologies.

Integrating Services
With public sectors offering an increased number of services, the focus is shifting from *what* kinds of services are provided to *how* they are provided. In several countries, a host of services are not only being provided, but are increasingly coordinated and customized to fit the needs of the citizens. Back-office oper-

ations are no longer the decisive factor of where the citizen needs to go; instead these operations are tied together by either integrating early in the value chain or by bundling services together in a single entry point for the citizens. Regardless of whether action is targeted up or downstream, the result is integration in products and services offered by public authorities. In the Philippines, gender and development mainstreaming efforts saw the creation of the Davao Medical Center, which in turn set up the Women and Children Protection Unit (WCPU)—a one-stop family crisis intervention centre, which provides legal, psychiatric and medical services to its patients. In Brazil, the Bahia's Citizen Assistance Service Centers (SAC) bring together federal, state, and municipal agencies in a single location to offer a multiple of government services. The centers have been placed in locations convenient to the public, such as shopping malls and major public transportation hubs. The concept of the SAC one-stop shop has been successfully adapted by a number of developed as well as developing countries, such as Portugal, Mozambique and South Africa. Within this category, there are several innovations, including client-focused one-stop service delivery for social services as well as mobile service delivery for multi-service clients in remote areas, innovative business registration, e-procurement and other similar practices.

Decentralizing Service Delivery
Bringing services and public officials closer to people (e.g., from national to regional level) often ensures a higher level of responsiveness and customization—and thus increased satisfaction on behalf of citizens and businesses. Decentralized service delivery also allows for a greater involvement of citizens in providing feed-back on public services and therefore for a better match between local services and local needs. In economic terms, maintaining a solely centralized system of service delivery and monitoring also tends to curb development outside of urban centres due to prohibitive transaction costs for either the supplier of services (i.e., government) or the users (i.e., citizens and business). In Morocco, for example, the PAGER project which brings water to the rural population, would not be feasible was it not for the devolvement of operation and maintenance of water facilities to local communities. So far the project has substantially increased the rate of the rural population with access to drinking water from 14% in 1994 to 55% at the end of 2003. In a knock-on effect, apart from the obvious benefits of clean water and adequate sanitation, PAGER has also had a huge impact on primary school enrolment in rural areas, where the attendance for girls has surged from 30 to 51 percent with young children, in particular girls, previously supplying families with water.

In another example from Morocco, the establishment of regional control facilities for controlling fresh exports of fruit and vegetable had a significant impact on the competitiveness of the sector. Previously, business incurred prohibitive costs to compete successfully in the international market because of high rejection rates of products having to be transported to a small number of centralized facilities far away from the source of processing. In Indonesia, in the Tanah Datar district in West Sumatra, decentralization has been carried out in 2001 and as a result policies were implemented by the District Education Department in Tanah Datar to increase the quality of teaching in schools with the aim to improve the condition of students from poor families. Particularly innovative were the policies to limit the number of students in each class, to create a reward-system for high performing students and teachers and to institute a performance-based contracting of headmasters.[7] In general, recent innovative strategies include decentralized policy development, implementation and evaluation; as well as decentralized budgeting and expenditure management assessments.

Utilizing Partnerships

Public-private partnerships as well as joined-up government or inter-agency collaboration are all becoming more common with the general public expecting greater participation, better utilization of resources and increased efficiency in service delivery. This often requires innovative approaches considering the lack of precedents compared to previous "silo" administration. In Greece, for example, the 1502 Call Centre takes advantage of the expertise of the National Telecommunication Agency by letting operators within a special service of the Agency provide information regarding available services of providing government certificates. In addition, the responsible Ministry has made special arrangements both with the Agency and the Postal Services in order to keep prices affordable. Also, the establishment of consultative groups/committees, which include public officials and members of the business community and deal with policy/budgeting issues, is now rapidly being adopted by other countries.

In Jordan, the National Network for Poverty Alleviation, established in 1998, has connected government ministries, national commissions, non-governmental organizations and activists into a productive network and demonstrated the dramatic impact that multi-disciplinary groups can have in promoting national poverty alleviation and social development. In the United Republic of Tanzania, the "safer cities approach" encourages partnerships between national governments, city governments, neighbourhoods and citizens. The approach, which was launched in 1996 by the United Nations Human Settlements Programme (UNCHS), aims to provide local authorities (cities, municipalities and towns) with technical support to develop sustainable ways of preventing violence and crime. In a collaborative effort, priorities were identified which eventually led to the development of a crime prevention strategy that has created awareness, improved relations between the police and the population and committed local authorities to continuous action.

Engaging Citizens

Citizens are being increasingly engaged in providing inputs to government's policy formulation and monitoring processes. A number of countries have developed strategies to encourage the active participation of citizens in, for example, budgeting and the fiscal processes.[8] In Thailand, the Constitution has been reformed to ensure public hearings in public programmes. In Australia, the State Government of Queensland has established a Community Engagement Division within the Premier's Department to engage the community in relevant policy deliberations to ensure social justice, equity and relevancy in public policies and programmes, especially at the regional level. Online consultations through the ConsultQLD are also available facilitating open public consultation on critical issues currently being considered by the Government. In India, the Government of the National Capital Territory of Delhi established an innovative citizen-government approach to governance. Through the Bhagidari Cell, networks of local groups have grown from 20 citizen groups in 2000 to more than 1,600 citizen groups representing about 3 million people today. These networks discuss problems hampering effective delivery of services with government representatives and then produce joint workable solutions in areas such as water supply, sanitation, schools, power supply and urban transport. Further, many countries, especially at the city level, now practice what is known as "Citizen's Report Card System—a citizen-based monitoring and public accountability system.[9]

Taking Advantage of Information and Communication Technologies

As the 2003 United Nations World Public Sector Report[10] points out, the use of internet-based services as a way to cut red tape or to spread digital infrastructure has expanded rapidly throughout public sectors in recent years. In Cameroon, for example, a new personnel and payroll data system (SIGIPES) allows better control of procedures, including the elimination of "ghost workers." ICT applications, in general, have been introduced to upgrade service delivery in terms of wider access to services, enhanced efficiency and timeliness, a more "citizen-centered" approach to services, and greater effectiveness, relevance and quality of services. Broadband[11] access policies, for example, are on most governments' ICT agenda since they are considered a key enabler of economic growth, distance education and make possible specialist treatment of people in remote areas where advanced medical care is scarce. The Republic of Korea, for instance, expects pervasive broadband to increase industrial efficiency, create e-business and jobs, improve global competitiveness, and add the equivalent of several thousand dollars to per capita GDP.

Yet, internet-based service is also a means of advancing and consolidating transparency and democracy into the overall practice of public administration.

The application of ICT in local government operations, for example by establishing electronic public information offices, has enabled local governments—policy makers and public officials—to better interact with the public, particularly individual citizens. This enhanced interaction may support government responsiveness and relevance by allowing citizens to better express their needs, participate in and influence policy-making, comment on policy implementation, provide feedback on government services (on and off-line services) and file complaints, among other activities. In Mongolia, for example, a model online consultation facility has been created for engaging citizen participation. The site includes a legislative forum designed for citizen comments on the specific laws posted on the site and a policy forum for discussion about existing or proposed policies.[12]

Seeking Solutions that Work

Innovation can be induced from an outside actor (such as the case of the European Union and its accession policy) or it can be internally driven. Both are important triggers of change. Innovations can occur at all levels of government, i.e., central and local levels. They can also be jump started by citizens with the government playing only a facilitating role. There are a number of examples where people have come together to solve a problem affecting the whole community. In Croatia, for instance, the collaboration between judges, law professors, lawyers and law students, working together in an NGO, has resulted in a web-based legal information infrastructure called the Judges' web, which improved the transparency, efficiency of and access to Croatia's judicial system. The Judges' web is considered one of the most innovative practices in the Croatian judicial administration, and its efforts have been recognized and praised by the Ministry of Justice to an extent where the project has been incorporated into the overall legal reform strategy. Studies have also shown that there is no direct link between political orientation and good government practices.[13] In fact, it is possible to identify innovative programs regardless of the party in favour. The same can be said about size and population. It has been recorded that good government practices occur in small municipalities, as well as in heavily populated areas and that size is not a determinant factor for innovation to occur, nor are financial resources as we will see later on. It is also often argued that innovations require political support, but evidence has shown that this is not always true. If the innovation is structural or systemic (e.g., innovative anti-corruption agency), then it must start at or be accepted at the top; if it involves a change in process and it is functional, it can start at a mid-management level and therefore it is not necessarily separated nor tied from politics.

Innovations occur for different reasons: a crisis, regime change, new leadership, opportunities or challenges. In general, people do not start out by deciding that they are going to innovate; they start by solving a problem in a way that they or others later realize is innovative. Experience shows that key factors in the success of an innovation include:

- Effective leadership (but "invisible," i.e., the leader chooses not to personalize the innovation);
- Inclusiveness, empowerment and commitment of all stakeholders (building teams and partnerships);
- Setting targets and establishing a conducive environment in which these targets can be reached;
- Monitoring mechanism to measure change against established benchmarks; and
- Reward system that establishes accountability, enhances creative thinking and unleashes innovative abilities that erstwhile could not express themselves.

Captains of innovation usually take risks without knowing the end result of their actions. In some cases they achieve successful results, but when they do not, failures can be disruptive for an organization that relies on continuity and a certain degree of stability and strict accountability. This has a tendency to restrain innovation in the public sector sphere. Factors that can hinder innovation in government include: lip service and administrative formalism (adopting an innovation because it looks modern, but without anything behind it); a change in a law or adoption of a practice without reference to contextual variables; structural/institutional barriers that inhibit the implementation of an innovation; institutions that do not allow risk-taking (although it should be noted that government is based on minimizing maximum loss, not maximizing maximum gain); "personalization" of the innovation by the leader or inertia of public officials who view an innovation as an exclusive prerogative of top managers in the organization. Financial resources cannot be counted as a factor that hinders innovation. In fact, many cases have proven that it is precisely the lack of funds that has triggered creativity and led to innovations in governance. As much as innovations are important, it is also necessary to focus on the *organizational dimension* that leads to innovations as mentioned in Chapter 2.

Getting from A to B

Innovation in government involves agents of change, processes and mechanisms, as well as value systems and normative orders, technology and resources (not necessarily financial). The will of the people implicated in solving a problem as well as leadership are critical components of the process. The process of innovation implies the following steps:

- Definition of the problem (as fundamentals, characteristics, principles, values, key features) relative to context;
- Establishment of a strategic plan framework;
- Agreement upon and adoption of guidelines;
- Documentation (circumstances, characteristics, results) in broad and diverse forms (e.g., video cameras to document case studies);
- Dissemination of results;
- Monitoring of implementation;
- Coordination and integration into the policy framework;
- Sustainability of the innovation (institutionalized rather than linked with a particular person); and
- Innovation can be prospective (rational and intentional) or retrospective ("muddling through").

Helping and Hampering Innovation

Everyone is for innovation; yet it is very difficult to conceive and implement. It takes time and energy and public servants have enough trouble coping with their current responsibilities. As Galimberti points out: "Once identified as an innovation that works and the risk now diminished, innovations can spread rather quickly and are often improved or expanded."[14] A number of factors are critical to building an enabling environment for innovation, including:

- Effective leadership;
- Organizational culture supportive of innovation;
- Promotion of teamwork and partnerships;
- Promotion of lifelong learning;
- Promotion of diversity;
- Monitoring the implementation of innovation; and
- Knowledge-sharing and networking.

Table 1.3 summarizes some of the factors that facilitate or hinder innovation in government.

Table 1.3   Factors That Hinder or Facilitate Innovation in Government

Hindrances	Facilitators
• Demand for error-free government (risk adversity)	• Autonomy/empowerment
• Negative attitudes toward innovation	• Leadership
• Legal structure/laws/legislation	• Inclusiveness and participation (building teams)
• Lack of access to information	• Legitimacy
• Media predisposition to report negative news	• Networks/access to information
• Deference to authority	• Support (civil society)
• Lack of autonomy	• Resources
• Lack of professionalism	• Scholarly literature
• Resource limitations (human or financial)	• Teaching innovation in university/government training institutions
• Auditor general/oversight agencies and risk adversity	• Documenting innovations through easily accessible case studies
• Resistance to change	• Rewarding risk-takers/recognition of innovators
• Low regard for public administration	• Media reports on innovation

Source: Alberti and Bertucci, 2006

Creating an Enabling Environment

As mentioned above, effective leadership is critical for the success of any innovation in governance. Strategic leadership capacity-building is an important tool to foster innovations in governance. Schools of public administration can play a key role in this respect, as well as international organizations, centres on innovation in governance and academic institutions. Advocacy and awareness building activities, including conferences and workshops on innovations, can also be of critical importance. Generally speaking, awareness needs to be built around the concept of what it means to be a strategic leader in the public sector. Experience has shown that strategic leaders encourage responsible risk-taking at mid- and other levels/front lines and are open to good ideas whatever their source—whether emanating from citizens, inside the government or from other governments. It has also been demonstrated that the type of leadership affects the sustainability of an innovation. If an innovation is based on a leader and it is not institutionalized, the innovation will die as soon as there is a change in leadership. The role of an effective leader is thus to build capacity and devolve responsibility and authority so that the innovation introduced can survive his/her departure. Accordingly, leaders that have avoided the "I syndrome" and used more inclusive language (my community) have achieved more sustainable results as in the case of the Mayor of Bogotá in Colombia who involved the whole community in addressing the shortage of water in the city.[15]

Another critical factor for the development and diffusion of innovation in public service delivery is well-educated and well-trained public sector employees. Public officials should be trained to embrace a culture of learning and to see themselves as active agents of change as underscored by the United Nations Committee of Experts on Public Administration at its first meeting in 2002. It is impossible to introduce innovations in public organizations without continuous upgrading of employees' knowledge and skills, as well as without them having access to recent developments in their respective areas of expertise. Currently, distance learning offers enormous cost-effective opportunities for continuous education. Diversity can also be a source of innovative ideas and creative solutions to problems since it brings together different backgrounds and ways of thinking.

With regard to the organizational culture supportive of innovation, a new mind-set or organizational culture which places emphasis on thinking about the possible rather than the obstacles encountered in tackling specific problems should be promoted through different mechanisms, including recruitment mechanisms, socialization upon entry in the public service; training; fair performance appraisal system, rewards, recognition and latitude to experiment. To build a culture supportive of innovation, it is necessary to promote an organizational environment based on shared leadership and trust, i.e., an organization that promotes a sense of leadership and ownership among all employees who are seen and act as leaders in their own sphere of competence and feel empowered to take proactive measures. If public servants perceive their jobs as repetitive and mechanic, i.e., with no margin of autonomy, innovation and new solutions become less likely. On the contrary, when they feel empowered and take responsibility, the organization as a whole benefits and the public servant's professional pride and satisfaction are enhanced. In this culture, managers do not categorically reject new ideas as interruption, thus giving a strong negative message. Instead, they welcome new ideas and new approaches and are ready to consider their potential value. It is also vital that governments provide information about innovation within government itself and externally. Access to information about government action is crucial, and governments should actively support, encourage and reward networking to share knowledge and ideas. New means and/or processes for sharing ideas and knowledge across traditional boundaries (across departments, other government orders/jurisdictions with other agencies) should be developed. Knowledge management through the exchange of information and experience is central to promoting excellence in government. Governments need to improve their image by fighting insularity and by being seen to adapt outside good practices to inspire inquisitiveness. In other words, governments need to work hard to create a positive image in the media (at all levels) despite the fact that it is a difficult endeavor given the propensity of the media to highlight only negative events.

With respect to promotion of teamwork and partnerships, it is well-known that teams bring together people with complementary skills and experiences that exceed the capacity of any one of the members, or of the members collectively but working independently. Teams facilitate the breaking down of barriers between genders, age groups, races, ethnic groups, and geographic biases. The communication skills and network that successful teams develop creates a capacity to respond quickly and flexibly to new problems and changing environment. However, team-work is not easy, and training on team-building and how to negotiate partnerships should be encouraged in the public sector, as well as new organizational arrangements to work in partnership with civil society and the private sector. Building trust, as well as legitimacy and partnerships are critical to the feasibility and sustainability of innovations in governance. As such, a peer-to-peer exchange rather than a traditional top-down donor-recipient scenario is preferable for sustainability of innovations. In a number of cases it has been shown that asking the population to be involved in the solution of a pressing problem from the beginning and making it part of the solution has brought about impressive results. There is strong evidence that impositions from above (such as imposing drastic solutions on the population by limiting the water supply at intervals of time) are not as effective as changing the habits of citizens through participatory mechanisms. One way of effecting cultural change is by changing patterns of behavior; this can be done through, for example, the use of narratives, i.e., explaining through different means of communication (including newspapers and television) why the innovation is being introduced, what people can do to help achieve the desired goal and what processes are involved.

Innovation must be oriented to achieving measurable progress. Without a well-planned and managed approach, the routine of day-to-day operations takes over. One response to this may be developing benchmarks against which to judge the success of innovation efforts. For example, the Ministry of Government Administration and Home Affairs of the Government of Korea has developed in 2005 a Government Innovation Index, which is a tool to gauge the level of innovation of organizations in the public sector. The index helps organizations to diagnose levels of innovation, identify weak areas, and develop action plans to fortify their innovation capacities.[16] The overall results of the index can serve as a reference for national innovation strategies. Documenting progress in innovation efforts can provide material for reference to other innovators, within and outside a specific country, who wish to learn from others, successes as discussed in the following pages.

Finally, in order to encourage innovation in public administration it is very important to include this subject in executive programmes, i.e, university curricula should expose and encourage innovation. It is also crucial to improve the body of knowledge about innovation and public sector challenges. In this respect both universities and international organizations can play a key role. Universities also have a fundamental role in encouraging young people to aspire to public service by highlighting that it is an honorable and noble profession which is challenging, stimulating and rewarding, as well as conducive to personal growth.

Transferability of Best Practices and Innovations

Sharing of information *per se* is not enough to enable countries to adapt innovations to their own administrative system. Successful practices are usually documented by example, resulting in only limited transfer of knowledge and ideas between countries and a tendency to "reinvent the wheel." In order to maximize the benefit of sharing successful practices among countries and to provide more effective assistance to governments interested in replicating specific innovations in public administration, it is necessary to develop a set of tools and methodologies to identify the validity and transferability of national practices and experiences, and the steps and requirements of the implementation process.

For a country to adapt an innovation from another context (or whether the federal level within a country can benefit from an innovation at the local level or vice-versa), it is necessary to evaluate:

- Whether that particular experience is indeed successful,
- Whether it is transferable to another country,
- Whether the country on the receiving end has the capacity to implement such practice, and
- To identify suitable approaches and methodologies for the replication of successful practices.

Transferring Innovations

Transferring innovations and successful practices is about knowledge transfer. It implies transferring ideas, as well as know-how, skills and lessons learned in the implementation process of an innovation. The transfer of an innovation may be described as "a structured learning process based on knowledge derived from experience coupled with human expertise capable of transforming that knowledge into social action."[17] In line with this definition, the *idea* behind a specific innovation is more important than the innovation itself. Although an innovation in government may be in relative terms a successful practice within a specific country, it might not lend itself to being replicated in other parts of the world because of the unique attributes of the case. It could be that a particular innovation has been implemented to respond to a very specific need within a certain administration and that the same needs are not felt in other administrations. Or it could be that because of the very particular characteristics of a central or local government administration, the best practice is not transferable. Therefore, practices, which were successful in one country, should not be blindly reproduced in another. Instead, their merits should be studied and tailored to local circumstances. There is evidence that a good practice is transferable when it is generic, adds value and involves simple processes, quick wins, is cost-effective, addresses an expressed or felt need among replicators and is effective. That is to say, if others have the same problem and the innovation has the potential to be useful, then it is transferable. Thus, transferability implies matching demand with supply for knowledge, expertise and experience. Finally, documenting successful practices through case studies is crucial in order to raise the awareness among different governments, and different levels of government within a country, about the existing innovations, i.e., solutions that are available and have already been tried and have succeeded.

Improving Transferability

In order to enhance the transferability of innovations and best practices, it is necessary to share knowledge by, for example, posting relevant information on the Internet through web portals such as the Global On-line United Nations

Network on Public Administration—UNPAN. Access to information is necessary but not always sufficient; information must be documented and disseminated. The documentation of a best practice implies that the people, communities and organizations directly involved in their implementation take part in documenting the practice. The promotion of a standardized reporting format is also very useful, as well as the documentation of perceived problems, obstacles and how to overcome them, roles, responsibilities and the various contributions of different actors, as well as the factors leading to sustainability. In addition, it is beneficial to document and analyze promising policy options. Best practices should also be thoroughly assessed before being transferred through validation processes (verifying that the practice exists on the ground), technical assessment (groups of experts) and normative assessment.

As part of the effort to disseminate information about innovations in government, case studies can be used as teaching/learning resources in executive training and leadership programmes. To promote the dissemination of information, it is also necessary to document practices that have not been described yet because of a lack of resources or capacity to do so, to translate into different languages for maximum exposure the available practices, and to disseminate information through autonomous networks. In fact, another important avenue to promote transferability of innovations is through networks of innovators. The Ash Institute on Democratic Governance and Innovation at Harvard University is playing a critical role in this respect through the Global Government Innovators Network. Other universities and research centers, and international organizations, can play an important role by disseminating information on innovations in government and transforming information into knowledge, as well as providing training for managers and public officials. The establishment of global partnerships that run programmes bilaterally in a number of different areas of the world would also increase the transferability of best practices.

Awards programmes for excellence in government such as the United Nations Public Service Awards, the International Dubai Awards, the CAPAM Awards and the Ford Foundation Awards Program, can also perform a very important function in terms of dissemination of innovations and best practices. For example, the Gawad Galing Pook Awards Experience from the Philippines recognizes innovation and excellence, inspires replication of innovation and excellent practices, and advocates citizen awareness and participation in innovative and excellent local governance programmes. In terms of disseminating information about innovations, it is worthwhile mentioning that the Public Management and Citizenship Program, created in 1996 in Brazil by the Ford Foundation and *Fundação Getulio Vargas* (FGV-EAESP), with the support of the National Bank for Economic and Social Development, has established an online database containing cases from more than 180 prize winners and many more cases that have not received awards. The CIDE Programme of Mexico has also been very active on this front. The Regional Network for Local Authorities for Asia & Pacific (CityNet) is also devoted to sharing innovative ideas and solutions, as well as strategies for adaptation (decentralized cooperation, networking, partnerships, information technology), with particular reference to local governments. CityNet has promoted city-to-city transfers and by doing so has replaced donor-to-recipient transfers (better matching supply and demand and promoting technical cooperation).

Finally, more attention should be given to up-scaling and transferring best practices, to combining best practices with good policies and legislation, and to mainstreaming national best practices knowledge systems as a policy tool. In sum, one of the most important elements in fostering transferability of best practices is the establishment of a knowledge management framework. Its objectives should be to build networks, create awareness, and share information; build learning tools; promote capacity building; peer-to-peer learning; and foster policy development. The target audiences and users could include the public, the media, media professionals, decision makers, practicing professionals, and training and leadership development institutions.

Absorbing and Implementing Best Practices

Innovation requires processes of adaptation, anticipation and openness to change. It is change that provides the opportunity to achieve new and different approaches. A precondition for replicating a best practice is that the government that is implementing it has the necessary capacity to do so. Each organization is different and faces varied situations at particular points in time. The techniques required to promote organizational innovation must therefore be context specific. In other words, one size does not fit all.

Successful Adaptation

In order to adapt a successful practice, a number of steps can be followed, including:

- Ensure that the information about the successful practice, both in terms of its components and expected outcomes, is disseminated among those who will be responsible for its implementation and those who will benefit from the innovation;
- Put in place teams to replicate the practice;
- Formulate a clear adoption policy and process; and
- Measure and report progress on the implementation process to assess sustainability.

With reference to sustainability, there is broad agreement that innovations can be sustainable only if the new practices are integrated and embedded into daily operational procedures. This implies the following:

- Practices are institutionalized;
- Ownership by stakeholders is promoted;
- Capacity-building is undertaken before introducing the practice (recruitment, placement, training, motivation);
- Sustainable economic resources, regardless of external funding, are guaranteed;
- Communication networks are established; and
- A balanced and equitable distribution of benefits across the community is established in terms of socio-economic classes, gender, geographic areas, ethnic groups and other criteria.

Moreover, it is necessary to institutionalize monitoring and evaluation procedures within the implementation and evaluation processes and establish a quality assurance system. It is also very important to have in place long-term and flexible objectives that lend themselves to change and amelioration. Finally, it is necessary to internalize and integrate practices within the local social textures and institutional structures and cultures.

In terms of selecting what to replicate, it should be the recipient entity to define the characteristics of the innovation it can use. There are also different degrees of transfer which include copying, emulation, mixtures, inspiration, etc. A number of instruments can be used to absorb a successful practice, including institutions/facilitators of the learning process as well as tools and guidelines. It is also useful to encourage adaptation rather than adoption, foster integration of monitoring and evaluation, take into account cultural considerations when designing transfer plans, and celebrate incremental successes. In general, an innovation will be successfully adopted in other contexts if the social and political actors in the recipient context see the problem addressed as a relevant public issue.

Building Capacity for Improved Adaptation

The ultimate goal of building capacity for adaptation of best practices should be creating an environment that encourages the generation of innovations and not only the adaptation of innovations from other experiences. In order to build capacity for adaptation of best practices, it is necessary to promote self-sufficient institutions that are rich in social capital and human capability and to integrate participatory democratic practices in the initiation and implementation procedures so as to ensure ownership and commitment. Other elements that could contribute to building capacity include documenting, monitoring and assessing innovations in order to derive lessons learned and facilitate their replication in other areas; as well as utilizing integrated communication systems (mass communication and interpersonal communication channels) to spread awareness about best practices.

The adoption of the "management by objectives" approach to ensure mutual commitment in the implementation between policy makers, civil servants, constituents and the various community and social actors is also a key factor in any transfer plan. So is the establishment of decision-making mechanisms that distribute decision power and share risks of innovations in order to encourage innovators to propose new ideas, novel practices and solutions without personalizing or over-exposing one party or individual to potential failure (i.e., using committees and other forms of participation in decision making inside the various organizations). With regard to the evaluation of best practices, integrated monitoring and evaluation mechanisms that benefit from independent entities could be useful in ensuring sustainability of the transfer at hand. Lessons learned for the future planning and revision of current practices as well as a continuous learning approach in the evaluation process is also very important. Finally, qualitative indicators could be useful to assess the absolute merit of innovations as compared to their relative merit in order to evaluate their sustainability and transferability to other contexts.

The knowledge factor in adapting a successful practice is also quite important. This relates to how officials are trained, to their experience, their tolerance for change, and other factors. Capacity-building requires tools and techniques that can build the ability of public officials to understand their own context and to achieve higher self-awareness of innovation possibilities and constraints within their organization. When selecting a specific innovation as a possible solution to a perceived problem, the organization that adapts the innovation is simultaneously part of the dissemination process and of the creative process. Yet, if local conditions are not ripe, taking innovations from other contexts will not result in successful innovation adoption and diffusion. In order to absorb a best practice or the idea behind a best practice, the following elements should be taken into consideration: Political culture (will and commitment); Administrative culture and heritage; Reform initiation among local actors (ideology, personal qualities); Human resources; Legal framework and regulatory issues; Leadership (charismatic vs. visionary), etc.

Replicating What Works

Successful practices and innovations can be effectively transferred to other jurisdictions and there is ample evidence that it can be done.[18] In order to facilitate the replication of an innovation (and once all of the above criteria have been satisfied), interested governments need a set of tools that can assist them in the transfer process and on how to use the acquired knowledge, as well as put it into practice. The creation of knowledge networks where successful innovations are arranged in categories such as service delivery, regulation, consultation and partnership, governance, horizontality, etc. including the contact information of the innovators, can be a first important step. The transfer process begins by matching demand with supply by documenting and exchanging successful solutions through an intermediary, including international organizations, that is knowledgeable about successful practices. The following approaches and methodologies for the transfer of best practices may be used:

- Practitioner-to-practitioner—engaging in different jurisdictions (peer-to-peer);
- Information sharing;
- Problem-solving teams/workgroups—multi-dimensional team with one member familiar with the innovation/problem;
- Transfer guidelines;
- Capacity-building/knowledge-based training;
- Hiring experts; and
- Awards.

Table 1.4   Strengths and Weaknesses of Transfers of Best Practices

Strengths	Weaknesses
Practitioner to Practitioner	
• Comparative experience	• Costly
• Practical solutions/convey knowledge nuance	• Borrower/lender—time constraints
• Mutual trust/personal high-level investment	• Scale limiting/not scalable
• Creates sustainable network	• Not present at implementation, thus nuances lost
• Creates opportunity to institutionalize connection	• Lack of criteria/standard retraining given focus on success of innovation
• Expands access to experience	• Lack of tactical tools
• Builds capacity for both parties	• Not all dimensions are covered
• Helps define responsibility	• Dependent on an individual staying in a position

Table 1.4 *(Continued)*

Strengths	Weaknesses
Information Sharing	
• Can be done through awards	• Access to information (if held privately)
• Relatively inexpensive	• False information/incorrect/misleading
• Can be peer-to-peer	• Language barrier (may be easily overcome)
	• Necessarily incomplete information
	• Lack of background country for innovation
	• Lack of legal infrastructure to support information sharing
Problem Solving	
• Similar to practitioner-to-practitioner with additional group dimension	• Language barriers/isolation
• Wider impact/richer information	• Risks being inconclusive (can over-come through institutionalization)
• Better ideas possible	• Remote locus of responsibility
• Cooperation oriented/conflict diversity resolution/overcomes positional bias	• Time consuming
• Collective learning process	
Transfer Guidelines	
• Possibility of developing strong framework	• Can give passive role to recipient
	• False sense of security
Training	
• Systematic/clear knowledge transfer	
• Rapid deployment	
• Adaptable to any stakeholder in the process	
Experts	
• Can be deployed quickly	• Can be inconclusive
	• Likely lacks knowledge of nuances
	• Supply driven

Source: Alberti and Bertucci, 2006

The strengths and weaknesses of each of these approaches and methodologies are outlined in Table 1.4.

As can be inferred, each of these approaches has strengths and weaknesses. Therefore, when adapting an innovation, and as mentioned earlier, an analysis of the different approaches should be undertaken in order to determine the right mix of ingredients. Tools and processes to be used in a replication process must encourage adaptation, not adoption, of the exemplary practice. It is also important to mention that transfers may vary in scope. Policy change is usually harder as there is greater resistance from politicians and/or bureaucrats, and thus it typically takes more than two or three years.

Concluding Remarks

The analysis of what innovations and best practices are; when and how they can be transferred as well as what methodologies exist to favour effective transfers is intended to provide useful mechanisms to worldwide policy makers and civil servants. Developing policies for public sector innovation is also critical to more effective public administration. The chapters that follow will provide in-depth analysis of the various issues examined throughout this chapter. With this chapter we have attempted to provide an overview of the main issues and approaches to replicating what works in government.

PART ONE

Innovation in Governance: Perspectives, Challenges and Potential

Chapter 2

Understanding Innovations
and Best Practices

Imraan Patel

This chapter aims to improve the understanding of how to enhance public sector innovation. It begins by introducing two conceptual models for innovative processes within the public sector. The chapter then reviews concepts of best practices, innovation, and improvement; determines whether these are helpful; and analyses selected issues associated with the transfer of innovations. It highlights why it is important to focus on the organizational context rather than on single innovations. The conclusion offers suggestions for the methodology on transferring innovation, improvements, and best practices in governance and public administration.

Characteristics of Innovation and Best Practices

Many of the world's nation states are involved in major efforts aimed at reforming and improving their governments (Kamarck, 2003). As a consequence, "innovation is used ever more frequently in the rhetoric and discourses of public service improvement" as a result of the "positive resonances" associated with this concept (Albury, 2005). However, it is important to recognize that innovation is not an end in itself but a means to an end. Innovation must be judged by its ability to create what Moore (1995) describes as "public value."

In this context, Moore (2005) introduces two very different models to understand innovative processes in the public sector. The first model is based on specific breakthrough innovations while the second model focuses on innovative organizations and continuous improvement. Further, he poses the question of whether the study of innovation in government is about: a) the processes that generated a breakthrough innovation and ways to spread that idea throughout the world or b) the creation of innovative organizations that continuously innovate and learn whereby small changes result in significant changes over time.

Despite the overlap between innovative ideas and their dissemination on the one hand and the creation of innovative organizations on the other, Moore argues that these two models focus on slightly different things. With breakthrough innovation, the key question is what constitutes a significant innovation and what processes enable it to spread. In the case of innovative organizations, the questions are slightly different and center on issues such as organizational structures, financing, cultures, etc. (Moore, 2005).

Notwithstanding these two approaches to innovation, attempts to facilitate its transfer should include strategies that deal with the innovation itself as well as crucial organizational issues. To explore this question in more detail, it is useful to briefly unpack the concepts of innovation, improvement and best practices.

Improvement versus Innovation

To achieve widespread improvements in governance and service performance, including efficiencies, in order to increase public value (Hartley, 2005), we should not only satisfy academic rigor but also make sure that the terminology used contributes in a practical way to improving democratic governance.

The word innovation is generally regarded as something positive and conveys images of renewal, commitment, improvement and progress. The academic literature, quite rightly so, has argued for the need to define innovation in a way that helps analysis and policy. Specifically, it is argued that innovation must be separated from general improvement. For example, Hartley writes that innovation and improvement need to be seen as conceptually distinct and not blurred into one concept (2005).

Combining improvement and innovation in a two-by-two matrix, Hartley illustrates that it is possible to have innovation without improvement as well as improvement without innovation. Within this framework, four scenarios are possible as shown on the following page.

Quadrant 1 occurs in highly stable environments where innovation is not needed because there is a close fit between that environment and its organizational processes, systems and stakeholder needs. Alternatively, the organization may be experiencing inertia and not identifying a need to either innovate or improve to meet new needs and changing circumstances.

Quadrant 2 represents organizations which focus on small incremental changes in order to improve. It must be noted that small changes can collectively lead to substantial changes over time.

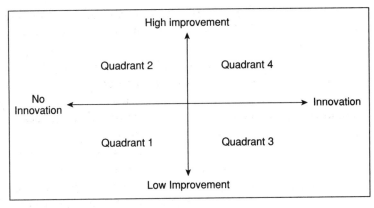

Figure 2.1 Innovation and Improvement
Source: Hartley, 2005

Quadrant 3 occurs when there is innovation that does not lead to improvement and may even lead to deteriorating performance. Situations associated with this pattern include: innovations that do not succeed, and innovations that lead to more choice but no real improvement for users.

Quadrant 4 represents a desirable situation whereby an organization innovates, resulting in noticeable improvements in outputs and outcomes (Hartley, 2005).

Conceptual clarity is important when undertaking academic studies on innovation. Yet, if innovation essentially involves the application of new ideas (White, 2003), then differences between innovation and improvement are less important since the methodologies developed to enable the transfer of innovation can also apply to a general improvement. Because of its positive connotations, innovation as a concept can be used to encourage and facilitate improvement and change. Definitions of innovation differ according to the perspective and approach of those who use it (White, 2003). For example, for an international awards programme like the United Nations Public Service Awards, a stricter definition is more appropriate as it helps isolate groundbreaking innovations. A public manager who aims to create a learning organization and who places a high premium on ongoing problem-solving will instead choose a definition that facilitates continuous improvement through incremental innovation—with a groundbreaking initiative seen as an added bonus.

Therefore, definitions differ depending on the purpose for which they are being used. In addition, definitions may change when dealing with the same activity but in two different settings. For example, a country with well-established innovation award programmes, such as the Innovations in American Government Program in the United States, would opt for a stricter definition of innovation as opposed to a country in transition where innovation award programmes are just being implemented. A country implementing an award programme for the first time might have more success by adopting a less strict definition. As the award programme develops and grows, the definition can always become clearer and stricter. Adopting various definitions of innovation has another advantage. As highlighted earlier, innovation has tremendous emotional value and depends on perception. A shifting definition together with suitable incentives can therefore help to create an environment where officials strive to raise the bar of what is possible. The present discussion has important implications for programmes and activities aimed at creating public value through "innovation." A variable definition highlights the need to focus on the conditions that facilitate learning from the experiences of others. As such, the details and practice of knowledge-sharing and replication become crucial.

Best Practices—Do They Make Sense in the Public Sector?

A second issue of terminology relates to the concept of best practices. This chapter supports the view of the Fourth Meeting of the Committee of Experts on Public Administration (CEPA) of the United Nations Economic and Social Council (ECOSOC) held in April 2005. Several members of CEPA argued that the concept of best practices is problematic in relation to public administration and governance. The best practices concept was popular in the 1980s, particularly in the private sector, where consulting houses favoured the approach that there were best ways of doing things. This standard one-size-fits-all approach was popular for a while, but soon lost favour as private sector companies realized that best practices in fact reduced a firm's competitive advantage and its capacity for innovation. In addition, some practices were difficult to implement because they were not easily transported to environments with different cultures, values, leadership and legal environments.

The concept of best practices has lost favour particularly among developing countries that were advised to adopt standard economic prescriptions by the World Bank and the International Monetary Fund (IMF). It is important to underline that most innovations in governance and service delivery are implemented within complex social and economic systems. Thereby, the approach of "differential diagnosis" used by Jeffery Sachs (2004) in relation to economic development solutions can also be applied to service delivery improvements and innovations. A systematic approach and a good diagnosis are critical in identifying problems that require the development of a solution (Sachs, 2005). Using differential diagnosis means that it is more suitable to talk about good practices (if these have an element of superiority) or, as argued during the

Experts Committee, to talk about successful policy options. Moving away from the concept of best practices has the additional advantage of avoiding fashionable trends and embracing instead an approach that values problem definition as the starting point for action whereby good practices, innovations and improvements are part of a menu of options for addressing that particular problem or challenge.

What Drives Innovation?

To better understand the opportunities and limitations of "replication," it is useful to know why innovations happen. Borins (2000) tried to provide an empirical explanation for this question by reviewing the winners of the Innovations in American Government Program and identifying the key conditions leading to innovation. Through a survey, innovators were asked to identify the conditions and challenges associated with a particular innovation. The conditions identified by innovators fell into five groups:

- **Initiatives resulting from the political process and system**, including an election mandate or pressure by politicians;
- **A leadership change**, including appointments from outside of the organization as well as new internal choices;
- **A crisis**, either current or anticipated, particularly with the potential for negative publicity;
- **A variety of internal problems**, including failure to respond to a changing environment, inability to reach a target population, inability to meet the demands of a programme, resource constraints, or an inability to coordinate policies; and
- **New opportunities** created by technology or other factors (Borins, 2000).

A less formal but similar analysis conducted by the Centre for Public Service Innovation (CPSI) on innovations in South Africa reveals a similar set of conditions, with one important addition. Following democratization in 1994 and the integration of South Africa into the global economy, a significant number of innovations occurred as a result of adopting and adapting successful models from other countries. These innovations were new but not necessarily original, discovered rather than invented (Hannah, 1995). In many cases, the transfer of models occurred in tandem with changes in leadership and shifting political conditions. On reflection, several of the innovations imported to South Africa either attempted to address an internal failing or resulted from a new opportunity created by new technology or processes.

Type of Innovation

Governments can and do innovate in a variety of different ways. Developing a suitable typology of innovations is central to efforts to transfer them. For example, it is easier to transfer a new design of a sanitation system (like ventilated pit latrines) than to transfer one-stop government centers, because the latter has significant legal, institutional and technological prerequisites. Geography and spatial issues will also affect the innovation. Various writers have attempted to advance different types. The CPSI developed four types of innovations: innovations in service delivery, innovations in citizen engagement and democracy, innovations in government processes (planning frameworks, budgeting, etc.) and innovative arrangements to reach a certain goal (for example, unique public-private partnerships or public-community partnerships). Drawing on several of these writers, Hartley identifies seven types of innovation. In practice, it is important to bear in mind that a particular change may result from the application of more than one type of innovation. The major types of innovation identified by Hartley are:

- **Product:** New products; for example, using television to deliver training content to teachers and nurses;
- **Service:** New ways to provide services to users; for example, the introduction of on-line forms;
- **Process:** New ways of designing organizational processes; for example, re-engineering business processes;
- **Position:** New contexts or users; for example, addressing the tax needs of informal enterprises;
- **Strategic:** New goals or purposes of the organization; for example, community policing;
- **Governance:** New forms of citizen engagement and democratic institutions;
- **Rhetorical:** New language and new concepts; for example, congestion charging in major cities (Hartley, 2005).

From the above typology, it is easily inferred that the type of innovation will affect the process of transfer, including how the innovation is documented and the methodology for sharing the innovation.

Focus on the Broader Trend

There is a fair degree of consensus that wholesale adoption of particular innovations or improvements is rarely possible. Experience has shown that the adoption of a particular innovation is part of a broader trend and trajectory and that an innovation tends to be affected by "previous patterns" (Farah, 2005). These trends and trajectories can be universal or may be specific to certain regions or countries that share common political, social and economic features. As a consequence, when evaluating an innovation, a detailed analysis of the trend or trajectory within which the innovation occurs is crucial. Once the trend has been identified, it becomes easier to determine whether, if transferred, the innovation will be successful and whether there is a need to consider additional innovations or changes.

Patterns of Innovation

As highlighted earlier in this chapter, innovation transfers are more effective when there are measures in place to increase the overall innovation capital of public sector institutions and systems. To illustrate this point, four issues are reviewed in the following sections, including patterns of innovation, problem types, as well as barriers to and opportunities for innovation. Glor (2001b) identified patterns of innovation based on three dynamics:

- **Individual motivation:** This can be either extrinsic or intrinsic. Intrinsic motivation arises from within the individual, for example, a commitment to a programme because of a personal identification with it. Extrinsic motivation arises from outside of the individual, for example, managerial control or some form of outside reward or incentive. Intrinsic motivation enables greater levels of problem-seeking and problem-solving as compared to extrinsic motivation;
- **Organizational culture:** This can be either a bottom-up culture or a top-down culture;
- **Challenge:** This can be either minor (for example, posing a low risk to individuals or organizations) or major (high risk to individuals and organizations).

Taking the two extreme points for each dynamic, that is, the top-down and bottom-up perspectives, and combining these, yields eight "innovation patterns." The patterns are as much about innovations as they are about organizations (Glor, 2001b). The patterns that emerge as a result of combining these three dynamics are summarized in Table 2.1.

While *reactive* and *buy-in* innovation produces fewer ideas and less variability between the ideas, innovations are easily approved, implemented and integrated. *Active* and *proactive* innovation, on the other hand, produces more ideas although of less variability. These innovations are accepted at the local level, but enjoy little support at the central level. *Necessary* and *imposed* innovations receive mixed

Table 2.1   Patterns of Innovation

Pattern	Motivation	Culture	Challenge
Reactive	Extrinsic	Top-down	Minor
Buy-in	Intrinsic	Top-down	Minor
Necessary	Extrinsic	Bottom-up	Major
Imposed	Extrinsic	Top-down	Major
Active	Extrinsic	Bottom-up	Minor
Pro-active	Intrinsic	Bottom-up	Minor
Transformational	Intrinsic	Top-down	Major
Continuous	Intrinsic	Bottom-up	Major

Source: Glor, 2002

support. They receive easy approval but encounter difficulties in implementation. While the center supports the innovation, the innovator does not enjoy support at the local level. Only *transformational* and *continuous* innovation engages the individual and creates major challenges to the status quo. *Transformational* innovation produces many ideas with high variation from the status quo but less variation between the ideas. Culture provides some support to the innovator, who accepts change and readily implements it. Long-term integration is, however, more difficult. Only *continuous* innovation engages the individual, the collectivity, and management. It creates an environment where many new ideas are introduced and the innovations are generally well-received, easily implemented and integrated because they arise from within the culture.

Innovation patterns help practitioners identify the issues they should pay attention to during the implementation process. A systematic analysis of the patterns can help identify stable and unstable innovations and can therefore predict the long-term chances of success. Each pattern is characterized by a different mix with regard to the "creativity of the innovation." In this instance, creativity is a measure of the number of ideas generated by each pattern as well as the variability of ideas (Glor, 2001b). These enable an understanding of key implementation issues associated with each pattern. Table 2.2 combines these two issues. Key factors associated with the implementation environment include ease of approval, ease of implementation, support provided to the innovators and central support provided to the innovation. Glor (2001b) concludes that there is a dilemma inherent in innovations based on the following observations.

The first six patterns (i.e., all except transformational and continuous) resulted in low creativity and minor impacts. For the remaining two, where high creativity and major impact occur, this happens in one of three ways: through the use of power from the center, through ongoing cumulative changes that produce a continuous impact, and through discontinuous large

Table 2.2 Implementation Consequences of Innovation Patterns

Pattern	Creativity of the Innovation		Ease of Approval	Implementation Environment		
	Number of Ideas	Variability of Ideas		Ease of Implementation	Support to Innovator	Central Support to Innovation
Reactive	Low	Low	High	High	Low	Low
Buy-in	Low	Low	High	High	Low	Low
Necessary	High	Medium to Low	High	Low	Low	High
Imposed	Low	Medium	Low	Low	Low	Low
Active	Low–Medium	Low	High	Low	Low	High
Proactive	Medium–High	Low	Low	Low organizationally, high locally	Low	Low
Transformational	High	High (from status quo); Low (between each other)	Medium–High	High	Medium	High
Continuous	High	All Kinds	High	High	High	High

Source: Glor, 2001b

leaps (Glor, 2001b). Glor's analysis, presented in abridged form in this chapter, highlights the need for a greater sense of innovation self-awareness by organizations wishing to transfer and customize innovations. Organizations that find this analysis useful are encouraged to review this study in full.[1]

Problem Types

According to Yapp (2005), the desire to find a new way to deal with a problem is a source of innovation. Thus, it is important to understand the nature of the problem that a group or team of organizations is dealing with. On this basis, he proposes a two-by-two matrix to facilitate the process of thinking about problems. The same two dimensions are used on both axes: whether an organization knows where it is going and whether the organization knows how to get there (see Figure 2.2). The implications of the Problem Types model are summarized below.

Operational management applies to an organization that knows where it is going and how to get there. In this case, a budget and resources are available and the innovator or team needs to get on with the task and be accountable for outputs. Too often, organizations mistakenly believe that they are in this quadrant and try to apply basic operational management without much success.

Concept creation is the task in cases where the organization does not know where it is going or how to get there. The focus is on finding a big new idea. Failure to get to the big idea results from organizations demanding project plans and cost implications too early in the process, hampering the need for staff to undergo iterative learning.

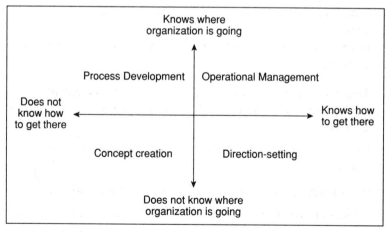

Figure 2.2   Problem Types
Source: Yapp, 2005

Direction-setting is needed in cases where the organization does not know where it is going but has some idea of how to get there. This is fairly common in the case of improvements that can be achieved by the application of new and emerging technologies, where the potential benefits are fairly obvious but integration into current strategy is not always clear.

Process development is required in cases where the organization knows where it is going but does not know how to get there. In this case, there is a need to clarify how the goals can be achieved (Yapp, 2005).

The Problem Types model highlights two important issues concerning the transfer of innovation. First, of all four problem types the last three depend on strong leadership to support imagination and concept creation to clarify direction and to design and develop processes to support improvement and innovation (Yapp, 2005). Second, the introduction of an outside idea can move from one of the last three quadrants to the first. When this point is reached, it becomes important to vet the new idea or improvement by applying operational management.

Barriers to Innovation

The proliferation of innovation awards programmes indicates that innovation is flourishing in the public sector. In many cases, however, innovation has not been able to prosper. White (2003), focusing on the South African experience, identifies a number of reasons why innovation fails to thrive, including: a) lack of access to resources for development and testing; b) lack of understanding about how to initiate innovation or what to do with new ideas or project possibilities that present themselves; c) inability to attract funding for long-term implementation; d) difficulties in finalizing arrangements for public-private partnerships; and e) inability to replicate and mainstream innovations. Albury (2005) identifies another set of barriers, including:

- Short-term planning and budget cycles of government (the move by governments to medium-term cycles in addition to annual cycles is positive);

- Poor skills in active risk or change management and a culture of risk-aversion;

- Few rewards or incentives to innovate or adopt innovations;

- Cultural or organizational constraints in using available technology;

- Over-reliance on a small pool of high performers within the organization as sources of innovation;

- Reluctance to close down failing programmes of innovation, i.e., what Hartley (2005) terms "exnovation"; and

- Delivery pressures and administrative burdens.

Opportunities for Innovation

In reviewing the innovation literature to enhance the operations of the Centre for Public Service Innovation (CPSI), White (2003) draws useful lessons for practitioners seeking to drive innovation. These include:

- **Innovation is contextual:** As such, the form and shape that it takes is largely dependent on circumstances and the prevailing needs of the time;

- **Innovation is a means of expression:** It arises to varying degrees in the presence of specific factors as well as specific combinations of these factors;

- **An environment for innovation can be created:** As a result of the patterns of innovation developed by Glor (2001b), this will require strategies that address how public servants are motivated, how the internal culture of the organization is shaped, and how the organization responds to external challenges;

- **Innovation does not need to wait for a challenge or a crisis:** Evidence on event-based innovation shows that an organization can induce conditions that inspire employees to initiate innovative solutions; and

- **Creative ideas arise by bringing together groups of people who produce intellectual capital:** An organization that is serious about innovation should enable and support communities of interest and networks that foster organic thought development.

Partnerships encourage successful innovation. Even where an individual has developed a solution, implementing or sustaining an innovation requires the buy-in of the department, access to internal or external funding, and in some instances the attention of policy-makers. In addition, innovations need tolerance for failure in order to prosper and grow. This requires a level of organizational maturity whereby a failure does not necessarily imply poor performance. Reflecting on two models for understanding the context within which innovation arises, White concludes that innovation occurs even without mechanisms to initiate it. Specific institutional mechanisms are required, however, to accelerate the speed at which innovation occurs as well as the frequency of occurrences (White, 2003).

Transfer of Improvements,
Good Practice and Innovation

The final section brings together some of the issues raised earlier with a view to highlighting suggestions that could help develop methodologies and tools to facilitate the transfer of improvements, good practice and innovation. These issues are explored only briefly as they are addressed in much greater detail in other chapters of this volume. For ease of reference, the word innovation will be used in this section to mean improvements and good practices as well as innovations. The Best Practices and Local Leadership Programme (BLP), a programme of UN-Habitat, proposes a useful definition of transfers, i.e., "a structured learning process based on knowledge derived from real-world experience together with the human expertise capable of transforming that knowledge into social action" (You and Kitio, 2005).

Innovation Self-Awareness

Innovation within the public sector is complex and challenging (White, 2003). As highlighted by Moore (2005) and Glor (2001a), ongoing systematic improvements can facilitate major changes. They also underscore that for constant innovation to occur, the public sector must evaluate its capacity to innovate and manage change. Innovation requires tools and techniques that can build the capacity of public officials to understand their own circumstances and to achieve greater self-awareness of innovation possibilities and constraints within their organizations. It may be more valuable to develop imperfect tools that improve public officials' abilities to design solutions that work in their contexts than it is to develop detailed tools that attempt to provide a unified model for transferring innovation.

Focus on the Problem

It is widely accepted that the starting point for many innovations is a process of drawing on the experiences of others. Public service institutions tend to find an innovation and look at how it can be transferred. Using the Problem Types model proposed by Yapp (2005), this may work when the task is operational management, i.e., when the organization knows where it is going and how to get there. For the remaining three problem types, however, it is more appropriate to start by defining the problem and then to search out approaches taken by others to solve a similar problem. These approaches could include groundbreaking innovations, incremental changes or even going back to basics. Box 2.1 provides an agenda that can assist in this task.

Box 2.1   Decision-Flow Agenda

- What is the service delivery/governance challenge that I am trying to solve?
- What have others done to address a similar challenge?
- What level of success was achieved through the implementation of the specific solution?
- What did it cost and how long did it take to implement?
- What were the prerequisites for the implementation (particularly legal, administrative, and financial in the original context)?
- Are there alternative solutions that could be proposed by employees of my organization or the recipients of services?

Source: Patel, 2006

The above does not suggest that organizations remain closed to alternative approaches and only seek them out once the problem has been defined. Continually reviewing alternative approaches provides organizations with new ways of looking at problems. In fact, the stimulus for many innovations has come from solutions that were only remotely associated with the organization's initial requirement. Reviewing solutions should be an ongoing organizational competence for innovation, together with strategic planning and future thinking.

Learning and Knowledge

As highlighted throughout this chapter, learning and knowledge-sharing lies at the heart of attempts to create innovative organizations and in transferring and adapting innovation. What is required, however, is a more detailed exploration of the process of knowledge-sharing and learning. Innovation suffers when the knowledge that an organization has amassed (either from its own practice or collated from elsewhere) is not able to be carried forward (Bhatta, 2003). Diffusion can fail because of impediments to the flow of information (whether engineered or inadvertent) or a mismatch between ideas generated in one context and the goals, capacity and incentives prevalent in another context (Donahue, 2005). Case studies, study visits and peer learning are traditional ways of sharing innovations. These, however, do not pay adequate attention to the key prerequisites that enabled the innovation (legal, economic, social and institutional issues) or to information on costs and resources required.

A conceptual model for thinking about learning and documentation as it applies to the transfer of good practices and innovation needs to look at information required for different purposes. For example, there are different information requirements for idea creation, action, and reflection/adaptation (as illustrated in Box 2.2). As argued by Galimberti (2005), "the idea behind a specific innovation is more important than the innovation itself" and, as such, the key to the successful transfer of new ideas is the "establishment of a knowledge network on innovation" (Galimberti, 2005). Establishing such a network requires looking at both the supply and demand sides for knowledge.

Box 2.2   Changing Learning and Information Requirements

Given the potential offered by new technology as well as the lack of government contact points in areas that were formally disadvantaged, South Africa identified integrated one-stop centers as having significant value. As part of the process of establishing these centers, the Citizen Assistance Service (SAC) initiated by the State of Bahia, in Brazil, was identified as an innovative model that offered value. A brief look at the changing information requirements of this project highlights some conclusions that could be of relevance to other examples.

There were three distinct phases of learning in localizing and customizing the SAC innovation to the South African context. The first was getting a thorough understanding of the project. At this stage, the project was identified through knowledge dissemination by UNDESA and this allowed the South Africans to assess whether it was relevant to their own context.

On this basis, the SAC concept was integrated into strategy documents and action plans. Using the high-level idea contained in the brief case study enabled the South African project team to generate enough buy-in into the concept. Then, the team began to implement the idea in South Africa. At this stage the project team needed to grapple with a range of institutional, financial and design issues. The brief case study was no longer useful in guiding the project team and it was felt that a physical visit to the project was required. Conducting the visit to Brazil was therefore the second phase of the learning journey. This study tour was facilitated by the United Nations Department of Economic and Social Affairs through one of its Regional Centres, the Bahia International Centre for Innovation and Exchange in Public Administration. Having the visit at this stage was important for two reasons. First, the people in charge of the implementation benefited from the study tour. Second, the project team could ask very specific questions that addressed real concerns and difficulties in adapting the SAC to South Africa.

The project is now entering a third phase whereby the requirements for information-sharing are ongoing and of a deeper technical nature. Learning strategies include ongoing communication for problem-solving and even technical assistance where people involved in the implementation process in Brazil work with the South African team.

Source: Patel, 2006

Using the Experiences of Others

How an existing experience is going to be used determines what information the receiving organization requires as well as how it interacts with the organization responsible for the original innovation. An established innovation or good practice can be of value to others in three ways:

- **Learning:** Learning takes place when the recipient organization has a good sense of the nature of the problem to which they seek a solution.

- **Benchmarking:** In this case, a country or agency looks at what it has in place or is implementing and compares this with other established practices. Benchmarking is mainly at the level of results or outputs and focuses on how the innovation has managed to achieve them.

- **Replication:** Based on careful assessment, a decision is made to introduce the innovation with minor modifications and customization. The assessment will include looking at the context, the nature of the innovation and its suitability.

The different uses of an experience are at the foundation of two decision matrices: Context-Risk (Figure 2.3) and Fit-Success (Figure 2.4). The Context-Risk matrix is more useful at the analytical and learning stage whereas Fit-Success is more useful at the implementation stage, particularly when committing time and resources. In terms of the Context-Risk matrix, replication requires strong context alignment and low risk. As there is never a case of complete context alignment and zero risk, replication will still require customization and modification.

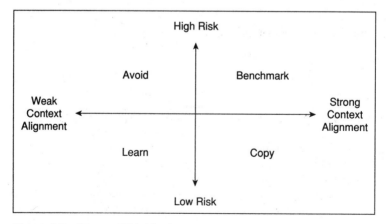

Figure 2.3   Content-Risk Matrix
Source: Patel, 2006

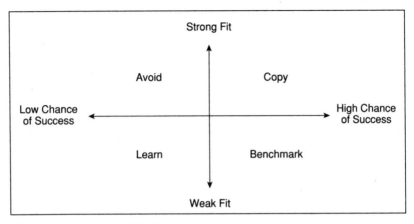

Figure 2.4   Success-Fit Matrix
Source: Patel, 2006

Another way of assessing how to use the experience of others is to plot chances of success with the fit of the innovation to the receiving organization and country. Determining fit and assessing success are not easy processes and will require the application of traditional tools of planning, i.e., cost-benefit analysis, institutional analysis, etc.

Concluding Remarks

The need to find ways that more effectively create public value in an environment of constant change has become an ongoing project for nation states and public services. Within this context, the global flow of ideas and approaches between and within countries has assumed greater importance over time. The ability to transform these ideas into successful action requires intervention on two fronts. The first is the development of tools and approaches for the assessment and transfer of innovation. The second is related to the enhancement of the innovation capacity of public service institutions. This chapter was a small contribution on both fronts.

Chapter 3

Learning from Best Practices in Public Management

A Methodological Approach

Juan Carlos Cortázar

The possibility of drawing lessons from a specific experience in public management and applying them fruitfully to other contexts and situations is doubtless one of the most important concerns within the field of public management (Rose, 1993). The nature of public management, as a field of knowledge that focuses on solving *practical questions* about managing public policy and organizations, shows how critical it is to transfer one country's or region's best practices to another. Clearly, the United Nations and other international organizations, including the Inter-American Development Bank, have an interest in fostering this type of learning, because it provides important leverage for promoting economic and social development. This chapter begins by proposing a concept of public and social management practices that makes it possible to learn from them. Then it briefly outlines the methodological approach that the Inter-American Development Bank's Social Development Institute (SDI) has been using to study social management practices in recent years.[1] We believe that this methodology makes a valuable contribution to understanding the development and operation of public management practices, as well as to producing lessons about best practices that can be applied rigorously in other contexts. The framework developed by the SDI is based on the approach developed during the past few years by Professor Michael Barzelay of the London School of Economics and Political Science.

Management Practices

We define management practices as methods that public managers use when dealing with problematic situations in the public sphere and/or the performance of public organizations and programmes which we expect produce certain valuable results.[2] We would like to clarify three aspects of this definition. First, we believe that management practices deal with situations that the actors involved see as *problems* rather than conditions; that is, as unsatisfactory social or organizational situations that call for change and for which change is possible through public policy or management intervention (Kingdon, 1995; Barzelay, 1998, p. 143).[3] Second, we believe that management practices are intended to create *publicly valuable* results. In this regard, we are taking the perspective offered by Moore (1998), which holds that public managers create public value when they produce solutions that effectively solve important problems for certain direct users, while at the same time responding to citizen aspirations and needs, which are generally articulated through a system of political deliberation. Third, we believe that management practices are *processes*. A process is a sequence of events that unfolds over time in context (Pettigrew, 1997, p. 338). The procedural nature of management practices demands that they be studied as a whole: in other words, holistically. A process can only be understood as a configuration of events that interact closely with the dynamic context in which they take place. On the contrary, focusing solely on the behavior of certain aspects (variables) of the process would impede the reconstruction of the complex interaction among actions, time and context (Ragin, 1987). It is precisely because of the need for a holistic perspective that case studies are an appropriate strategy for analysing management practices. They allow us to investigate contemporary phenomena within their real-life context and to consider their multiple dimensions and characteristics (Yin, 1994, p. 13).

Analysing the "Best" in Management Practices

When is a management practice "best"? Within the rich but not very systematic discussion of best practices in public management, we believe that it is possible to clarify what makes them best from at least two points of view. One is to ask to what extent the practice achieved the proposed results or whether it achieved better results than did other alternative practices. Another is to ask how the practice worked and also why it did or did not work well. The answer to the first question clearly pertains to evaluation of results and impact. The answer to the latter question, on the other hand, pertains to the area of *analysis of practices*. Our methodological approach clearly falls within the second area.

Given the focus on learning about best practices in a specific context in order to transfer lessons learned to another context at a later date, the reader may think that what is most important would be to evaluate the results actually obtained. But is it possible to apply what is learned about one practice in another context without a prior understanding of how and why the practice was able to develop and operate appropriately in its original context? We do not think so. Because the contexts are not equivalent, it does not make sense to merely copy a practice, which is why Bardach (2004) proposes to extrapolate it, that is, to apply our conclusions about a practice in its original context to a different context. To do this, it is essential to understand how and why the practice developed and operated in its original context so that we can subsequently clarify (taking into account the differences in the context that receives the practice) whether it will be able to operate in a different situation. Therefore, the causal reconstruction of the process that enabled it to operate well or not is essential in assessing whether it may be useful in a different context.[4] We do not think, however, that the evaluation of results and the analysis of practices run contrary to each other. Indeed, from the point of view of extrapolating what is learned about best practices in public management both are necessary since it does not make sense to extrapolate what has been learned from one context to another if the practice in question does not promise good results.[5] In short, the purpose of the methodological approach presented here is not to evaluate management practices from the standpoint of their impact on resolving social problems. Our interest, which is complementary, lies in explaining how these practices *develop* and *operate*, in order to draw relevant lessons regarding the practical problems that public managers confront in various contexts and situations.

The Function of Management Practices

In order to draw lessons from the analysis of practices that will be useful for the field of public and social management, certain generalizations must be made regarding the development and operation of the practices that managers perform on a daily basis. Given that such practices vary considerably and have different purposes, we must adopt a conceptual framework that distinguishes types of management practices according to whether theoretical questions about their development and operation can be applied. We propose to identify various types of practices, based on their function as part of the management process. Eugene Bardach suggests that the study of a management practice involves particular attention to that practice's function. Thus, he proposes that the functional characterization should operate as an abstract definition of the end or result that must be obtained by this practice within a functioning system (2000). If we understand management of a public policy or programme to be a functioning system, it then becomes possible to break down the management process into subgroups of practices designed to achieve different ends or results within the system. Figure 3.1 proposes a functional view of the public management process based on general management literature that focuses specifically on strategic management.

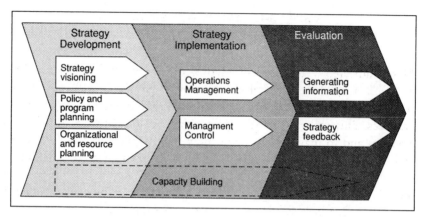

Figure 3.1   A Functional View of the Public Management Process
Source: Barzelay and Cortázar, 2004

If we take this functional point of view, we understand management practices as methods of action by which managers perform and become responsible for functions related to developing, implementing and evaluating strategy.[6] In performing these functions, managers confront the public and management problems to which we referred before.

The practices for developing strategies change or reproduce the basic value approaches that guide the operation of a policy or programme. Therefore, it is necessary to devise a strategic vision, plan the courses of action, and anticipate the organizational mechanisms and necessary resources for putting them into practice. The practices for implementation put the processes and planned activities into action, using the anticipated resources and organizational mechanisms to produce the goods and services to be delivered to users. This assumes that productive activities are carried out (operations management), as well as activities that regulate the proper functioning of the productive process (management control). Finally, evaluation practices make it possible to assess the public value that has been produced, and to contrast the results and impacts achieved with the proposed objectives. The intention is to provide feedback for the future performance of the remaining management functions. Moreover, while carrying out these three major types of practices, it is always necessary to develop essential organizational, technical or social capacities. A functional classification of these practices makes it possible to compare practices carried out in different contexts or situations, thus enabling us to arrive at "limited historical generalizations" (Ragin, 1987) regarding the development or operation of *types of management practices* in various contexts and situations. Clearly, the potential for generalization is valuable to those who are interested in transferring lessons about best management practices from one context to another.

A Methodological Approach
for Studying Management Practices

As we indicated in the previous section, our approach consists of analysing specific management experiences as a way of producing systematic knowledge about the development and operation of public and social management practices. This makes it possible to identify various types of management practices and to draw lessons about how they would apply in diverse contexts. The case studies that Stake (1995) terms instrumental are suitable for this proposal, because—rather than centering on the singularity or intrinsic special characteristics of a particular historical experience—they focus on the experience as a way to address a concern, question, or set of problems that goes beyond the specific experience in question. In an instrumental case study, the researchers have research interests that go beyond the intrinsic value of the experience, yet require an analysis of that experience in order to be able to produce knowledge and learning about questions or topics that are relevant to developing a field of knowledge, such as public and social management. Therefore, the methodological design must be appropriate for this type of case study. For that reason, our approach is based on two fundamental components: the narrative approach to the experience being studied, and an analysis of management practices that is simultaneously institutional and procedural.

A Narrative Approach

In order to rigorously produce and present empirical evidence about the public management experiences that we wish to investigate, we propose to use a narrative approach. A narrative approach is very sensitive to the components of a process, that is, the sequence of events that unfolds over time in context (Abbot, 2001, and Polkinghorne, 1988). Because we understand public and social management practices as processes, the narrative focus is suitable for our purposes of understanding and transferring lessons about best management practices. The narrative focus applied to the study of public and social management practices assumes that researchers will produce a narrative about the experience they would like to understand. The narrative is a way of representing a particular experience by organizing into a logical sequence the events of a process according to their contribution to the overall development of that process (Polkinghorne, 1988). A narrative is undoubtedly different from a chronology, whereby the actions and events are organized exclusively according to their position in the timeline. It is also different from a report, which offers a static view of specific events without including them within a coherent whole.

In order to produce a narrative that rigorously presents evidence about the experience under study, researchers have to consider the two major components of a narrative: the events and the plot. An event is a group of actions or occurrences organized according to their meaning within an overall experience. Clearly, events are not objective realities recorded by the researchers. They are conceptual constructions that researchers use to organize the flow of events according to the research interests that guide them. How do the researchers organize the events? They do so according to the meaning given to the events within the overall narrative, that is, according to the plot devised for the narrative. The plot is the medium through which specific events acquire coherence within the overall body of events, as one event is linked to another in order to show the development of the process under study. In other words, the plot is the organizing principle of the narrative, which identifies the meaning and role that each event plays within it. The plot transforms a chronology or list of events into a narrative by emphasizing and recognizing the contribution that certain events make to the development and result of the process (Polkinghorne, 1988).

Both the plot and the event are conceptual constructions produced by the researchers, based on their research interests and the theoretical framework being used. The plot is produced through a process similar to that used to produce the hypothesis: researchers propose an assumption that is contrasted with the events, and observe whether it is able to explain them. In this way, the researchers' assumptions interact with the evidence from the events, and this interaction constantly refines the plot until it is able to explain the events under study. A suitable organizational structure for the events in the narrative emerges only after various encounters between the events and the plot, during which the researchers try to adjust both components (Polkinghorne, 1988). The researchers do not try to impose a previously established plot on the events. Rather, the researchers engage in a dialectic process between the events and the organizing principle of the narrative, which is what reveals the events' meaning and enables them to be part of a single narrative.[7] The task of producing a narrative may seem relatively simple. Experience, however, shows us that it is not easy to narrate a management experience by trying to explain the process it followed. The flow of events to be considered tends to be vast and in constant motion, which usually results in the researchers becoming lost in a tangle of events, dates and actors. It is also easy for the researchers to lose sight of what they want to explain, which creates tremendous confusion with respect to which events are truly relevant to the research and which are not. In addition, the narratives frequently end by focusing more on the social or political context of the management processes than on the management process itself.

The narrative structure is a simple instrument that allows the researchers to get an overview of the body of experience under study and at the same time focus on its specific components. This tool enables the researchers to approach three tasks in a systematic, iterative way: a) formulate the different types of events that comprise the experience being studied; b) establish significant relationships among these events, based on the overall plot of the narrative; and c) propose relevant research questions. The first task consists of breaking down the complex experience under study and organizing the dynamic flow of its constituent events into events of a particular type. A first step is to identify those events that are directly related to the management process or practice under study. We call this body of events the episode under study (see Figure 3.2). The episode then comprises a body of events whose development and interconnection are precisely what the researcher wishes to explain. We previously pointed out, however, that in order to explain a process, it is necessary to refer to the context in which that process took place. Our interest lies not in explaining the context but in explaining the episode, yet in order to do this we must take the context into account. Following that, a second step consists of identifying those events that were not part of the episode but had a significant influence on it or were themselves influenced by it. We will designate as previous events (PE) those events that occurred prior to the episode and had significant influence on it. Contemporaneous events (CE) are events that also influenced the episode but occurred at the same time. We will designate as related events (RE) those events that were influenced by the episode and occurred at the same time. Finally, later events (LE) are events that were influenced by the episode but took place after it. Figure 3.2 shows the various types of events that we propose to formulate, organized along a time line. The arrows indicate the direction in which the influence flows among them.

A second task that the narrative structure may help researchers carry out consists of identifying relationships among the events (and even among the sub-events within an event). As noted in the previous paragraph, establishing

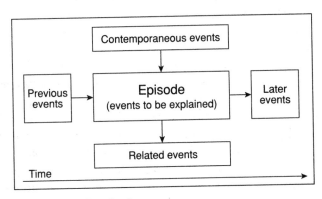

Figure 3.2 Narrative Structure
Source: Barzelay and Cortázar, 2004

how the various events affected each other is a fundamental step in the task of explaining a narrative. Given that it is possible to establish numerous connections among the events under consideration, researchers must identify the relationships that seem most significant in order to explain the process. What can be used as a guide for selecting which relationships among the events are the most relevant? It depends on the researchers' own conception of the process's narrative thread, that is, the plot.

The third task is that of formulating good research questions. As we indicated before, our focus is on developing instrumental case studies, in which studying a specific experience is useful because it enables us to respond to a concern, question or set of problems that goes beyond the experience in question and also helps develop the field of knowledge about public and social management. If this is the purpose, the first type of question (which, to follow convention, we will designate as Type A) must refer not to the specific experience we wish to study, but to the theoretical topic we wish to address by studying this experience (see Figure 3.3). If the theoretical topic and its related question(s) transcend the specific experience under study, it then becomes possible to address the question by conducting a comparative study of various specific experiences. As we already noted, by conducting a systematic comparison of various experiences revealed by developing or using a particular type of management practice, it is possible to develop what Ragin (1987) calls limited historical generalizations. These enable us to arrive at general arguments that are applicable to a specific type of management practice (be it strategic development, implementation, or evaluation of public policies and programmes). Clearly, then, these questions are important not only for comparing various specific management experiences, but also for transferring (extrapolating) what is learned based on how one or more specific experiences are understood.

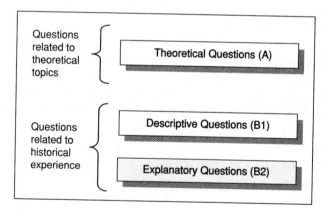

Figure 3.3 Types of Research Questions
Source: Barzelay and Cortázar, 2004

A second type of research question (which we will call Type B) must refer to the actual experience under study. Some of these questions will have a more descriptive character, investigating what events or sub-events took place, who initiated them, and how they developed. Other questions are more explanatory in character, investigating why the events occurred in the way they did. We will call the first B1 and the second B2. It is important to remember that the questions regarding the experience under study must do more than explain what happened within the experience. (If this direction were followed, the study would be intrinsic, not instrumental.) Rather, they must also indirectly address the theoretical questions related to the topic being researched (Type A questions). Suitable coordination between these two types of questions is critical to conducting a successful instrumental case study: as Figure 3.3 suggests, the Type B questions serve as support for the Type A questions.

In summary, the process of identifying events and the relationships among them—that is, building a narrative structure—enables researchers to devise relevant questions about the experience. These questions must be consistent with the questions related to the researchers' theoretical topic. With a good narrative structure and relevant questions, researchers can design and carry out the field work necessary for producing information that will enable them to produce a rich narrative about the management experience under study.

Analysis of Management Practices

A narrative that presents empirical evidence about the management experience under study makes it possible to analyse both the development and the operation of the management practices, examining them in the context of the types of management functions to which we referred in the previous section.

We previously defined management practices as processes, that is, as a sequence of actions that unfold over time in context (Pettigrew, 1997, p. 338). Consequently, the objective of focusing on the analysis of practices is to achieve a dynamic understanding of the actions performed by a management function. This demands that we take into account how such actions interact with the institutional framework and their overall context, given that they are influenced by it but exercise influence over it as well. Because we focus both on the procedural nature of the practices and the institutional framework in which they unfold, we call this focus institutional processualism (Barzelay and Gallego, 2005).

The actions that make up a practice result in part from the design and planning efforts made by those who initiated the practice in question. The actors use this design to guide their actions, taking into account the ideas, rules, tasks and approaches that it involves. The direction that these actions actually take, however, does not fully correspond to that envisioned in the design, because the actors are themselves immersed in a group of specific institutional frame-works and immediate events that we will call a situation in motion. These events force the actors to refocus, revise or modify the direction planned for the actions, in order to make them viable and therefore enable the actors to achieve the planned ends or results. In turn, the situation in motion develops according to the actions carried out by the actors, but also according to a broader context involving a vast combination of political, institutional, ideo-logical and public-policy factors. In order to understand how the actions com-prising a management practice develop and operate, it is necessary to analyse the complex interaction among the four components we have indicated: the actions, the design of the practice, the situation in motion, and the context. Figure 3.4 proposes a conceptual model for analysing and comprehending this interaction.

As the diagram shows, the actions occur within the situation in motion (which becomes their immediate context). The design of the practice has a powerful influence on the actions (1), prescribing the direction they take and their operation. That said, the actions are also influenced by the situation in motion, which forces the actors to modify the plan for their activities, under-take actions not planned in the design, or not to undertake certain previously established actions (2). The situation is also affected by changes that result from the actions undertaken (3). In this way, a complex interaction is established between the actions and the situation in motion, which transforms both pro-gressively and simultaneously. No doubt the interaction between these two components is influenced by the overall context (4), which in turn is modified to some extent by the changes in the situation in motion (5). Moreover, the experience of modifying the course of action leads the actors to provide feed-back regarding the design of the practice (6), which is also modified by the

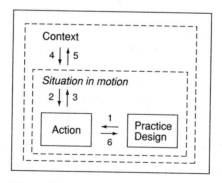

Figure 3.4   Institutional Process Analysis
of Management Practices
Source: Barzelay and Cortázar, 2004

process of implementing the practice.[8] By using the proposed analytical model, researchers can offer an explanation for the direction taken by the practice under study or its operation. Doing so—as we shall see—they will be in a position to clarify the potential for transferring (extrapolating) what is learned from the experience under study to different contexts and situations.

Concluding Remarks:
Proposing Lessons to be Transferred

Based on the type of explanation offered by the institutional processual framework, researchers may arrive at conclusions that provide an understanding of how a particular practice performs one or a number of management functions. The conclusions are explanatory arguments related to the theoretical topic that guides the research, which means that they must contribute to address Type A questions. But the researchers' conclusions, which are based on the study of a specific experience, cannot fully address Type A questions. That would require analysis and comparison of various experiences related to the underlying theoretical topic. In accordance with our overall goals, when analysing a practice the following elements should be considered:

- The trajectory exhibited by the practice in performing one or a number of functions; that is, the path of progress, consolidation, crisis, stagnation or recovery that the practice has taken; and/or

- The operation of the practice, that is, the functioning that has enabled it to suitably perform the management functions for which it was designed, or that has impeded it from doing so.

- The objective of the kind of research we propose, however, is to produce knowledge that will be useful not only in the academic world (as can happen with the conclusions from a study) but also for the effective practice of public and social management. By proposing *lessons*, researchers should thus offer *practical arguments* concerning what public and social managers can do to enable a management practice to function and develop in a way that is suitable for its work environment. The fundamental task of the conclusions is to offer an understanding of the experience and topic under study, while that of the lessons is to offer *recommendations* regarding how to improve the performance and development of management practices. The lessons enable public managers to learn by understanding a particular experience, which allows them to *extrapolate* from the specific context in which the experience occurred to the context in which they work.

In summary, the work of researchers must end by proposing a set of conclusions and lessons. The conclusions consist of explanatory statements regarding the aspects of the practice (direction or operation) that interest researchers from a theoretical point of view. These statements are analytical in character and offer answers to questions such as "why did it happen" or "how did it happen." They are mainly targeted at an academic audience and are based on conceptual frameworks that are connected to various fields of knowledge. The lessons are statements that are proactive in character and have to do with what social and public managers can do to carry out the practice under study in a suitable way within its immediate context. Thus, lessons have a prescriptive character and offer answers to questions such as "why do it" and "how to do it." They are clearly intended for an audience of people working in the field (managers) and are based on different perspectives with regard to management knowledge. This would include, for example, the body of propositions produced by a particular school or trend of thought regarding management that encompasses the appropriate performance of a management function or the body of propositions that the SDI has produced regarding the role of social managers in Latin America and the Caribbean.

A good set of conclusions and lessons should thus prevent the mechanical replication of management practices that are considered "successful" or "good," opening up for us the more fruitful and complex field of *management and organizational learning,* to which we have tried to contribute in the preceding pages.

PART TWO

Transferability and Adaptation of Innovations and Best Practices

Chapter 4

Diffusion and Adoption of Innovations
A Development Perspective

Donald E. Klingner

Innovation requires processes of adaptation, anticipation and openness to change. Change provides the opportunity to achieve new and different approaches to governance and development. Replicating a successful practice in public administration requires government capacity to overcome barriers to innovation diffusion and adoption. Among other things, capacity implies a favourable policy environment, leadership support, stakeholder involvement, adequate funding and an appropriate transfer plan. It also implies the capacity of the organization to constantly adapt to changing circumstances both internal and external. Not long ago, an assumption existed that the technology, administrative systems, policies, and processes of developed countries were inherently better than those of developing nations and could be simply transplanted abroad with little or no adaptation. Structural, contextual, and other considerations that impeded the successful transplantation of the above were often overlooked with all too obvious results. This chapter examines and critiques the utility of best practices in development administration. It establishes the importance of innovation to governance in general and development administration and implementation in particular; explores the relationships among organizational learning, knowledge management, and innovation diffusion and adoption; and presents guidelines for the adoption of innovations.

Diffusion of Innovation in a Development Context

After World War II, the success of the Marshall Plan at rebuilding Europe and a global interest in economic development for least developed countries (LDCs) led to the creation of a new field of study and practice (Seely, 2003).

Development administration emerged as an amalgam of development economics and public administration aimed at improving economic conditions and governance systems in LDCs by replicating Western concepts and techniques. It generally presumed that the laws, policies, structures and procedures in developed Western countries were superior to those indigenous to developing countries because of their greater rationality, efficiency and relationship to democratic ideals (Rostow, 1971; Fredland, 2000). Their diffusion and adoption was considered both automatic (given the "evolutionary superiority" of reforms introduced by Western consultants) and purposive since Western lenders often mandated administrative reforms as a condition of continued credit (Adamolekun, 1999). However, this traditional notion of economic development has by and large been abandoned because it did not achieve the desired results (Heady, 1998). It did not decrease the gap between rich and poor nations, nor reduce global poverty (United Nations Development Programme, 1998). One scholar clearly summarizes this failure as reported by United Nations:

> The United Nations' Human Development Report, 1999, notes that between 1980 and 1996 gross national product (GNP) per capita declined in no less than fifty-nine countries. It reports that the income gap between the fifth of the world's population living in the richest countries, and the fifth in the poorest widened from 30 to 1 in 1960 to 74 to 1 in 1997.
>
> —Hoogvelt, 2001, p. xiii.

In response to the now discredited traditional approach to development administration, three analytically separate yet interdependent approaches have emerged: comparative administration, development management, and international public management. *Comparative administration* began as a social science discipline intent on correcting the two fundamental intellectual flaws of traditional development administration: ethnocentrism and ignorance (Riggs, 1968; Klingner and Washington, 2000). Its adherents are primarily scholars and researchers who believe that traditional development administration failed because development administrators tended to automatically and erroneously assume that Western techniques and structures were superior to their indigenous counterparts (Fredland, 2000); and because they were unaware of the unique historical factors that had led to the success of Western management techniques (Riggs, 1968). In contrast, comparative administration is the more value-neutral study of public administrative systems across countries and cultures (Riggs, 1980 and 1991; Rutgers, 1998). It examines alternative governance models as outcomes of cultural contexts (historical, economic, political and social), and evaluates the relative capacity of administrative systems based on underlying trends and conditions (Peters, 1988; Van Wart and Cayer, 1990; Heady, 1996). Its intellectual antecedents are political science and sociology. Its primary purpose is to compare alternative systems in order to understand how they have evolved and why they function as they do, rather than to evaluate them, describe their shortcomings or prescribe recommendations to improve them. The sub-field of *development management*, which encompasses the management of particular development efforts as well as the indigenous process of development, broadened in the 1990s.

All over the world, demands for development and democratization through *international public management* have pressured governments to make good policy decisions and use scarce resources effectively (Dilulio, Garvey and Kettl, 1993). Government capacity—or the lack thereof—is perhaps the most obvious factor affecting perceptions of governance (Klingner, Nalbandian and Romzek, 2002). In developed countries, governance usually means *maintaining* government's ability to coordinate policy, gather information, deliver services through multiple (often non-governmental) partners, and replace hierarchical bureaucracies with more flexible mechanisms for managing indirect government (Brudney, O'Toole and Rainey, 2000; Kettl, 2002). In developing countries, it probably means *establishing* government's ability to deliver vital public services (through core administrative functions like budgeting, human resource management and programme evaluation) while simultaneously focusing on more fundamental changes (e.g., citizen participation, decentralization, innovation and entrepreneurial leadership; Kettl, 1997) necessary for effective political systems.

Innovation Diffusion and Adoption

The term "innovation diffusion and adoption" describes the spread of new products, values, policies or processes beyond the locus of their original success. If viewed purposively, this spread can be described as both organizational learning and knowledge management (Sabet and Klingner, 1993). If viewed descriptively, innovation diffusion and adoption includes the intended and unintended consequences of complex and symbiotic relationships between producers and consumers that occur across organizations (Schrage, 2004), countries (Beatty, 2003) and regions (Mavhunga, 2003).

Innovation diffusion and adoption, organizational learning and knowledge management can also be viewed as aspects of public policy and administration, in that they relate conceptually to policy-makers' ability or willingness to learn from exogenous experience, and adapt it as best practice public policy or administration in new settings (Rich, 1997). From within the framework of public policy, Knott and Wildavsky (1980) scale the use of university research in government agencies using six stages: reception, cognition, discussion, reference, effort, and influence. They point out that their scale is cumulative in nature, each stage building on the previous one. This scale is described in Table 4.1.

Lester and Stewart (1996) classify different types of factors that researchers suggest affect knowledge utilization by public officials. The first category is

Table 4.1   Stages of Knowledge Utilization

1. Reception	"I received the university research pertinent to my work."
2. Cognition	"I read and understood the university research that I received."
3. Discussion	"I participated in meetings for discussion and popularization of the aforementioned university research."
4. Reference	"I cited university research studies as references in my own professional reports or documents."
5. Effort (adoption)	"I made efforts to favour the use of university research results."
6. Influence	"University research results influenced decision in my administrative unit."

Source: Adapted from Knott and Wildavsky, 1980; cited in Landry, Lamari and Amara, 2003, p. 194

technical factors—primarily the availability of information and the appropriate rational/technical organizational resources to use it (Julnes and Holzer, 2001, p. 695). Second, *contextual factors* influence the appropriate use of information. This includes politics (Julnes and Holzer, 2001) and organizational culture (Julnes and Holzer, 2001; Landry, Lamari and Amara, 2001; Landry, Lamari and Amara, 2003). Third, *human factors* are important. Several researchers have found that such individual attributes as professionalism (Sabet and Klingner, 1993), education (Landry, Lamari and Amara, 2003), type of position education (Landry, Lamari and Amara, 2003), and decision-making style (Webber, 1987; Webber, 1992) influence organizational policy adoption decisions. These findings are summarized in Table 4.2.

Guidelines for Adoption of Innovations

Within this general history and context, we may present several key guidelines that apply to successful adoption of innovations. These guidelines relate to time orientation; sovereignty and capacity; empowerment and accountability; and adaptability, flexibility and incrementalism.

Time orientation: The length of time required to adopt innovations depends upon the nature of the objective and the circumstances. Within these contexts, it is important to remember that successful innovation diffusion and adoption, even under favourable circumstances, usually takes years, and often decades. Thus, organizational commitment to policy objectives almost always extends beyond the involvement of any one programme director or elected official.

Sovereignty and capacity: In many cases, diffusion and adoption of best practice innovations takes place in fragile states where either sovereignty or

Table 4.2.   Summary of Explanatory Variables for Innovation Diffusion and Adoption

Political	Organizational	Social/Interaction	Technical	Human
• Internal interest groups[a] • External interest groups[a] • Unions[a]	• Risk taking[a] • Attitudes toward change[a] • Focus on users' needs[b] • Users' context[b] • Work relevance[b] • Policy relevance[b] • Federal/State agency[b] • Number of employees[b]	• Adaptation of products[b] • Acquisition efforts[b] • Linkage mechanisms[b]	• Goal orientation[a] • Information[a] • Resources[a] • Qualitative products[b] • Quantitative products[b] • Theoretical products[b] • Focus on advancement of scholarly knowledge[b]	• Graduate studies[b] • Function of position[b] • Decision-making style[c]

Source: Adapted from Landry, Lamari and Amara, 2003
[a]Julnes and Holzer, 2001
[b]Landry et al., 2003
[c]Webber, 1987

capacity may be problematic. Creating new national sovereignty is different from, and harder than, building government capacity (Pollitt and Bouchaert, 2000; Kettl, 2002).

Empowerment and accountability: Successful organizational change relates to empowerment and accountability (Blair, 2000; World Bank, 2002). Empowerment is the increased ability of the poor to make political, social or economic choices, and to act on those choices (Kabeer, 1999; Narayan, 1999). This ties with accountability because it relates to results-oriented and customer-focused applications of New Public Management to managing development programmes (Hirschman, 1999). The key to both is to develop a multi-lateral development assistance plan and a multi-national, multi-institutional framework for financing development over a long period of time (Brinkerhoff and Coston, 1999), all supported by a participative and client-centered development management process (Dale, 2003; Goldspink and Kay, 2003).

Adaptability, flexibility and incrementalism: Innovation diffusion and adoption occur within the context of complex systems that are increasingly difficult to model with any accuracy. The more a policy decision is imbued with values, the less applicable the rational method, where inputs cannot be quantified as accurately. Another duality to ponder is that of theory versus practice. While theoreticians look for an all-encompassing model, a practitioner might find other processes to be more efficacious. Borins (1998) and others (Jones and Kettl, 2003) argue that although problems seem similar across nations, types of solutions that are effective in one public sector context may not succeed in another political, economic or social setting. Lindblom (1959/1979) assesses rational models of the decisional processes of government; rejects the notion that most decisions are made by rational, total-information processes; posits that the policy-making process is defined by a series of incremental decisions as a response to short-term political goals; and argues that decision-making is much more dependent on events and circumstances than the will of policy-makers. More to the point, however, the composition of the critical mass of stakeholders is specific to the context and may not be generalized for application elsewhere beyond a few observations. In this respect, Bardach (2000) and Barzelay and Campbell (2003) argue that smart practice development programme administration is not so much a toolkit of ideal practices, but an operational guideline that emphasizes reducing mechanisms and factors that inhibit adaptation to contingency. Particularly in high security risk environments, adaptation to contingency is essential—without it little or no progress will be obtained and the policy context will be appropriately characterized as fraught with "wicked problems" that by definition defy resolution (Roberts, 2000).

Concluding Remarks

Adoption of innovations is best viewed as a complex process involving organizational learning and knowledge management. Because these are heavily influenced by contextual variables, this is an indigenous process rather than one of transfer and absorption. It is best viewed as some smart practice guidelines rather than as a uniform toolkit. Diffusion and adoption of smart practice innovations in governance, public policy and public administration depend on a clear understanding of the mechanisms involved in transfer, and the contextual variables that affect its successful implementation. Such guidelines should include provisions for allowing a sufficiently long-range time orientation to accommodate changes in organizational culture and learning. Another important component would be to recognize and respond to the need to build either (or both) national sovereignty or government capacity, depending on the context as well as focus on empowerment and accountability as key indicators of local buy-in. Moreover, maintaining an adaptable, flexible and incremental approach to innovation diffusion and adoption—including use of smart practice rather than best practice public policy and administration should also be part of the guidelines. Finally, consideration should be given to ensure sustainability through a "balanced scorecard" approach that assesses the impact of proposed innovations along a range of economic, political, social, cultural, environmental and administrative criteria.

Chapter 5

Transferability of Governance Institutions

The Ombudsman and the Independent Commission against Corruption

Ladipo Adamolekun

This chapter reviews the experience of transferring two governance institutions on a worldwide scale—Sweden's Ombudsman and Hong Kong Special Administrative Region of China's Independent Commission against Corruption (ICAC). After an overview of the spread of the two institutions, attention is drawn to the factors that have made the transfer possible, including a distinction between formal institutional transfers and their effective functioning in different countries. The key messages of the chapter are summarized in a concluding section.

Transferability of Governance Institutions

One of the issues that featured prominently in the literature on the decolonization process in Africa and Asia from the late 1940s through the 1960s was the extent to which political and administrative institutions were successfully transferred from former colonizing powers to the successor states. In Africa, the emergence of one-party and military governments in place of democratic governmental systems during the first two post-independence decades led many observers to conclude that transfer efforts had failed. Some observers noted that only the forms of government were transferred without the values that underpinned them. Attention was also drawn to the inconsistencies and contradictions between the autocratic and arbitrary features in the operation of the colonial political and administrative institutions and the democratic institutions that were supposed to have replaced them during the decolonization process. The steady commitment of a few countries in Africa (for example, Botswana and Mauritius) and India in Asia to the maintenance and nurturing of demo-cratic governmental institutions were the exceptions.

Notwithstanding this poor record, the worldwide democratization wave of the early 1990s was accompanied by an ambitious programme of transfer of governance institutions in both the developing and transitional countries of Central and Eastern Europe. It is also noteworthy that throughout the entire period under review (from the late 1940s to the 1990s) there was an ongoing transfer of governance institutions among the developed countries. For exam-ple, the ombudsman system spread from Sweden to the Scandinavian countries and then to a significant number of Western democracies from the 1950s through the 1960s to the 1970s and beyond. Regarding the transfer of gover-nance institutions to developing and transition countries, there were two influ-ences at work: one was internal while the other was external. The internal influence was strongest in countries where reform-minded political leaders pushed for the promotion of good governance as a key issue during electoral contests and proceeded to establish appropriate governance institutions after winning elections.

The external influence was determined by donor governments making the promotion of good governance one of the conditions for providing develop-ment assistance. The most explicit case is the political conditionality of the European Union requiring transitional countries to introduce specific gover-nance institutions, including both an ombudsman and an anticorruption body. In Africa, some countries have introduced the two institutions at the instiga-tion of external donors and with their support and that of others that intro-duced them on their own initiative. These countries have also benefited from the support of external donors in financing the cost of running the institu-tions.[1] Only a few countries in Southern and Northern Africa have introduced the institutions on their own initiative, and they are financing the cost of run-ning them with only minimal external support.

Below, we examine the evidence of the spread of the two institutions. This is followed by a discussion of the factors that have been conducive to their suc-cessful transfer.

Ensuring the Rights of Citizens Worldwide[2]

When the first ombudsman was appointed in Sweden in 1810, his responsibil-ity was to review the acts of government officials and administrators in order to ensure that citizens' rights were properly protected. Arising from this origi-nal role definition, an ombudsman is commonly referred to in the literature on the subject as "the citizens' defender." A summary of the worldwide spread of the ombudsman system is provided in Table 5.1.

Table 5.1 Diffusion of the Ombudsman Institution

Years	1809–1959	1960–1969	1970–1981	1982–2005	Total
Number of countries	3	5	19	93	120
Number of African countries	..	2[a]	4	20	26

Source: Adamolekun, 2005

[a] The two pioneer countries in Africa are Mauritius and Tanzania.

Although the ombudsman institution was first established in Sweden during the first decade of the nineteenth century, it did not spread to other Scandinavian countries until the twentieth century: Finland (1919), Denmark (1955) and Norway (1962). By 1981, the institution had spread to some Commonwealth and European countries, including France (1973), New Zealand (1962), Nigeria (1975), Spain (1981), Tanzania (1968) and the United Kingdom (1967). There were also ombudsman institutions at the provincial and state/regional levels of government in a few other countries, notably Australia, Canada and the United States.

The rapid expansion in the number of countries with ombudsman institutions coincided with the worldwide democratization wave of the 1990s. In addition to the significant number of African countries highlighted in Table 6.1, the institution was also established in many Latin American and Asian countries, as well as to transition countries in Central and Eastern Europe. It is also important to mention the creation by the European Union of an ombudsman under the Maastricht Treaty. The first European ombudsman was appointed in 1995. An important variation on the ombudsman theme that also originated in Sweden is the appointment of ombudsmen with responsibility for specific aspects of governance. By 1980, Sweden had created four specialized ombudsmen: an anti-trust ombudsman (1954), a consumer ombudsman (1970), a press ombudsman and an equality ombudsman (1980). By 2004, the most common specialized areas of governance assigned to ombudsmen in many countries were protection of human (or civil) rights and consumer protection. Some other countries have also appointed ombudsmen to protect citizens against maladministration in specific areas of governmental administration, such as local government administration, police administration and health management (for example, the United Kingdom).

It is also worth mentioning that the International Ombudsman Institute (IOI), created in the 1970s, has promoted the spread of the ombudsman institution. IOI operates as an international network with continental and sub-networks; its primary objective is to promote collaboration among member countries and experts. Currently, the Institute has over 100 member countries. It has produced a handbook for the training of newly appointed ombudsmen worldwide. Another factor that has helped the spread of the institution is the demonstration effect provided by regional and language-based associations of ombudsmen. Two examples that involve African countries are the African Ombudsman Association (2003) and the Association of Francophone Ombudsmen and Mediators (AOMF) established in 2001. The third annual conference of the AOMF was held in Tunisia in 2003, attended by 63 ombudsmen and mediators.

Focusing on Anti-Corruption

Although corrupt practices have characterized the operation of governmental institutions since their emergence in modern times,[3] the idea of creating specialized institutions to combat the problem is a recent phenomenon that many observers date from the establishment of an Independent Commission against Corruption (ICAC) in Hong Kong in 1974.[4] ICAC's success in achieving a significant reduction in corrupt practices within a short time turned it into a model for countries that sought to tackle the problem. As in the case of the ombudsman, it spread first within its geographical zone, notably Singapore and the state of New South Wales in Australia. Its spread to developing and transition countries did not occur until the 1990s for reasons stated in the Introduction. Taking sub-Saharan Africa as an example, the majority of anticorruption agencies in the region were created between the early 1990s and the present. In all, about 30 African countries have created anticorruption bodies, including Benin, Botswana, Burkina Faso, Cameroon, Ethiopia, Kenya, Malawi, Mali, Nigeria, Sierra Leone, South Africa, Tunisia, Uganda, United Republic of Tanzania and Zambia. A significant number of transition countries have also created similar bodies, modeled, in varying degrees, on the ICAC example.[5] By 2005, anticorruption agencies have been created in almost every transition country in Central and Eastern Europe, in most countries in Asia, and in a significant number of countries in Latin America. The author is familiar with the phenomenon of teams from some newly established anticorruption agencies in Africa undertaking study tours to ICAC and one or two other anticorruption agencies in Asia during the 1990s. In some countries in Africa and elsewhere, retired officials who had held key positions in ICAC have provided either hands-on assistance (for example, as pioneer directors of anticorruption agencies, such as in Botswana for some years in the 1990s) or advisory inputs (for example, in Kenya in 1999).

Transparency International—an international Non-Governmental Organization (NGO) that acts as a pressure group to get countries to adopt and implement strategies for tackling corruption—has contributed to the spread of anticorruption agencies worldwide, beginning with its biannual anticorruption conferences started in 1997.[6] ICAC is almost always highlighted as a model anticorruption agency during these conferences. One sub-regional organization in Africa that has contributed to the spread and strengthening of anticorruption agencies among its member countries is the Southern Africa Development Community (SADC). In 2003, the SADC secretariat developed a common strategic plan for improving the functioning of anticorruption agencies in the Community's member countries.

Because combating corruption is an integral part of enforcing accountability, some countries have sought to include the fight against corruption in the mandate of an ombudsman. In the two cases known to the writer (India in the 1980s and Namibia from the 1990s to 2003), the idea of institutional fusion was eventually abandoned and a distinct anticorruption agency was created. Without question, the transferability record (in terms of diffusion) of the two institutions summarized in the preceding paragraphs is very strong. The next section focuses on the factors that have made transfer possible, including a distinction between formal institutional transfers and their effective functioning in the different countries.

Factors Conducive to Successful Institutional Transfers

The first point to make is that the two governance institutions are widely acknowledged as being relevant to the promotion of good governance. The ombudsman ("the citizens' defender") makes government accountable by allowing the citizen to be a direct actor. An anticorruption agency focuses on a complex problem that is at the heart of enforcing accountability in political and economic management and in social life. The obvious difference between these two institutions, which is also reflected in the degree to which transfer can be described as a success, is the specificity of the mission of the ombudsman in contrast to an anticorruption agency that is just one part of many interventions required to tackle the problem of corruption. This point is further elaborated below.

Transferring the Ombudsman Institution

The combination of a sharply focused mandate (mentioned above) and the simplicity and flexibility of the institutional arrangement has contributed significantly to the spread of the ombudsman. The ombudsman could be a single individual (with support staff) or a multi-person commission—a three-person commission in unitary Tanzania and a commission of 37 in the Nigerian federal system.[7] Strong evidence of the flexibility of the institution is the fact that some countries appoint as an ombudsman individuals with a legal background while in other countries the ombudsman could be a former civil servant or an educator. Ombudsmen can also be members of either the legislative or the executive branches. In some countries, an executive ombudsman is obliged to submit his/her annual report to the legislature, thus bridging what some would see as a divide. Of course, there is a conceptual distinction between a legislative and an executive ombudsman to the extent that the former is also seen as contributing to the idea of holding the executive accountable to the legislature. (In parliamentary systems where the ombudsman is regarded as a "parliamentary commissioner," citizens route their complaints to the commissioner through their members of parliament.) Both the legislative and the executive ombudsman can serve effectively as a citizens' defender, depending on the exact definition of his/her mission, the statute governing his/her operations and the resources made available (Adamolekun, 1984). Because the ombudsman is required to deal directly with citizens, the use of local languages facilitates such contacts in multilingual societies. Usually, the ombudsman's office would include staff that understands the main local languages either to take telephone calls from citizens who speak those languages or to translate complaints written in local languages. This is another dimension of the flexibility of the ombudsman.[8]

Notwithstanding the salient factors that have contributed to the transfer of the institution, the extent to which ombudsman institutions have functioned effectively or performed satisfactorily has varied significantly in both developed and developing countries. For example, in parliamentary systems where the Member of Parliament (MP) "filter" is the norm, overall success in the performance of the parliamentary commissioner (ombudsman) would depend on the dedication of individual MPs. This might not be a good practice for young democracies to imitate given the trust gap between parliamentarians and their constituents in many of these countries. In many young democracies, a fundamental problem of governance is poorly performing governmental administrative institutions. Since the majority of complaints are against the errors of omission and commission by the officials of these institutions, it follows that the level of effectiveness of ombudsmen in obtaining redress for citizens would be low (Burbridge, 1974).[9] Existing studies of ombudsman institutions also show that the degree of autonomy enjoyed by ombudsmen and the resources made available to them have a significant impact on their performance. While the countries that adopt the institution are generally familiar with these factors for success (thanks to study tours and easy access to information through the internet), internalizing them and making them operational has lagged behind the speed of formal adoption. The obvious explanation is that progress toward deepening democratic political culture and strengthening administrative capacity happens over a longer timeframe and, of necessity, countries will improve at different paces. Consequently, a systematic comparison of the performance of ombudsman institutions in the developing and transition countries where they have been created since the early 1990s is certain to reveal major differences in the levels of their performance.

Transferring Anticorruption Agencies

To a great extent, it would be correct to assert that strong evidence of how corruption undermines development efforts (including the effectiveness of development assistance) is at the root of serious international attention to tackling the problem since the mid-1990s. And it is also true that the undisputed success of Hong Kong Special Administrative Region of China's ICAC as an instrument for achieving significant reduction in corrupt practices within a relatively short time, and its continued usefulness in containing the problem, has turned it into a model anticorruption agency. Unlike the specificity of the ombudsman role as citizens' defender, however, the complexity of the problem of corruption (economic, political and social) means that anticorruption agencies are only part of several instruments that need to be coordinated to tackle the problem. Again, as in the case of the ombudsman institution, study tours and the internet have made it possible for interested countries to learn about the factors for success in countries where anticorruption agencies perform well.

Existing studies on the functioning of anticorruption agencies confirm the same observation made with respect to ombudsman institutions: success in rapid spread is one thing and effective functioning of the agencies is another. And because both institutions focus on aspects related to the enforcement of accountability in public governance, the performance of anticorruption agencies would be enhanced in countries that make progress toward deepening democratic political culture and strengthening administrative capacity. As already mentioned, progress would be over a long timeframe and countries will, of necessity, improve at different paces. A critical dimension to the effective functioning of anticorruption agencies that is absent from the ombudsman role is the critical importance of simultaneous progress in the case of economic reforms that would remove opportunities for rent-seeking, and the introduction and implementation of specific administrative reforms such as open and competitive procurement procedures and practices, as well as strong controls in auditing and financial management. It would also make sense to mention the need to develop and implement an ethics reform agenda. A comparison of the findings contained in studies about how anticorruption agencies have performed in Africa, Asia, Latin America and transition countries of Central and Eastern Europe would shed considerable light on the points underlined in this chapter.

Concluding Remarks

As a conclusion to this chapter, I would like to highlight three key messages. First, there is an important distinction between an impressive transferability record of the governance institutions considered here in terms of spread on the one hand and the actual functioning of the institutions in the countries that have adopted them on the other. In both cases, implementation progress has been slow compared to the rapid speed of spread, especially during the last two decades or so. The second message, closely connected to the first, is that the factors for "success" in spread are different in significant respects from the factors for ensuring effective functioning (that is, implementation) of the governance institutions in the different countries concerned. The third message is the need for comparative research on the actual performance of the two selected governance institutions that have been widely transferred across continents, to focus on improving the enforcement of public accountability. The results of the proposed research (to be undertaken by multiple teams) would enrich the understanding of both scholars and practitioners of existing and possible approaches and methodologies for the assessment and transfer of successful governance institutions.

Chapter 6

Dissemination of Innovations
Learning from Sub-National Awards Programmes in Brazil

Marta Ferreira Santos Farah

This chapter contributes to the discussion of innovation and dissemination in government and the public sector using examples from innovative programmes promoted by sub-national governments (primarily municipalities) in Brazil. It focuses on lessons learned about innovation and dissemination processes that extend beyond national and local contexts. It also emphasizes the importance of staying linked to the real world, that is, the national and local realities that necessarily play a role in any consideration of practice versus theory.

The examples presented here are based on experiences gathered by the Public Management and Citizenship Program, created in Brazil in 1996 by the Ford Foundation and the Fundação Getulio Vargas (FGV-EAESP), a school of business and public administration in São Paulo, with the support of the National Bank for Economic and Social Development (BNDES). Focusing on sub-national governments in Brazil, the Program awards innovations in public administration and policy that improve citizens' lives; it also helps to disseminate these innovative initiatives. Now in its tenth year, the Public Management and Citizenship Program has a database of almost 9,000 innovative programmes from different regions of Brazil that emphasize sectors such as health, education, children and youth services, public security, gender, local development, poverty alleviation, environment, budgeting, e-government and digital inclusion. These programmes, 180 of which have received awards, provide insights into: a) government and public sector innovation trends in Brazil in recent decades; b) the innovation process in government and the public sector; and c) the dissemination or diffusion of innovative experiences.

Innovation in Brazil: A Historical Perspective

Innovation is not a new phenomenon in government and the public sector. Although innovations occur all the time, it is possible to identify specific periods in which some countries have experienced an "innovation trend." These innovation trends are associated mainly with important changes in the role and functions of the state at all levels. Secondarily, innovation trends are also affected by technological advances, which provide opportunities for changing how public services are delivered and the public sector is organized. In Brazil, for instance, there is a parallel between a first period of innovation beginning in the 1930s and a more recent period beginning in the 1980s. Before the 1930s the state or federal government came to assume a new role, i.e., initiator of national development. The thirties and following decades in Brazil were marked by institutional innovation and new practices in public administration. The federal government created new institutions and procedures in an attempt to overcome traditional patrimonial practices and to build a public sector that represented all Brazilians, not only the elite.

The more recent innovation trend in Brazil began in the 1980s, with the democratization of the country after some 20 years of dictatorship. In the democratization process, the sub-national governments—mainly the municipalities—became the new face of Brazilian federalism, which was institutionalized in the Constitution of 1988. The new role of municipalities coincided with a more comprehensive phenomenon that affected many countries: globalization and the reduced role of federal or central governments, followed by an emphasis on decentralization and local government. Changes in the role of the state include a redefinition of *what* government does as well as *how* government implements its policies and programmes. Usually, these changes are associated with a critical view about government processes in a previous period.

In Brazil, the periods of innovation mentioned above were oriented to new ways of "doing" business in government and public administration. During the first period, some of the critical issues related to government processes included: a) the need to fight against patrimonial tendencies in public policies and public administration; b) the excessive decentralization and fragmentation of the Brazilian government at the beginning of the twentieth century and the absence of a national agenda; and c) the need to bring modern principles of impersonality to public administration. During the second period, in the last decades of the twentieth century, the main criticisms to the Brazilian government and public administration included:

- Excessive centralization of the federal government;
- Non democratic formulation and implementation of public policies and programmes;

- Exclusion of important segments of the Brazilian population from access to public services and social policies;
- Unresponsiveness of public policies, programmes and governmental agencies to citizens' needs;
- Lack of social control and evaluation; and
- Lack of accountability.

As a result of this second period, we are witnessing changes in what government does and how it does it. As occurred during the 1930s, innovation and new institutions are on the rise. Two main factors stimulated Brazil's more recent movement of innovation: The *democratization process*, which in Brazil led to greater decentralization, and the *fiscal crisis*. After two decades of dictatorship, Brazil adopted a democratic regime in the 1980s. Redemocratization included a process of decentralization followed by innovations in public policies and programmes. With the Constitution of 1988, municipalities assumed new responsibilities. At the same time, there was strong demand for a new way to define and implement public policy—which should include democratic and participative mechanisms. The main actors and institutions that influenced the innovation process were national. Since the late 1980s, the fiscal crisis affected the capacity of the state to meet society's demands, especially in the area of social policy. Severe limitations on financial resources led to the introduction of government and public sector innovations intended to make policies more efficient. The actors and institutions that influenced fiscally prompted innovations were national and external.

Since the 1980s, the new role of municipalities in Brazil has required new institutions and practices. On the one hand, this innovation movement includes new policies and programmes (innovations in the products of government and the public sector). On the other, it involves innovation in the decision-making process—or the formulation of public policies—and in the process of implementation. Despite the specificity of the Brazilian context, one can identify similar trends in other countries, especially within Latin America. Other regions can also benefit from analysing the relationship between innovation and the role of the state. For example, it could be useful for countries whose main challenge is not linked to changes in the role of the State, but rather to efforts to build national or local governments in scenarios of post-independence, post-war or post-civil war, or the redefinition of national boundaries and identities. The following sections present some ideas about the process of innovation dissemination. These ideas were developed by looking at local innovation experiences in Brazil and their dissemination from one local entity to another in recent decades (Farah, 2004; Sugiyama, 2004; Farah, 2004b).

Dissemination of Innovations

The present chapter uses an innovation-dissemination framework, which suggests an active selection and incorporation of ideas and practices, to explore the mechanisms by which innovations spread. To understand why dissemination occurs and why, often, it does not, the following dimensions must be considered.

Intrinsic Characteristics of the Innovation

The first element that makes an innovation a potential candidate for dissemination, i.e., one of several alternatives considered by other countries or local entities, is its capacity to provide an effective answer to new problems or its capacity to answer an old problem in a new and successful way. The innovation, as described earlier in this chapter, can be a new policy or programme or a new procedure. In the case of Brazil, we can choose from a diverse group of innovative initiatives at the local level.

A first example is the Rose Woman House (Programa Casa Rosa Mulher) from the municipality of Rio Branco in the state of Acre in the Amazon region. This 1996 programme provides a "shelter house" for girls and women who are victims of sexual or domestic violence or are at risk for prostitution and drug trafficking; importantly, Rose Woman House also offers integrated services including psychological and legal support, health assistance, education, and job opportunities. As well as being one of the first programmes in Brazil with this focus and the first in the Amazon region, Rose Woman House was the first to address this newly recognized social problem with an integrated approach for reintegrating these women into the community. A second example is the Save Time programme (Poupatempo), created in 1996 by the state of São Paulo. Through this initiative, the government brought together more than 30 public services and established a new paradigm for delivering services to the public, guaranteeing efficiency, quality of services and quality of interaction between public servants and citizens. The innovation in this case is essentially one of public service procedure. The perception that the innovation is able to address relevant issues is as important as its capacity to solve problems. For some authors, the perception is even more important than the innovation's capacity to solve problems (Weyland, 2004; Melo, 2004).

The Nature of the Problem Addressed

A second characteristic relevant to the analysis of innovation transferability is the nature of the problem addressed. If the problem addressed by the innovation is present in other local entities or countries, the innovation has the potential to be useful to these places. Another example from Brazil is the School

Grant programme (Bolsa-Escola), which was implemented simultaneously in the mid 1990s in the Federal District and Campinas, in the state of São Paulo (where it was called Renda Mínima, or Minimum Grant). Bolsa-Escola and Renda Minima are minimum grant programmes for low-income families that have children attending elementary school (every child between 7 and 14 must attend school). The programme is based on the assumption that long-term poverty eradication requires a break in the cycle that keeps multiple generations of families in poverty. Ensuring that children of poor families have access to education is one tool to help break the poverty cycle. This innovation was disseminated to many municipalities throughout the country, initially on a horizontal basis from one municipality to another, through networks established by political parties, politicians, public servants and professional communities linked to the social policies sphere. Then, the federal government adopted the innovation as a federal programme implemented and managed at the municipal level, which helped to strengthen the process of dissemination. Currently, the programme is spreading to other countries seeking to eradicate poverty, mainly in Latin America.

Perceptions of the Relevance of the Problem Addressed

The existence of a similar problem in other communities is not sufficient to stimulate the transfer of an innovation. Other locations will adopt the innovation only if social and political actors in those places see the problem it addresses as a relevant one that deserves an answer and a search for new responses. This point highlights the importance of the "recipient" countries' internal elements in the transference of innovations. The definition of a problem as a social and political issue in these countries is a pre-condition for the adoption of innovative initiatives in the public sector. In the example of the Bolsa-Escola programme, transference from one municipality to another was based on the selection of poverty and elementary education as relevant social and political issues by the local entities that adopted and adapted it. The same process occurs in its transference to other Latin American countries: in 2000, the Tenth Ibero-American Summit of Heads of State and of Government in Panama recommended the adoption of Bolsa-Escola by Latin American countries, which suggests that both the problem and the innovation were considered relevant.

Convergence of Policy Agendas

It is also important to consider the innovation in relation to the public policy agendas of other countries. If the problems addressed by the innovation, as well as *how* it addresses them, are convergent with the policy agendas of the local entities to which the innovation can potentially be disseminated, the innovation has a chance of being chosen by those involved in public policy formulation and implementation. The influence of local agendas on the process of dissemination cannot be overestimated. If the local agendas do not emphasize a specific issue, the intrinsic characteristics of the innovation are irrelevant: the recipient entity does not *want* it, because it is not a political and social issue in this context. Local policy agendas are shaped by a number of factors, including:

- Structural factors, such as globalization and fiscal crisis, which create specific and new challenges to governments;
- The influence of external agencies, especially financial agencies by placing conditions on access to funding as well as disseminating ideas in international forums; and
- The influence of social and political internal actors, such as politicians, bureaucrats, experts, partisans and social movements.

The literature on innovation dissemination in contemporary public policy emphasizes the influence of external actors, especially external financial agencies, through two primary mechanisms: a) coercive mechanisms, such as putting conditions on access to financial support (Melo, 2004; Cooke, 2004; Weyland, 2004); and b) knowledge mechanisms, through the agencies' influence on the diffusion of ideas by "academia," epistemic communities and through international public policy networks (Melo, 2004). Other analysts, however, believe that this emphasis on external actors has minimized endogenous factors such as the influence of internal actors on public policy (Farah, 2004; Melo, 2004; Weyland, 2004).

Cooke (2004) underscores the influence the World Bank had on the incorporation of the participatory management paradigm into the policy agendas of many developing countries. In a recent article about administration development and management, Cooke defends the thesis that developing country agendas and thinking are controlled externally by institutions of the developed world, such as the World Bank. Such a perspective minimizes the active presence of internal actors, who have the capacity to influence the construction of a national agenda (Farah, 2004) and who interact with external actors. In the specific case of the participatory paradigm, since the 1970s, strong social movements have demanded citizen participation in public policy as an important component of democratization.

Access to Information About Innovations

The dissemination of innovations also depends on the existence of information. Information can be disseminated through a direct relationship between the innovator and other countries or municipalities, following the paths of similarity (Weyland, 2004) and generally based on a previously established relationship between the local entities. Usually, the diffusion of information presupposes the existence of networks. Networks can be composed of specific participants, including bureaucrats and experts, political parties, NGOs, academic working groups, and awards that publicize innovative governmental programmes—or a combination of different actors (Sugiyama, 2004). It is important to disseminate information about innovative programmes from organizations outside the mainstream that are not known beyond their own borders. Both internal and external actors who are interested in broadening the spectrum of policy alternatives for countries and municipalities can play an active role in achieving this type of dissemination.

In discussing the influence of external actors, Weyland encourages the direct transmission of information by third parties, preferring it to the "promotion of models." He considers as third parties entities from outside the innovating and recipient locations. Analysing the diffusion of policy-reform models in Latin America, he considers that the presence of third parties—mainly international organizations—has the advantage of broadening the spectrum of innovation alternatives by bringing experiences from countries not in direct contact with the recipient country. At the same time, however, this indirect transmission can "push" uniform solutions that are not appropriate for specific contexts (Weyland, 2004, p. 14). Some analysts emphasize information above all other factors and perceive the diffusion or dissemination of innovative policies as a strictly cognitive issue, "the diffusion of policies being seen as just a problem of making information available" (Melo, 2004, p. 4). In fact, information is an important but incomplete part of the dissemination process, as suggested by the analysis of the internal diffusion of innovative programmes in Brazil, such as the Bolsa-Escola and Participatory Budgeting (Sugiyama, 2004; Wampler, 2004). One must also consider the active role of political actors in the recipient countries and local communities (Melo, 2004; Sugiyama, 2004).

Selection of Innovations by Policy-Makers

Social and political actors in recipient countries or municipalities play an active role in the dissemination of innovations in government and the public sector. This means that the conditions mentioned above are important, but cannot sufficiently explain the transference of innovations or the lack thereof. Internal policy-makers *act* to incorporate an innovation—they can also reject or ignore it—and thereby influence the process of dissemination. Melo highlights this active role:

The adoption of an innovation, in this perspective, is seen not as an automatic mechanism, as in many studies about diffusion, but rather as the result of a choice. In fact, domestic actors in the process of diffusion search actively for public policy models and also use external actors in a strategic way. In many cases, as pointed out by Ikenberry (1990), these actors engage actively in the search for external solutions, as these can help executive bureaucracies to implement policies they defend.

—Melo, 2004, p. 5[1]

In turn, these actors are conditioned by institutional and structural factors; they do not interact in a vacuum (Melo, 2004).

Decision-Making Constraints at the Local Level

The various dimensions of dissemination pointed out above affect the choices that internal actors make. Similarly, the following institutional and structural constraints on decisions at the recipient's level are also relevant.

Political incentives: The adoption of an innovation can be influenced by political incentives linked to its potential in terms of political benefit. This perspective is favoured by the rational choice approach, which emphasizes the competitive scenario of opposing parties and politicians in a democracy (Walker, 1969; *apud* Sugiyama, 2004). The innovation will be adopted if it is seen as a means to re-election. Recent studies on the dissemination of innovative programmes in Brazil (School Grant, Participatory Budgeting and Family Health) suggest that this contributes to dissemination, but not as an isolated factor (Wampler, 2004; Sugiyama, 2004).

Financial incentives: Similar to political incentives, the existence of financial incentives can affect the decision to adopt an innovation. In Brazil, the choice of some innovations at the local level is influenced by financial transfers made by the federal government and linked to local implementation of specific programmes (Sugiyama, 2004). For instance, the Family Health programme emerged as a local initiative and later transformed into a federal programme conditioned on voluntary adoption by municipalities, but dependent on access to federal resources. Another example is qualification programmes for elementary school teachers, strongly stimulated in Brazil by the creation of FUNDEF;[2] this federal fund for the development of elementary schools stipulates that 60% of the resources transferred to each local entity must be spent on courses for teachers. The same influence is seen when international agencies pressure countries to adopt certain innovations; that is, the agencies establish the adoption of some "social technique" as a condition for accessing financial resources. The influence of this kind of incentive is important, but as with the others, it does not act alone. In addition, financial incentives are affected by the level of dependency (or autonomy) of the recipient local entity on external financial resources.

Institutional framework: The adoption of an innovation can be facilitated by the existence of an institutional framework that opens the way for the implementation of new procedures, institutions and practices. In Brazil, the institutional framework established at the federal level by the Constitution of 1988 is an important stimulus for many local innovative programmes and institutions. One example is the adoption of innovative programmes for children and adolescents that are supported and facilitated by a national regulation called the Children and Adolescents Code. This phenomenon also occurs in the health-care sector, where innovative initiatives, including preventive care and the integration of different levels of attention, are strongly linked to a federal policy framework, the Unique Health System (Sistema Único de Saúde—SUS). An institutional framework can be seen as an incentive to the adoption of innovations consistent with the framework's main principles. In other cases, the absence of an adequate institutional framework can be an obstacle to the adoption of innovations. For instance, innovations cannot be transferred at the local level in some countries, if the municipality in these recipient countries does not have the institutional autonomy to assume responsibility for public policies.

Structural characteristics of the recipient entity: The adoption of an innovation depends on the administrative capacity to "make it work" and to adapt it to local conditions. For instance, some innovations require the recipient local entity to have financial capacity. If the innovation is costly to execute, it restricts the spectrum of countries or entities that can select it and adapt it to their needs without external financial support. The same can be said about the technical and administrative requirements of an innovation. An example from Brazil is the Digital Municipality programme in Piraí in the state of Rio de Janeiro. Over the course of three years, this programme developed a communications and information system that connects municipal governmental agencies, every school and public library, community internet access centers, urban companies and rural producers. The municipality offered citizens 25,000 free emails, more than Piraí's total population. Although this was not an especially expensive programme, its dissemination required a certain degree of local technical and administrative capacity, as well as some financial capacity.

Path dependency: The selection of an innovation in the field of public administration is also affected by previous policy patterns in a specific country. This means that, in the same country or municipality, hypothetically it can be more difficult to incorporate an innovation in the educational policy, for instance, rather than in healthcare, due to the history of these different sectors in that specific country.

Ideology: The adoption (or rejection) of an innovation by politicians can also be affected by ideological alternatives. A recent study about the dissemination of innovative programmes in Brazil (Sugiyama, 2004) suggests that the ideological affiliation of politicians and administrators linked to a government "limit the range of policy choices and priorities" (ibid., p. 15). This conclusion is important because it explicitly introduces a political component into the decision-making process linked to the adoption of an innovation.

Concluding Remarks

Although there have been innovations in the public sector throughout history, the past few decades have seen a distinct trend of innovative initiatives linked to the redefined role of the state in contemporary society. This recent innovation trend is associated with a new role for sub-national government that facilitates new policies, institutions and practices. Governments who face increasingly complex challenges look for solutions that have worked in other contexts, that is, with the expectation that it is possible to learn from others without having to "reinvent the wheel." Knowing what innovations have been developed by different countries is important as a starting point for the dissemination process. Conditions that contribute to the dissemination of innovative initiatives include the intrinsic characteristics of the innovation as well as many other factors related to the countries and local entities that can potentially adopt it. These include cognitive elements, such as the transmission of ideas and information; structural elements, such as external conditioning to change and the countries' financial and administrative characteristics; and institutional and political elements.

Given the complexity of the dissemination process, it is important to recognize that the influence of external actors is limited. Nevertheless, external actors can play a useful role by broadening the spectrum of available initiatives. The three main challenges in this area are: a) including in the information process all initiatives identified as innovative by governments and public administrations themselves and by an expanded network of NGOs, local policy networks, awards programmes and others; b) translating initiatives into more languages to broaden their accessibility; and c) strengthening autonomous networks, which permit the exchange of information and evaluation (technical and political) of innovations by all interested parties.

Chapter 7

Adaptation of Best Practices
The Experience of the Institute of Public Administration of Canada

Joseph Galimberti

This chapter discusses best practices and innovation drawing on some of the experiences of the Institute of Public Administration of Canada (IPAC). It distinguishes between best practices and innovation. Best practices are considered successful government practices that have evolved over a long period of time and continue to evolve by adjusting to changing situations and contexts, as opposed to an innovation, which is a new practice or experience. Under best practice, the chapter describes the successful adaptation of Canadian best practices by other jurisdictions in Lithuania and China, and suggests how the success of these transfers can best be measured. The section on innovation uses material from the IPAC Award for Innovative Management established in 1990. It describes the award, looks at how innovations spread, and relates some successful adaptations of Canadian innovations to other jurisdictions. The chapter concludes that the idea behind a specific innovation is more important than the innovation itself and calls for the establishment of a knowledge network of innovation to facilitate the successful transfer of new ideas.

The Lithuania-Canada Government Reform Project

In the late 1960s and early 70s, the Canadian federal and provincial governments began developing decision-making systems that integrated priority setting, policy-making, budgeting and planning systems. These systems, which have evolved over time and are still changing, are designed to help governments deliver their mandates and keep their promises (Bernier, Brownsey and Howlett, 2005).

Lithuania sought assistance from the Ontario government and IPAC in 1997. Its euphoria over independence was dissipating. Per capita incomes had fallen to two-thirds of pre-independence levels. Income inequality was rising. Governments lasted, on average, one year. Lithuania's Baltic cousin, Estonia, had been selected for fast-tracking in the EU; Lithuania had not. Cabinet meetings went on and on, dealing mainly with trivial matters and not priorities. The Ministry of Finance avoided requests for new funding of priorities and continued funding questionable programmes. The Prime Minister indicated that he did not know what happened with Cabinet decisions. The government of Lithuania was trying to avoid the excessive centrism it had experienced with Moscow but instead had retreated too far in the other direction, preventing the delivery of the government mandate. Lithuania sought help from the Ontario government and IPAC as a result of an Ontario government employee of Lithuanian origin having taken a leave of absence to work for the Lithuanian government in the early 1990s.

The resulting reform project was funded by the Canadian International Development Agency (CIDA), with IPAC as Executing Agency. By the fall of 2000 an integrated policy and fiscal planning system was in place, which subsequent governments have retained, institutionalized and improved. The following four key features define the system (Evans, 2005, pp. 9–10):

A **strategic planning committee** (similar to Ontario's Policy and Priorities Board), chaired by the prime minister, to oversee the priority-setting and budget process and review major policy issues.

A **strategic planning system** (modeled on Ontario's business planning system), including:

- A government priority-setting exercise in advance of the budget process; five strategic policy priorities were approved by the Cabinet in spring 2000;
- Preparation of individual ministry strategic plans to reflect the government's strategic priorities and ministry service-delivery priorities; and
- Public release of ministry strategic plans and agreement in future to report publicly results achieved versus the plans' targets.

An **integrated fiscal-planning system,** including:

- A macroeconomic plan developed in tandem with the priority-setting exercise; the plan included realistic aggregate revenue, expenditure and deficit targets, as well as a fiscal envelope to fund the strategic priorities;
- Individual ministry budget ceilings accompanying the budget circular's instructions to ministries and agencies; and
- Instructions requiring ministries to demonstrate how their budget requests supported the government's strategic priorities.

A **restructured Chancellery** to reflect a shift in focus from an administrative to a strategic/analytic organization. This included the creation of a Strategic Planning Unit to coordinate the planning process and liaise with the Ministry of Finance.

The project employed a practitioner-to-practitioner methodology. In the course of the project, 24 senior Ontario government officials, including the Secretary to the Cabinet, traveled to Lithuania to work with their counterparts in central and line agencies. A total of 23 Lithuanian political and administrative officials visited Canada. In the process, countless workshops were delivered and documents exchanged. Does this constitute a best practice? Gordon Evans, who was secured as the lead consultant to the project shortly after leaving his post as Assistant Secretary to the Cabinet in Ontario's Executive Council, notes:

> To the degree that the Ontario-Lithuania collaboration is representative, it infers that interactions between two public services, with one assuming a mentor role, gravitate towards a best practices model. We export the system as it should be, warts removed. This arises not from any desire to over-claim, but from the practical consideration that less than stellar moments should not be emulated.
>
> —Evans, 2005, p. 32

What was perhaps an exemplary practice for the Ontario government was a substantive reform for Lithuania. But how do we measure the success of a government reform such as this? Are there measures that capture the quality of policy management (Evans, 2005. p. 11)? Evans looked for measures that capture the quality of policy management at the Organisation for Economic Co-operation and Development (OECD) and New Zealand, UK and Canadian Cabinet Offices without finding any practical performance measures. As a result, Evans, along with Nick Manning of the World Bank, devised a figure indicating stages of executive policy unreliability along with a summary of policy unreliability indicators (see Figure 7.1).

Using these indicators, Evans found that Lithuania had made significant progress from 1998 to 2002 on all stages. It should be noted that projects like the Lithuanian reform generate tools that are adapted from the assisting country; for example, Cabinet Memoranda Manuals, Minister's Handbook and impact assessment guidelines that could also prove to be valuable resources for other jurisdictions.

Public Policy Options Project China-Canada

The Public Policy Options Project (PPOP) is a responsive project designed to provide quick, targeted assistance to specific policy needs identified by the

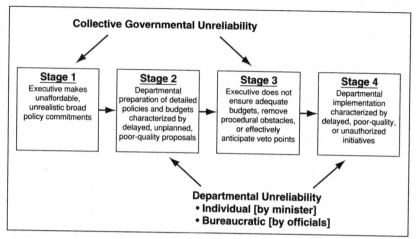

Figure 7.1   Stages of Executive Policy Unreliability
Source: Evans, 2005, p. 16

Chinese government. Each approved project must represent a policy priority of the Chinese government. Since the inception of the project in 1996, about 50 sub-projects have been completed. This project, funded by the Canadian International Development Agency (CIDA) is co-managed by IPAC and the Conference Board of Canada, whose role is to link Canadian exemplary practices and policies to the policy priorities of the Chinese government. Each of these projects has matched senior management and policy staff from Chinese state and provincial governments, research institutes and academics with senior Canadian executives from the public, private, academic and NGO sectors.

For each of the sub-projects, policy reports are prepared and submitted to higher authorities, in most instances the State Council headed by the Premier. Policy recommendations are based on field studies in China, Canadian expert presentations in Canada and China, study tours to Canada, Canadian participation in conferences and seminars in China and exchanges of actual policy documents (e.g., draft legislation).

Examples of Results

The following are examples (federal, provincial and municipal) of the results of three of these sub-projects (Fortier-Balogh and Lemaire, 2002, p. 26).

Support for Small and Medium Sized Entrepreneurs (SMEs) with partner Industry Canada. China recognizes that SMEs are a key engine of economic growth as well as a major source of job creation, the latter being particularly important because state-owned enterprises are dismissing large numbers of workers. The resultant policy document relied heavily on Canadian practices. The policy document issued by the State Council focused on: improving the legal and regulatory framework for the growth of SMEs; identifying appropriate ways for different levels of government to provide assistance to SMEs through credit guarantee programmes (83 municipal SME credit guarantee centers have been established); and the organization of community-based public-private support networks for SME development involving local banks, municipal government, educational organizations and community organizations.

Occupational Safety Regulations with partner Ontario Ministry of Labour. The State Planning Council of China enacted an Occupational Safety Law as a result of the partnership with the Government of Ontario. Among other things, the new law integrates Canadian concepts such as the notion of workplace training in occupational safety, self monitoring guidelines and better accident reporting.

Reforming Urban Utilities, The Shanghai Municipal Waterworks and the Cities of Vancouver and Toronto. The Shanghai Municipality and Shanghai People's Congress approved the Framework on Restructuring the Shanghai Running Water Utility, authorizing a two-stage process. The first stage eliminated operational losses and reduced government subsidies through the establishment of appropriate water rates. The second stage included the elimination of investment losses and the streamlining of operations. The Shanghai water system is used as a model for other Chinese cities.

The Lithuanian and Chinese examples show exemplary Canadian practices which have evolved over a long period and which have been successfully adapted by other countries. In these cases and all other experiences of IPAC, the adaptation of best practices has been on a responsive basis, with the recipient country looking to improve its policies or practices by learning from the experiences of others. Because the methodology is based on a practitioner-to-practitioner relationship, mentor jurisdictions will remove the flaws in their current practices and advise on difficulties that the receiving jurisdiction can expect in implementation. The process is both capacity-building and knowledge-transferring.

IPAC and the Award for Innovative Management

IPAC's experience with innovation is based on its Award for Innovative Management, currently sponsored by IBM Canada, KPMG and the Public Service Commission of Canada. The Award was launched in 1990 to enhance the image of the public sector; to recognize organizations and individuals for creative and innovative ways of doing things; to identify and publicize success stories in the public sector worthy of emulation; and to foster innovation. Table 7.1 outlines the annual themes and the number of submissions generated by each theme.

Table 7.1   Awards for Innovative Management

Year	Theme	Number
1990	Service to the Public	57
1991	Empowerment	68
1992	Partnership Management	103
1993	Better with Less	114
1994	Re-shaping Government	111
1995	Making Diversity Work	82
1996	Mastering Change	115
1997	Connecting Citizens and Government	93
1998	Doing Things Differently	153
1999	Measurement and Recognition	49
2000	Collaboration: New Approaches to Policy and Management	106
2001	Developing the Public Service of Tomorrow	104
2002	Outside-In: Changing Government to Meet Client Needs	133
2003	In the Know: Managing Knowledge	95
2004	Pulling Against Gravity	98
2005	Public Service Without Borders	69

Source: Institute of Public Administration of Canada, 2005
(*www.ipac.ca/awards/innovation/index.html*)

The annual theme is based on the IPAC agenda, which is determined in part by a biennial survey of deputy ministers (heads of departments) of the federal and provincial governments as well as chief administrative officers of major municipalities, asking them to identify the key challenges facing public sector organizations over the next few years.[1]

Annual submissions are reviewed by a jury composed of five distinguished members of the public administration community. The jury selects seven or eight finalists for interview and determines the winners. The awards are given at the Institute's annual conference attended by about 500 participants. The final seven or eight entries are featured in IPAC's magazine, Public Sector Management, and the executive summaries with contact points of all submissions can be found in the IPAC website's database.

Once identified as an innovation that works and with risk diminished, innovations can spread rather quickly and are often improved or expanded. The first gold winner of the IPAC Award in 1990 was Accès Montréal, a one-stop shop. Montreal reported that, as a result of winning the Award, it received about 250 enquiries and visits from interested governments from across Canada and around the world. New one-stop shops appeared soon after and IPAC had many submissions to its Award, posing difficulties to respective juries as to how significantly different a one-stop shop must be before it can be considered innovative.

The most recent one-stop shop to receive an IPAC Innovative Award was Victoria Connects (bronze award) in 2001 because it was multi-jurisdictional. It is an innovative storefront operation run by three levels of government, including 14 municipalities, to provide business start-up and development services, including business registration, licensing and tax payments and business development support (including information, training, workshops and counseling). The services are delivered electronically, by phone, or in person at the Victoria Connects Centre (Bernier, 2001).

How Do Innovations Spread?

The most important factor in disseminating innovation is recognition; awards programmes play a very important role. Recognition gets publicity and leads to presentations at conferences and seminars. Submissions provide an inside look at public sector management and become valuable research documents that stimulate research and writings on topics relevant to the work of senior managers and the teaching of public administration. Books using material from the IPAC Awards have appeared in Canada, the United States and Germany, and articles have been published in Canadian and international journals. The New Public Organization, by Kernaghan, Marson and Borins, published by IPAC in late 1999 and containing several chapters on the Awards, has been reprinted twice in both French and English. Professors use submissions in various ways as teaching tools in their classes. IPAC jury members, who are very senior public servants, are forced, as members of the jury, to take a careful look at submissions. They often circulate submissions of interest to their colleagues for attention. This is one of the reasons the jury is rotated on an annual basis.

Dr. Sandford Borins conducted a formal study of the spread of innovations from the top 90 submissions, identified by pre-screeners, from the first five years of the IPAC Award 1990–94. He found that:

- About 88% of the awards have received some media attention;
- 61% of the sample has been replicated; and
- 21% has been replicated internationally; Borins cites the Ontario Office of Seniors Issues (silver award, 1992), sensitizing people to the difficulties of the aged, has been adopted in the U.S., Japan and New Zealand; the Canadian ultraviolet index (1994 submission) has been adopted in the U.S., UK, Denmark and Germany; and the United Nations has adopted Parks Canada's accessibility programme (1992 submission) as the basis of its international standard (Kernaghan, Marson and Borins, 1999, p. 89).

Examples of International Replication

In relation to international replication, IPAC has been directly involved with several countries. In the CIDA-funded Canada-South Africa Provincial Twinning Project where Canadian provinces were twinned with South African provinces, Service New Brunswick helped establish in a remote community in the Province of Limpopo a one-stop shop for social services, business and a health nursing station. In a black township near Kimberley, Northern Cape, Service New Brunswick assisted in a one-stop shop that provides social services, seniors' services, a nursing station, an internet learning center and a place to pay electricity bills. In the same vein, the Province of Nova Scotia twinned with Indonesia in another CIDA-funded project, helping to establish fourteen one-stop shops.

In the area of service delivery, both the Seychelles and Qatar are in the process of adapting the award-winning Citizens First study. This is a survey of 60,000 households conducted every two years in Canada to assess the quality of government services as perceived by citizens and to compare the quality of public service with that of the private sector. Surveys have shown that the drivers of citizen satisfaction are, in order of priority: timeliness, staff competence, courtesy, fairness and outcome. Several governments in Canada have set service standards based on these surveys. The 2000 survey can be found on the United Nations Global On-Line Network on Public Administration (UNPAN) website. Qatar is conducting a similar survey to provide base-line data for its reforms on service delivery. Because of the number of guest workers in Qatar, the study there will be called People First.

In service delivery, some simple things can reveal a lot. Look at a telephone book. Citizens often do not know which level of government provides what service and which departments provide the service. If government listings are divided by level of government and the listings are by department and not by service, e.g., permits and licenses, taxes, marriage, divorce, etc., then government services are driven by the convenience of the bureaucracy and not the needs of the citizen. Barbados and Northern Ireland are revising their government listings according to service. We have had visitors to Canada who, when shown the government blue pages, have ripped them out of the telephone book saying that that is just what they need back home. Of course, Canadians borrow heavily from other jurisdictions. When Singapore came out with its life cycle of events (from birth to death), many jurisdictions rearranged their services and websites based on the life cycle.

It is not so much the innovation itself, but the idea behind the innovation that is most transferable. With respect to service delivery, it means looking at government from the outside in. This is the notion behind one-stop shops, Citizen's First, government blue pages in the telephone book or being able to register a new business in 30 minutes. The main difficulty in achieving these innovations or reforms is not so much the use of technology but getting different orders of government and different ministries and departments to work together to provide citizen-centered services and developing new governance structures and accountability regimes to accomplish this.

Horizontal Approaches

Another idea that has been behind many innovations has been the horizontal approach, or what is called joined-up government in the United Kingdom. It can be adapted to many different circumstances. The Neighbourhood Integrated Service Teams (NIST) initiative of Vancouver, which won a 2003 United Nations Public Service Award, was born out of a solution to one particular long-standing problem. Residents of a local neighborhood had been struggling for two years with a home on their block that was plagued by a seemingly never-ending string of noisy gatherings, brawls and troublesome tenants. Although police, building inspectors and health board representatives paid many visits, the problem only escalated. The answer was not providing more staff but rather co-operation, communication and team work between city staff and the public. In 1995, the City of Vancouver formally launched the NIST programme, which now consists of 16 teams representing local neighborhoods. Teams are drawn from library, parks, planning, police, fire and rescue, engineering, permits and licenses, and social planning departments as well as some schools and the health board. Once an issue is identified, the neighborhood team decides which members should handle it and which members of the community should be in the decision-making process (Linquist, 1997).

NIST won the IPAC gold award for innovative management in 1997. On the jury that year was the Associate Secretary to the Cabinet of the Province of Saskatchewan, who realized that the City of Vancouver had developed a horizontal solution to a perplexing issue. She invited the Associate City Manager of Vancouver to come to Saskatchewan to make a presentation to a meeting of Deputy Ministers. In 2002, Saskatchewan's Department of Intergovernmental and Aboriginal Affairs won the silver IPAC Award for its strategy for Métis and off-reserve First Nations people. It is a comprehensive, long-term, horizontal approach involving 12 Saskatchewan departments and focused on poverty reduction.

Taking horizontality a step further, the Vancouver Agreement is a unique partnership among the federal, provincial and municipal governments; community groups; and business to tackle serious problems afflicting impoverished neighborhoods. This innovative project won the gold 2004 IPAC Award and the 2005 United Nations Public Service Award. The Downtown Eastside of Vancouver is the Agreement's first focus because it is the poorest postal code in Canada and is beset by poverty, crime, and public health crises; an open drug scene; and economic decline (Dutil, 2004). Key words to describe this innovation would be horizontal, citizen-centric governance, poverty reduction, community-based and accountability regime.

The Vancouver Agreement is already sharing its expertise with a partner in Chile facilitated by CIDA funds. The Interdisciplinary Program in Educational Research (PIIE), a social service and research organization for communities on the fringes of the capital city of Santiago, recognized that it alone could not respond to community issues such as social exclusion of at-risk youth, poverty and inadequate educational opportunities for children and adults. PIIE, following an internet search, was attracted to The Vancouver Agreement because of its innovative governance arrangement. Vancouver and Santiago have subsequently collaborated through exchange visits, email and the exchange of documents. PIIE has approached Chilean federal, state and municipal government agencies and the private sector to discuss a possible multi-sectoral approach to dealing with the social, economic and educational challenges in the Chilean communities of Cerro Navia, Pudahel and La Pintance.

Concluding Remarks

In conclusion, to facilitate the transfer of new ideas to jurisdictions looking for solutions it is important to establish a knowledge network where successful innovations are arranged in categories, such as service delivery, regulation, consultation and partnership, governance, horizontality, etc., including contact information for persons involved with successful innovations. People who have taken risks and conducted successful innovations are proud of what they have achieved and are usually proud to share their knowledge. Placing the submissions on a database with a good search engine is not sufficient, since innovators focus on specific achievements and may not be aware of the broader implications of their innovation.

Chapter 8

Local Capacities for Adaptation of Innovative Ideas and Practices

Lessons from Municipalities in Mexico

Tonatiuh Guillén López

This chapter analyses the capacities needed to adapt innovations in governance based on the experience of the Mexico's Government and Local Management Award (GLMA). Processes of innovation and best practices in Mexican local governments have developed over the past fifteen years (Cabrero, 1995, p. 381) as a result of the country's democratic transition, which is moving Mexico away from the semi-authoritarian and highly centralized regime that predominated during most of the twentieth century. Beginning in the second half of the 1980s and especially in the 1990s, Mexican municipalities initiated a new phase in their history due to a number of reforms which introduced greater democracy at the local level and enhanced the municipalities' autonomy from federal and state institutions. In other words, innovation and the search for better administrative practices were an outgrowth of this new, more evolved era of municipal public management. Progressively, each innovation is helping build the modern image of the municipal institution as an entity continuously adapting and interacting with parallel processes of democratic reform, decentralization, local development and the evolution of intergovernmental relations, not to mention its impact on civil society (Guillén, 1996, p. 223).

Paving the Way for Innovation

The relationship between democratic transition and innovation in local management does not imply that, in general, every innovation depends on this political condition. Yet, in the case of Mexico, the new democratic scenario played a predominant role in creating an enabling environment for innovation given: a) the appearance of new political and social actors in the municipal arena; b) their incorporation in local governments' public affairs and processes; c) new parameters in the relationship between society and government; d) political and legislative changes in intergovernmental structures; and e) new ways to identify and solve local public sector problems.

The democratic process significantly modified the social and institutional structures of Mexican municipalities, paving the way for innovation. The greater interaction between citizens and local government, especially in the 1980s, made it possible to transcend traditional processes and practices by altering how public affairs were run, how previously unavailable material and social resources were used, and, finally, by improving the community's quality of life. It is important to note that the process of democratic transition is not over yet, either at the local or the national and state levels. Deepening democracy and modernizing the administrative structures of municipalities is part of that process. Despite important advances made to date, there are still significant challenges in this respect. In addition, the introduction of good government practices and innovative programmes is affected by the municipalities' institutional inheritance, which endures to some degree and inhibits the expansion of these initiatives. Hence, innovation grows within a complex relationship between the traditional institutional framework and the search for new ways to provide public services; as one might expect, this process is not free of tensions.

Resistance and Encouragement

The evolution of municipal government institutions and its innovations is affected simultaneously by two dynamics that, together, can act as inhibiting factors. First, there are the traditional aspects of the municipalities' institutional inheritance that support authoritarianism, discretionary decisions, corruption, inefficiency and social inequality. Second, processes that are external to the municipality determine its fundamental characteristics: the centralization of institutions and programmes of the federal and state governments, for example, or the preservation of regulations that limit the municipalities' capacity for public intervention or intergovernmental negotiation. Innovations simultaneously encounter forces of resistance and encouragement. In general terms, innovations develop within the context of the traditional molds of the state structure, the political system and culture—while, at the same time, they are also affected by more progressive factors within those institutions. In different degrees and forms, each innovation reflects elements of both modernity and tradition, a situation which is not surprising at this stage in the evolution of the Mexican state. From this perspective, innovations reflect the positive balance of this contradictory scenario. They are programmes that transcend their traditional limitations and replace inertia with action.

We conclude that, in Mexico, the process of democratic transition and its effect on the municipalities has generated great capacity for social and institutional evolution, even though it is developing in the context of the modern/traditional friction described above. Overall, we are talking about macro-social potential, which is present in different degrees throughout the country, albeit in a dispersed and fragmented fashion. Although innovation can be seen throughout the country's municipalities, it exhibits strong local features and is characterized by poor communication and dialogue with other experiences and municipalities. To better disseminate innovations, the municipalities must improve horizontal communication and collective learning among governments and local societies.

Innovation in Government and Best Practices

Innovation in Mexico is broad and diverse; its presence is felt in practically all regions of the country. At the same time, it is a profoundly individual process brought about by specific local factors. Although communication between municipalities has improved notably in the last few years—particularly through the creation of associations of municipalities[1]—the capacities and lessons of innovation have not developed to their full potential because of a lack of mechanisms for disseminating and transferring successful practices. The most noteworthy achievement with respect to improved communication is the work of the Government and Local Management Award (GLMA—*www.premiomunicipal.org.mx*) undertaken by the *Centro de Investigación y Docencia Económicas* (CIDE) and sponsored by the Ford Foundation. Even here, although its contribution is valuable, the Award's capacities are not sufficient to meet the municipalities' demand for horizontal communication that better systematizes and disseminates the lessons of innovative experiences.

The purpose of the GLMA is to identify, evaluate, acknowledge and disseminate the best municipal government experiences in Mexico and to promote academic research in this area. Each phase of the Award process involves different tasks that touch on a broad range of specialists (academics, professional experts and representatives of social organizations related to the municipalities), institutions from the federal government and the states related to the municipalities, and the municipalities and their associations. The Award has only a small administrative organization to promote all of these activities, with help from a Technical Council of Academics and a Council of Institutions. These institutions and individuals have built a collaborative network across the country that includes government, academic and research institutions, and civil organizations.

As a result of its activities, the GLMA has Mexico's broadest infrastructure and most extensive institutional network for achieving the tasks of identification, evaluation, analysis, acknowledgment and diffusion of best municipal government practices. Despite limited resources, the GLMA has maintained high quality work between 2001 and 2005. However, with additional resources, the GLMA could do more, particularly with regard to the diffusion of best experiences in order to increase their transfer potential. With this caveat, the innovations and best practices compiled by the GLMA can be considered a reasonable indication of the programmes that Mexican municipalities have produced over the last five years. Without doubt, the Award experiences database does not capture all of Mexico's innovative programmes; no statistical or documentary source offers such complete information. In any case, the registered programmes comprise a representative sample that allows us to find the best local practices and identify their actors, the priorities of their political agendas, their social bases, regional characteristics, and cultural and electoral variations, among other elements. The 1,760 programmes registered at the GLMA between 2001 and 2004[2] allow us to describe some general features of the innovation processes carried out by local governments in Mexico.

Determinants of Good Governance Practices

In political terms, innovations appear to be possible in practically all contexts and possibilities offered by the country's electoral framework. In Mexico, citizens are represented in municipalities by national political parties; the three main ones are *Partido Revolucionario Institucional* (PRI), the *Partido Acción Nacional* (PAN) and the *Partido de la Revolución Democrática* (PRD). The indigenous municipalities are the exception; in the state of Oaxaca they are able to govern themselves through traditional systems that exclude the national political parties. In general terms, as shown by the programmes registered by the Award, political orientation is not a variable that particularly constrains or promotes good government practices. It is possible to identify innovative programmes across the political spectrum; in general, innovation is not especially associated with a municipality's political orientation.

Similarly, the size of municipalities is not a determinant of good governance practices considering that such practices are found both in small, medium and large-sized municipalities. However, in recent years the participation by large municipalities, i.e., more than 500,000 inhabitants, has declined from 30 per cent in 2001 to roughly 10 percent in 2004. The programmes registered by the Award describe creative experiences whose quality does not depend on the magnitude of social, economic or material resources, but rather on the particular arrangements that lead to more efficient public goods and services. In this respect, the scale of a programme is not equivalent either to its quality or its capacity to meet social demands. Additionally, the locations of innovative programmes are distributed across the southern, central, and northern regions of

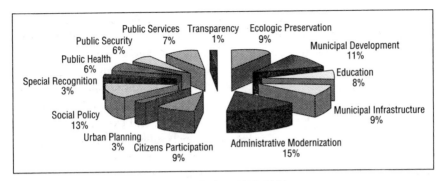

Figure 8.1   Participation in Awards, by Policy, 2001–2004
Source: Centro de Investigación y Docencia Económicas (CIDE)

the country with the central region accounting for approximately 50 per cent of the programmes. Figure 8.1 describes the innovative programmes based on the type of public policy they affect. The 13 categories used to classify the programmes reveal a wide spectrum of public functions that are the object of innovative practices. Although patterns can be identified in the distribution, the relevant fact is the thematic broadness of the innovation efforts.

Capacities for Innovation and Best Practices

Looking at Mexico's political, demographic, regional and public policy variables, we conclude that there are potential innovations with universal appeal to all municipalities, although bringing them to fruition is not automatic or spontaneous. In other words, innovation factors as well as catalysts able to convert them into a good practice exist in every context. It is important to note that although the factors that stimulate innovation and good practices are present in virtually all municipalities; this potential is not necessarily translated into innovative practices. Certain conditions are required to turn these possibilities into realities, which we will discuss later. For now, suffice to say that qualitative analysis is required to identify innovative factors and the conditions that can catalyze their development. The previous reflection is relevant to the identification of capacities that allow for the generation, dissemination and replication of innovations. At least latently, social, institutional, political and cultural capacities exist in all of the country's municipalities, although not all of the same scale or type, considering the extreme heterogeneity that characterizes municipal societies. That said, despite having different interests or collective objectives, municipalities do still share many common characteristics. For the moment, we want to assess whether those capacities are present, even in basic forms.

A municipality's capacities refer to how it deals with the various factors of the innovation process. These factors, whether social or institutional in nature, require certain capacities—knowledge, abilities, organization, resources—that, together, can make the innovation happen. The large number of programmes in Mexico suggests that these factors and their respective capacities exist in practically all municipalities in the country. What explains whether an innovation occurs or not is how capacities are brought together and energized. In other words, certain social actors who are closely affiliated with a given project must orchestrate the productive use of these capacities. The process can be initiated by local governments or local societies and organizations; it can also be promoted by external sources. The critical issue is that the set of actors, their respective capacities and the institutional framework proactively combine to make the innovation process happen. Consequently, the first challenge in generating and replicating innovative experiences is to identify the local capacities and the institutional or social actors who display those capacities. The second and greater challenge is to generate or stimulate productive encounters.

From a structural perspective, innovation processes can be analysed according to their components, or factors. On the one hand, there are the social actors and their organizations, their social characteristics and the type of society in which they exist, among other elements. On the other hand, there are the institutional factors, which determine the specifics of local government, its structure and size, the characteristics of its political or administrative resources, its legal framework, etc. As one might expect, there are many such factors in each experience, because the fusion of elements in any innovation process is complex. Experience suggests that the availability of factors is not enough; as described above, the dynamic that stimulates their productive interaction is equally important.

In general, two circumstances are required to create this dynamic: a) a demand or concrete need, internal or external to the local government; and b) the simultaneous identification of that need by leading institutional or social actors. In the case of Mexico, the first circumstance is a constant in all municipalities. The second is less certain, and when it does happen it tends to come from the municipal president (also known as the mayor), owing to the extensive powers and responsibilities concentrated in this figure in city councils. For this reason, in Mexico, the dynamic that galvanizes the various factors of innovation is closely associated with the agenda of the municipal president, whose significant institutional capacities may be strengthened further by personal charisma.

The Experience of GLMA Programmes

The GLMA programmes that we analysed re-enforce the notion that the municipal president plays a key role in activating the factors of an innovation.

Although the municipal president is not the only actor who can generate this dynamic, his or her contribution is instrumental to the success of the overall process. In other words, the leadership quality of this political figure is quite relevant to the generation, diffusion and replication of innovative programs. Clearly, it is not ideal for an innovation to be so dependent on the leadership of the municipal president. This situation is the result of Mexico's political and electoral system, which imposes additional conditions that restrict factors for innovation; these include, in particular, a ban on the immediate re-election of elected officials (making it impossible to accumulate experience and improve the performance of municipal political and administrative bodies). Another limiting condition is the electoral system's reinforcement of the political parties' monopoly in citizens' representation, thus disabling alternative social leadership. The characteristics of Mexico's political system severely limit the city councils' capacity to deliver innovation and good governance. Yet, the municipal presidents have been key actors in activating the factors of innovation, given their significant institutional powers. Regarding Mexico's capacities for municipal innovation, we conclude the following:

- Every type of municipality in Mexico has the potential to generate innovative programs, regardless of its social characteristics or the magnitude of its resources;

- Local capacities—social and institutional—that make good practices possible exist in every municipality, although in different degrees and types. Overall, the difficulty to generate and replicate innovative programs is not related to capacities (without underestimating their relevance);

- Structural analysis of innovative programs allows us to define their components as "factors," each with certain "capacities"; and

- It is not enough for a municipality to possess factors and capacities for innovation; these components require activation by key participants in the innovation process. This dynamic is fundamental to the growth of good practices.

Individual Innovative Programmes

Analysis of the innovation process becomes more complex when looking at individual programmes. As a starting point, we can identify four features of innovation in the municipal setting. First, within any municipal government, innovation is selective; that is, it is not undertaken simultaneously across all policies and programmes, but only in some of them. Second, innovation is the constructive answer to *specific, identified public demands*. Third, these demands stand out as *priorities* in the local agenda, which makes it possible to accept the innovation as a relevant alternative capable of garnering additional public resources. The fourth feature of innovation is its links with different social and institutional actors—it is not an isolated idea or programme. In addition to the general features, it is important to recognize that each individual programme has its own distinctive characteristics. Specifically, each innovation process depends on the influence of individual actors such as the heads of local government and social organizations who have the capacity to adapt their economic and administrative resources to the needs of a given programme. Through this mechanism, programme or policy content, resources and schedules can be adapted to local characteristics and needs. This adaptation to context is indispensable for local initiatives; they cannot be achieved by general programmes designed according to national or even regional criteria.

An overview of the GLMA programmes reveals the broadening of public functions in response to specific local needs, as shown, for example, by local government participation in programmes and policies of social, economic, environmental or educational development. We see municipal government becoming more engaged by social demands, thereby increasing the intensity and complexity of its interaction with municipal society. In addition, the expansion of public functions depends on the development of democratic governance, or at least the potential for this to occur. The intensification and broadening of functions and links between a municipality and society are not unilateral; in fact, they require integration and interdependence made possible by the development of democratic governance. We must emphasize that, although the relationship between a municipality and society is a necessary one, it does not happen automatically or without tensions. Once the broadening of municipal functions has begun, it requires careful nurturing by dedicated actors to sustain it, a phenomenon we can identify among the successful GLMA programmes.

In analysing individual programmes, two consistent components emerge. Specifically, innovators are driven in one of two directions, either a) from democracy toward governmental and administrative quality or b) from governmental and administrative issues to the quality of democracy. Characteristically, we encounter both elements on the same road, coming from different directions. The programmes compiled by the GLMA support our thesis that administrative quality develops the instruments of local democracy and, likewise, that local democracy stimulates the development of administrative quality. Although there are many paths to achieving such innovations, it is remarkable to see that all cases share this encounter. In other words, when the innovation comes from the side of democracy, it ends up within the scope of administrative quality; and if it comes from the side of an efficient administration, it ends up within the scope of democratic quality (Guillén and Rojo, 2005, p. 516). The innovation challenge, from this perspective, is not the entry point of the process, but rather the manner of entry and the decisions and consistency with which the innovation is undertaken.

Our work in this area leads us to conclude that the basic features of an innovative programme include: selectivity; the definition of a specific goal that is relevant to the local context; and a process that is designed by a network of relevant actors and appropriate to the local context. An innovative programme may furthermore strengthen the democratic base; stimulate the quality of local administration and government; and extend the municipalities' functions and services.

Documentation and Replication of Innovations in Government

Innovation processes can be evaluated only if properly documented; in other words, translated into useful information. Knowledge-building, diffusion and replication related to innovative experiences require a sufficient documentary base. However, documentation poses a great challenge for societies such as Mexico's, which are underdeveloped and characterized by emerging institutions. Mexican municipalities demonstrate great heterogeneity in their societies' populations and cultural roots. As such, we see urban municipalities with metropolitan characteristics, and we also find small rural and indigenous municipalities with populations of only a few hundred. The documentation experience is also heterogeneous: while in some municipalities it is almost nonexistent, in a few others it can be quite abundant. We must add that even in municipalities with plenty of resources, documentation is not always adequate to identify and evaluate innovation processes. In general, Mexican municipalities have not approached documentation as an institutional practice; even the preservation of this documentation is a common problem for local administrations.

Lack of documentation implies a great challenge in properly identifying innovation processes. In Mexico, there are three primary channels for identifying innovative experiences: academic studies; awareness-building by innovators; and the positive effect of awards and acknowledgments. The first two channels have had limited reach. The third has been more effective, in particular the contribution of the Government and Local Management Award. These three channels can also be used to classify the documentation of Mexico's innovative experiences. The most extensive database has been developed through the GLMA ceremony and its analytical and diffusion activities. As noted earlier, almost 1,800 experiences were compiled in the database between 2001 and 2004; in 2005, the database is likely to exceed 2,000 cases. In this sense, in Mexico, most innovation experiences have been documented by external actors, i.e., by people that are not part of the local process. This fact has implications for the collective knowledge on innovation and good government; that is, the database itself represents external information that is not always in a format that facilitates transference and replication. The preceding statement is not meant to invalidate systematic and detailed study—even by external entities—of innovation processes with an emphasis on social and administrative variables. The challenge is to transform this knowledge into recognizable information that can be integrated into one's own experience or by other actors who may learn from it and replicate it. If this transformation does not happen, there is a risk that there will not be sufficient documentation and information on good practices to be communicated.

Therefore, the documentation challenge is a major component of the innovation process and of an innovation's potential to generate transferable knowledge. The challenge lies in shaping a collective memory that reflects the particular identities of multiple actors, institutional frameworks, social needs, and public policy alternatives learned from different experiences and situations. The complexity of this challenge is quite imposing even in relatively homogeneous nations. The difficulty increases in multicultural societies with unequal regions, which is the Mexican case, and increases yet again at the international level. At this level, even simple communication about experiences faces obstacles of distance and language, as well as the fundamental challenge of communicating similarities between far-flung locations. Rich documentation of innovative experiences, while not an impossible task, is a specialized one that requires resources dedicated to this purpose. At present, innovation documentation in Mexico can be described as follows:

- The universe of innovation processes is insufficiently documented, resulting in minimal use of collective memory and knowledge;

- The format of this documentation makes it difficult to be communicated and recognized by other local actors to fit specific situations;

- Insufficient instruments of interaction for transferring this information from one municipality to another are an impediment to learning and replication; and

- Under these conditions, the dissemination and replication of good practices tends to be oral and circumstantial. Documentation must become more organized and systematic.

Originality and Replication of the Innovation

To identify and evaluate innovation requires criteria that allow us to distinguish it from any procedural and structural changes do are not important to the innovation's ultimate goal, i.e., to improve government for the benefit of society. As a consequence, these criteria must be linked to the innovative programme. Definitions used by international institutions are helpful in this regard, as are the innovation criteria established by Local Agenda 21, provided they are adapted to the national context where they will be applied. To be identified and evaluated as innovations, programmes must be compatible with the objectives of UN-HABITAT Local Agenda 21, since they reflect universal social interests (see Chapter 10). Based on the GLMA data, we can identify two useful complements to the criteria to evaluate and identify innovations: one is related to the immediate context, including the antecedents of this context; and the other is related to the horizontal scenario of other municipalities, including variables of local diversity. With reference to the immediate context, a programme can be called innovative if it differs from typical practices in similar or parallel areas, whether contemporary or not. Therefore, both the synchronic and diachronic dimensions are taken into account. Because of its innovative content the programme or process acquires an original profile that is noticed by the actors involved.

Another feature of the immediate context is related to whether the innovation is limited in scope. Thus, if the innovation is transferred to a broad range of municipalities—the horizontal context—it may lose its original intensity. In other words, an innovation in the immediate context can become an ordinary practice in other municipalities. The popularization of an innovation can contribute great social benefits, but may also cause the programme or process to lose its innovative character. The innovation becomes routine, without implying any loss of quality or the weakening of its social benefits and relevance. Thus, an experience can be described as innovative in the horizontal context if it contributes to the collective knowledge base. Innovative experiences, in their most evolved state, have demonstrable differences from both the immediate and horizontal contexts. Further, they incorporate not only theoretical but also practical elements that benefit local society and its institutions. For this reason, the concept of innovation must be distinguished from the concept of best practices, considering that lack of novelty does not imply that it is not a best practice. Innovation's diffusion, transference and replication are not the same as best practices; in our view, "best practices" correspond only to the initial phase of the experience and to its individual analysis.

Highly original innovations, which presuppose special conditions, resources and social actors, have a low probability of replication in comparison to more routine innovations. From the perspective of their contribution to the collective knowledge base, a highly original innovation is superior to a more mundane innovation. From the perspective of social benefit, both can be effective. The relative advantage of less original innovative experiences lies in the fact that they may be recognized more easily by external actors, given their common elements. In consequence, the cost of adaptation is lower, improving the likelihood of transference and replication.

If we look at the innovative experiences of other countries, developed or undeveloped, the seeming originality of the international cases will be increased simply because of the differences among respective national contexts. If there are few shared elements between the international experience and the potential actors interested in replicating the innovation, it will be more difficult to learn from the international case and, therefore, transference and replication will be limited. In this sense, the knowledge, analysis and communication of international experiences should be useful to replicators even designed for specific potential users. Thus, the originality of the innovation might reduce its probability of being recognized and replicated by others. In other words, the greater the original content, the greater the effort needed to document, analyse and adapt it to new contexts.

Concluding Remarks

The experiences described in this chapter allow us to draw some conclusions about capacities needed for the generation, diffusion and replication of innovative programmes and good local practices. Although derived from experiences in Mexico, they may be useful to other nations and regions. First, the presence of capacities among diverse local institutions and social actors is not the determining factor in generating innovations. Data from the GLMA show that these capacities exist in practically all municipalities in Mexico, large or small, in one region or another, independent of political or cultural characteristics. We must add, however, that these capacities always require development, even in areas with relatively more resources.

Capacities may be limited, especially in municipalities with small populations and minimal resources. Even under these conditions, however, the development of innovative programmes is feasible and can consolidate into good practices. The municipal profile largely determines the type of programme, how its objectives are prioritized, the level of resources and the social actors involved. But the municipal profile in itself does not determine if capacities exist or not. Each municipality requires specific programmes according to its local conditions, capacities and resources. In simple terms, no one would expect urban programmes to be adopted in rural municipalities, for example. Somehow, each local context defines a range of programmes based on its specific needs. In any case, this issue is separate from the debate on local capacities.

Our analysis implies that it is possible to generate, disseminate and replicate good local government practices in virtually all municipalities. The difference between one experience and another is determined by how these capacities or factors are combined; the productive interaction of capacities is the characteristic that distinguishes a successful municipal programme from one that does not succeed. The social or institutional dynamic needed to generate that encounter can be defined as a capacity in itself. Given its political and electoral system, in Mexico this specialized capacity tends to be concentrated in the municipal president (mayor).

Under these conditions, proposals for generating, disseminating and replicating good practices must be oriented toward this key figure of local government. It is not an ideal situation, since it tends to make the innovation process dependent on the abilities and personal qualifications of the municipal president. At least in the short and medium terms, strategies for promoting good practices must focus on the role of the mayor as the activator of the factors and capacities of innovation. For Mexico, this means upgrading the mayors' capacities.

In addition, the diffusion, transfer and replication of good practices depend on effective communication processes. The first challenge is to document the collective learning about the process, which must include content designed with the goal of transference and replication; this means that not all current documentation is able to help replicate good practices. In Mexico, the documentation of local government processes is slowly being compiled, but it is usually in a format that impedes diffusion and replication. Thus, any replication of good practices tends to occur through informal, oral and frequently circumstantial channels. In spite of the significant efforts of programmes like the GLMA, the task of adequately documenting good practices remains in its initial phase. The good news is that there is significant potential in the available information, which, with additional work, could become valuable documentation for transference and replication. At the international level, more efforts could be undertaken to properly document and share innovations and best practices for the benefit of all interested countries.

Chapter 9

Different Approaches to Policy Transfer

Carlos Conde Martínez

Policy transfer has received growing attention in political science literature. The frequency of development policies' transfers, as well as the intense policy cooperation between industrialized countries indicate that there is great interest in the concept of transfer, its mechanisms and the conditions for its success. The present chapter describes several models of policy transfer and analyses the main variables that contribute to explain the nature of this phenomenon.

Political Science Approach to Policy Transfer

Dolowitz and Marsh (2000, p. 5) define policy transfer as "a process in which knowledge about policies, administrative arrangements, institutions and ideas in one political setting (past or present) is used in the development of policies, administrative arrangements, institutions and ideas in another political setting." This is an ancient phenomenon; in particular, the field of public administration has plenty of examples of administrative reforms and innovations that have been transferred from one national or regional context to another.

We can mention some of the most well-known examples. The introduction of Napoleonic local administration in most of continental Europe was a perfect example of policy transfer during the nineteenth century. This immense institutional reform, whose basic trends still define the administrative structure of European countries and many of their former colonies, consisted of the adaptation to different national contexts of a radical reform originated in France. The success of this transformation was observed by the intellectual and political elites of different countries and inspired them to undertake the deep transformation of their own national structures. Closer to our historical period, the New Public Management reforms also can be analysed as a process of policy transfer. These reforms initially took place in one national context and, through different mechanisms of intellectual and political influence, traveled from one country to another. These two major examples of administrative transformations explain the critical importance to political science of the processes and mechanisms of policy transfer. Despite the interest of the phenomenon, the scientific treatment of this issue is recent and to some extent is still in the process of proposing hypotheses. In this section we will analyse, first, some typologies developed by different authors. Second, we will consider the scientific literature's main variables on policy transfer processes.

Initially, policy transfer was considered as an independent variable in the explanation of the processes of policy convergence as illustrated by the paradigm of modernization that became dominant in social science literature during the 1950s and 1960s. This theory has inspired the majority of development policies for decades and is still present in several approaches to the problem of development. Modernization is based on the assumption that some elements defining Western development (i.e., secularization, industrialization, urbanization, popular participation) should be transferred to the underdeveloped world as a prerequisite for progress, economic growth and social development. Under this assumption choosing the "right" model and implementing it in the "right" way would create the same effects. Optimism and strong belief in the possibility of political and social convergence through transfer of policies and practices were the prevailing sentiments in this period.

The practical aspects of transfer are not included in this picture. In fact, the transformation of local conditions is considered under these perspectives a matter of political will and material resources. The evolution of political science and public policy analysis in the last decades has shown the limits of these approaches. On the one hand, the attention devoted to practical aspects of policy-making underline the impact of institutional and contextual constraints in the phase of implementation, which explains the failure of a number of policies inspired by the modernization paradigm. On the other hand, alternative theoretical models to the rationalist approach, like the bounded rationality model, the incremental approach or the garbage can model have shown the complexity of policy processes.

Convergence as the Result of Policy Transfer

A review of the political science literature reveals that the notion of convergence and transfer is not limited to the analysis of the problem of development. In fact, public policy analysis makes reference to these concepts in the context of industrialized countries as well. The theoretical concern about convergence arises from the observation by specialists in comparative politics that industrialized states face similar problems and have a tendency to solve them in a similar way (Bennett, 1991). According to this author, convergence may be observed in different policy elements: political goals (environmental protection, inflation control), policy instruments (setting up autonomous agencies for public services delivery, provision of subsidies to different social categories), policy styles (emphasis on social participation in decision-making processes, territorial decentralization), etc. For this author, convergence is the result of policy transfer, and the level of convergence depends on the relationship among the different types of transfer. The Bennett model includes the main intellectual concerns about policy transfer: proposal of typologies in order to describe particular cases and analysis of variables that might influence results and impact. We will treat both questions by describing three typologies proposed by different authors and then by analyzing five variables influencing transfer. Bennett describes four different types of transfer: emulation, dissemination, harmonization and imposition.

Emulation: Knowledge about external models has frequently inspired internal decisions. This type of convergence is usual in international contexts as well as in federal ones. The current explosion of global communication and comparative knowledge makes this type of transfer a very common tool of political innovation. Emulation is by definition voluntary and is justified by the interest of the policy borrower.

Dissemination: This form of transfer requires the existence of transnational networks acting as platforms for the generalization of policy solutions. The mechanism is more sophisticated than mere emulation in the sense that it requires the previous existence of permanent formal or informal networks in which experts or practitioners share concerns, experiences and solutions. The similarity of solutions comes from the exchange of ideas and the frequent contact between some elites. These groups of politicians, civil servants or experts are confident in the use of transnational instruments for the solution of local problems. Some level of regional or cultural identity plays an important role in this category of exchanges, for example, the Latin American policies of privatization or the introduction of New Public Management instruments in Anglo-Saxon countries are significant cases (Halligan, 1995). A common educational background may be influential in dissemination processes. In this sense, the role played by some elite academic centers can be identified behind the generalization of policy options.

Harmonization: This type of transfer is based not only on the existence of a network of motivated actors with opportunities for interaction, but on the authoritative action of some international organization. Transfer, and eventually convergence, arises from the recognition of interdependence. The existence of common institutions supports the implementation of common solutions to common problems in the understanding that national isolated policies can be, first of all, less efficient, and second, can damage the interest of partner countries. Organizations such as the Organisation for Economic Co-operation and Development (OECD), the Council of Europe or the European Union are the best examples of organizations playing this role of transfer platforms.

Imposition: The transfer is defined by an external agent that sets the objectives, instruments, evaluation tools and even provides the necessary resources for the implementation of the policy. This category of transfer is the most common situation in the context of cooperation for development. International donors usually impose significant conditions in exchange for financial or technical support.

Institutional Conditions of Policy Transfer

Bennett's descriptive model is based on the hypothesis that policy transfer leads to policy convergence, a view which is not necessarily shared by other authors. The adaptation of general models to local conditions can produce a great variety of results. Bulmer and Padgett (2004, p. 106) consider that the level of intensity of the transfer and the agreement of the borrower country on all the details of the policy can lead to different situations involving several levels of success. This typology focuses on the content of policy more than the institutional conditions of transfer.

Emulation: This form of transfer consists of borrowing a foreign policy in all its terms, adapting its different elements to contextual differences. Bulmer and Padgett make a different use of the word emulation than Bennett. For them, emulation makes reference to the content of the policy, whereas Bennett describes the institutional context. As a result, emulation is in this typology the strongest form of transfer (identical policy in different context) in opposition to Bennett, for whom emulation is the weakest form (imitation without common institutional framework).

Influence: This form will occur when a foreign model serves as a mere inspiration for a new policy or an adaptation of an existing domestic policy. The difference with emulation is a matter of degree and intensity.

Synthesis: This mechanism is based on combining elements from different contexts. Synthesis implies a level of creation by the borrower and is in this sense the result of a process of study and analysis. Synthesis can be considered a system of policy formulation based on comparative study and adaptation to the local context of a set of policy criteria and instruments experienced in other contexts.

Abortive: The potential transfer is blocked by veto actors in the borrower constituency. This form underlines an important element in any process of transfer: contingency. Most studies focusing on contingency stress the importance of the local context for the final result. This is the case in the influential study of Dolowitz and Marsh (2000). For these authors, policy transfer can bring policy success or failure. The large variety of variables will explain the final result of the process of transfer: actors involved, object transferred (policy, programme or practice), origin of the transfer (international, local) and constraints of transfer. The quality of knowledge involved in policy transfer is the most common explanation for a failed or abortive form of transfer.

Political Factors of Transfers

Radaelli (2000b, p. 11) distinguishes four possibilities concerning government's commitment in the context of the European Union. For this author, political factors are the main element explaining the effective transfer of policies.

Inertia: This situation is defined as one which lacks commitment for change. Political will for innovation and reform does not exist because external models of change are considered dissimilar to domestic practice or preferences.

Accommodation or absorption: This mechanism involves change and adaptation with some extent of maintenance of essential local structures. Policy legacy and local context are important barriers to change; in this sense, modifications originated in a different context might face some degree of resiliency from the borrower institution that will introduce flexibility in the reception of transfer.

Transformation: This change occurs when the fundamental logic of political behavior changes.

Retrenchment: The mere attempt of transfer is counter-productive, as the final result is less adapted to the external model than the previous situation. The risk of change can have as a result the reinforcement of local actors opposed to change and reform.

Table 9.1 summarizes the main elements of the three typologies described.

Main Variables in Policy Transfer

The previous concepts offer a basis for the description of policy transfer processes. The different classifications are based on a number of variables that can contribute in different ways to analyse practical cases of policy transfer. The main variables involved in these processes are constraint, institutionalization,

Table 9.1   Policy Transfer Types by Main Variables

Institutionalization and Coercion	Similarity and Success	Political Commitment
Bennett, 1991	*Bulmer and Padgett, 2004*	*Radaelli, 2000b*
Emulation: Internal decisions are inspired by external models. The process is voluntary and the initiative local.	*Emulation:* A foreign policy, process or practice is borrowed in all its terms.	*Accommodation:* Transfer induces changes and reforms compatible with domestic institutions.
Dissemination: The existence of professional networks explains the sharing of knowledge and the generalization of solutions to similar problems.	*Synthesis:* Implies a process of policy creation by the combination of elements taken from different contexts.	*Transformation:* Transfer implies the modification of the previous pattern of action.
Harmonization: Based on the existence of common institutions. Mainly focused on regulation and policy design and implementation.	*Influence:* The foreign model serves as a mere inspiration. The process of policy design is basically local.	*Inertia:* Political will for change does not exist. Local constituencies follow previous patterns, avoiding external models.
Imposition: External actors impose objectives and provide resources. Dominant model in development policies.	*Abortive transfer:* The transfer is blocked by veto actors.	*Retrenchment:* Transfer is considered a threat, which strengthens local opposition to innovation and reform.

Source: Adapted from Bennet, 1991; Bulmer and Padget, 2004; Radaelli, 2000b

internationalization, political commitment and knowledge. Each of them deserves further explanation.

Intensity of Constraint

The intensity of constraint is a crucial factor in processes of transfer: is the transfer a result of voluntary action or is it imposed by external agents? Behind this simple question lay important questions for the analyst, theoretical as well as practical. Transfer of best practices or policies is usually considered a voluntary action inspired by rational behavior. Political or technical actors are committed to improving the quality of public services delivery or governmental performance in an overall sense; therefore, they are in search of successful innovations or reforms in order to implement them at home. Empirical analysis, however, more often will show scenarios of bounded rationality in which policy-makers are suffering different degrees of coercion that impose significant pressures on their behavior. We could distinguish three different categories of coercion behind policy transfer. First, situations of extreme need or urgency in which rapid solutions have to be given to compelling problems. This is a common situation for decision-makers who come to view external models as a source of inspiration for local action. Second, there are conditionalities related to foreign aid that usually impose important obligations of innovation and reform. Finally, the membership of international regimes is nowadays one of the most extended situations in which coercive change has to be introduced in national constituencies. Either under the form of supranational organizations imposing mandatory rules (i.e., the Council of Europe concerning human rights protection) or intergovernmental agreements involving mutual obligations (i.e., trade regimes), a wide variety of internal reforms arises from the international arena.

Some reflection is needed concerning the mechanisms of coercion. The mere expression of the concept of coercion is frequently perceived negatively as it is related to external imposition lacking correct information about local conditions or even political legitimacy. This attitude is common in developing countries as they identify external coercion either with a colonial past or with recent policies of modernization or structural adjustment. Despite negative attitudes, the existence of conditions related to programmes of external aid is a very present factor in development policies. This is a classic top-down mechanism of coercion based on sanctions or incentives. As we will see below, conditions in the administrative field are strong in the context of the relationships between the European Union and the Arab Mediterranean countries. Nevertheless, the coercion variable is quite complex and can be applied in the context of industrialized countries as well. In the context of international regimes (the European Union being probably the most visible), governments accept mutual obligations that can involve significant reforms including transfer of external policies or programmes. We can mention the setting up of general goals or standards or more compelling practices such as institutionalized peer review and evaluation. Under this modality, coercion is not an external imposition, but a mechanism of self discipline, inspired by the idea that international obligations reinforce capacities of reform. It is important to note that under this modality, coercion does not mean lack of participation in the decision-making process; on the contrary, obligations are the result of negotiations on which governments have substantial influence.

Degree of Internationalization

By internationalization we mean the intensity of relationships between a given constituency and the international environment. The existence of intense links between different national or local contexts facilitates successful exchange and transfer at the policy level. The frequency of transfer between different local or regional governments at the national level illustrates that deep relationships between decision-makers intensify the possibilities for circulation of policies or practices. Another illustration is the European case, as it is generally accepted that the intensity of trans-European exchanges in all fields (economy, education, population mobility, environmental challenges, security issues, etc.) provides immense possibilities for transfer. Therefore, the link between the national authority and the international context is a critical explanatory element concerning the scope of transfer: How frequent are international contacts? How institutionalized are they? How wide is the variety of contacts? Are they limited by regional, cultural or linguistic factors? Is the colonial link still predominant? The quality of previous international connections is crucial in this sense, as the complexity of policy and administrative innovations requires the existence of a cognitive community. Mutual understanding between lender and borrower of policy experiences seems to be a necessary prerequisite for successful transfer.

Measuring the level of internationalization is not an easy task, but some factors can be underlined. In particular, we will mention structural and subjective factors. Concerning structural factors, the density of exchanges (social, economic, political and academic) is an important element explaining the political commitment to adaptation in the international context. Civil society pressure over governments is an effective impulse for innovation. The exposure of national social or economic groups to more effective and successful policies and practices in other international contexts is a powerful stimulus to the introduction of these practices. Subjective elements related to the profile of decision-makers may play a role in the capacity for transfer as well. The attitude toward international integration depends on factors such as the weight of a country's historical legacy or the nature of its international situation (involvement or isolation). Some cultural factors (trust or mistrust toward the external environment) may contribute to explaining attitudes toward processes of transfer that necessarily involve an orientation toward learning from abroad. Positive attitudes toward internationalization increase the potential for policy transfers, whereas nationalist resistance to following foreign models, very present in countries submitted in the past to colonial rule, is a considerable obstacle to transfer.

Level of Institutionalization

No less important than structural or cultural factors are the legal and formal aspects of government interactions. Institutionalization is defined by the existence of common rules, organizations promoting cooperation, and the intensity and quantity of exchanges and interactions. Europe can be an example of this variable. The European political space is defined after World War II by the submission of national states to supranational institutions with mandatory capacities. Respect for supranational executives and judiciaries, and voluntary submission to common rules and institutions, guarantees mutual understanding. The generalization of collective action in several fields creates cognitive communities in several sectors of governmental activity that favour policy transfer. The European Union's strong modality of institutionalization is far from being the only experience of an institutional platform promoting policy reform and convergence. A larger European institution such as the Council of Europe plays a similar role in several fields, such as human rights protection or democratic development. The Organisation for Economic Co-operation and Development (OECD) is an influential platform for policy convergence between industrialized countries. More recently, in a totally different context, the New Partnership for Africa's Development (NEPAD) introduced an innovative institutional system of cooperation in several policy fields, including some elements of "soft" coercion as the peer review mechanism. In short, the existence of formal institutions, informal networks or any permanent and stable form of international interaction is a significant variable concerning possibilities for successful transfer.

Amount of Political Commitment

The willingness of national governments is obviously a crucial factor when considering the process of innovation and reform. Governmental motivation can be explained by a complex set of domestic and international factors. In the context of the European Union, Radaelli (2000a) considers that behind most of the European decisions intensifying cooperation, convergence or transfer there is a fear or an opportunity related to the process of globalization. The reinforcement of economic growth, the guarantee of the welfare state or the protection against global terror justifies further integration and common action. The necessity of providing citizens with concrete results in every sector of governmental intervention in a context of periodic electoral evaluation explains the strong will of policy innovation and success. On the contrary, when integration is considered a challenge to strong political preferences of national electorates (a threat to welfare provision by the accession of poorer countries), possibilities for transfer will decrease. Legitimacy plays an important role in transfer processes. Political legitimacy based on agreement between political actors for the introduction of innovations may be a prerequisite for effective implementation.

The Knowledge Factor

The assumption that successful experiences in one country must necessarily lead to success in a different country is generally contested. Dolowitz and

Marsh (2000, pp. 18–20) point out three factors that can produce policy failure in a process of transfer: a) uninformed transfer when the borrowing country has insufficient information about the innovation or policy transferred; b) incomplete transfer when crucial elements of the policy in the original country have not been introduced; and c) inappropriate transfer when the differences in economic, social, political and ideological contexts have not been taken sufficiently into consideration. The absence of accurate and sufficient knowledge is common to the three causes of failure. This gap may refer to different elements: bad information about the original policy or practice and the local conditions of its success; mistakes about the requirements of the process of transfer and the creative adaptation always needed; local conditions that can be misjudged or overestimated concerning the capacity of absorption of a given policy or practice.

The knowledge factor is a crucial element concerning policy capacities in general. The academic and professional profiles of decision-makers and bureaucrats are generally a factor with deep impact on capacities. In the case of transfers of policies and innovation, some elements must be considered in particular. The main question is: how sophisticated is the comparative knowledge and understanding of international and foreign constituencies? The answer to this question depends on many factors; among these factors, higher education systems and systems of professional training are the most influential variables. Empirical knowledge about this question is limited, but the existing data show that knowledge about the external environment is in general insufficient. The European case illustrates this situation. Despite the uncontested fact that European public administrations are probably the most internationalized in terms of international relationships and obligations related to the European integration process, the academic programmes concerning public administration, as well as the programmes of service training for civil servants, are mostly inward-looking and pay very little attention to comparative administrative knowledge and information about foreign public administrations (Verheijen and Connaughton, 1999). Available case studies show that, despite current conditions of globalization, comparative knowledge and information about foreign systems and international regimes are absorbed at a very slow pace by human resources systems in the context of public administration (Conde, 2004).

Finally, the management of knowledge in administrative organizations plays an important role in the capacities for successful policy transfer. How is information about successful policies and experiences gathered and distributed? Does the selection of models depend on information obtained accidentally or from systematic and critical systems of information? Is reception passive or proactive? Are public administrations in search of good models and practices or is this behavior outside of their institutional interest and capacities? The role of international networks and international organizations can be crucial in the provision of accurate and well-developed information with potential to become a management tool for decision-makers.

Concluding Remarks

We conclude this chapter by proposing some elements that public administrations should ensure in order to take advantage of the possibilities of partnership while avoiding the threats of dependency and stagnation. First, more knowledge about foreign and international models is required. International integration creates the conditions for the imposition of some economic and administrative models. Dominant models are being transferred to the local arena; this can be effective only if they are adapted to the local context. Capacities for understanding, influencing, anticipating, lobbying and getting information are crucial needs for recipients. As we have seen, one of the main causes of policy failure is the uninformed, inadequate or incomplete transfer. Second, transfer is a tool that makes up part of a larger policy framework. The mere concept of public policy is the result of the evolution of state functions and governmental intervention, as it was born hand-in-hand with the welfare state in the context of liberal participative democracies. The adaptation of policy instruments and programmes of action or administrative practices requires capacities for mobilizing resources and setting up coalitions of local public and private actors able to successfully implement structural reforms. These reforms are complex public policies requiring strong leadership with capacities for explanation, social mobilization and understanding of the local context, replacing the authoritarian tradition of a regulatory state. Real policy starts after the approval of a law or the signing of an agreement. Third, in the context of coercive modes of transfer, negotiation capacities to defend the interests of the national economic structure and the citizens of the country are required. International treaties and their implementation processes are the result of negotiation. Bargaining, mutual adjustment and the search for favourable agreements are necessary elements defining governmental and administrative action in the international arena.

PART THREE

Approaches to Transferring and Adapting Innovations and Best Practices

Chapter 10

Best Practices Knowledge Management Framework

Nicholas You and Vincent Kitio

The original call for best practices was launched in 1996 as part of the preparatory process for the Second United Nations Conference on Human Settlements (Habitat II) as a means of identifying solutions to some of the most pressing social, economic and environmental problems facing an urbanizing world. The international community defined what constitutes a best practice and adopted guidelines for their documentation and dissemination. The Habitat Agenda, adopted by the United Nations General Assembly, further decided that best practices be used as one of the two key instruments for assessing progress in achieving its twin goals of shelter for all and sustainable urbanization.[1] As a result of this decision the Best Practices and Local Leadership Programme (BLP) was established. It is made up of a global network of public, private and civil society organizations devoted to the sharing and exchange of lessons learned from experience. This chapter provides an overview of the concepts, definitions, methods and lessons learned to date.

What Are Best Practices?

Based on the "Report of the Preparatory Committee for the United Nations Conference on Human Settlements." presented to the General Assembly, "best practices": (1) Have a demonstrable and tangible impact on improving people's quality of life; (2) Are the result of effective partnerships between the public, private and civil society sectors; and (3) Are socially, economically and environmentally sustainable (UN, 1995, A/50/37). The General Assembly, based on the UN-Habitat Agenda, further recommends that best practices be used as one of the two key instruments for assessing progress in achieving its twin goals of shelter for all and sustainable urbanization (A/RES/S-25/2).

These three basic criteria have been expanded over time to include additional considerations in light of emerging issues and trends and to better differentiate between good and best practices. These considerations include: leadership and community empowerment; innovation within the local context; and gender equality and social inclusion. Best practices are used and promoted by UN-HABITAT and its partners as a means of:

- Improving public policy based on what works;
- Raising awareness of decision-makers at all levels and of the general public of potential solutions to common social, economic and environmental problems;
- Assessing emerging issues, trends and policy responses; and
- Transferring expertise and experience through networking and peer-to-peer learning.

How Are Best Practices Identified and Documented?

Initiatives are identified and documented through three principle means:

- Targeted search by a global network of institutions representing all spheres of government and private and civil society sectors;
- Calls for best practices using the incentive of the biennial Dubai Award for Best Practices as well as other award and recognition systems; and
- Ongoing research and development.

Best practices are documented by the people, communities and organizations that are directly involved in their implementation. They include all spheres of government, the private and civil society sectors, professional associations, etc.[2] The documentation of best practices is considered to be a capacity-building exercise and an exercise in self-appraisal. The global network of best practices partners plays an important role in this process, especially with regard to smaller municipalities, non-governmental and community-based organizations.[3] The documentation process makes use of a *standardized reporting format*. This format is the product of consensus between all partners of the network. It has evolved over time as a function of lessons learned and in response to emerging issues and trends. It is essential to:

- Facilitate the hand-holding and capacity-building functions of partners;
- Develop and disseminate a common set of guidelines;

- Facilitate the assessment process; and
- Enable comparative analysis and the identification of lessons learned.

The combined use of a common set of criteria and a standardized reporting format has been particularly useful in identifying and analysing lessons learned in terms of identifying:

- How people and communities perceive their problems and what empowers them to undertake or initiate change;
- Obstacles that people and their communities face and the approaches that are particularly effective in overcoming them;
- The respective roles, responsibilities and contributions of different social actors and partners;
- Contributing factors in sustaining an initiative, and conversely, the mitigating factors that cause initiatives to fail; and
- Promising policy options, effective institutional frameworks and governance.

How Are Best Practices Assessed?

The Best Practices and Local Leadership Programme uses a three-step process: a) validation, b) technical appraisal and c) normative assessment.

Validation involves the global network of partners representing relevant geographic and/or thematic expertise and experience. It is designed to verify that the information submitted is an accurate reflection of reality and to ensure compliance of the submission with the three basic criteria and the reporting format. The validation process relies on information communication technology and a dedicated intranet.

Technical appraisal is undertaken by an independent Technical Advisory Committee (TAC) composed of up to 15 regionally representative and gender-sensitive experts. The committee meets physically and its task is to differentiate between "good" and "best." The committee looks at each practice from the following perspectives:

- Compliance with the three basic criteria of impact, partnership and sustainability;
- Compliance with additional considerations of leadership and community empowerment, innovation, gender equality and social inclusion, and transferability;
- Absolute merit within a national and/or local context; and
- Relative merit in comparison to other practices in the same thematic area.

Normative assessment includes the Committee identifying approximately 100 best practices from an average of 600 submissions every two years. It is also charged with the task of identifying a short list of not more than 48 equally meritorious initiatives. The short-listed practices are forwarded to an independent jury made up of five internationally renowned individuals using a similar but more political approach in selecting 12 award-winning practices.

Best Practices and Knowledge Management

Documented and peer-reviewed best practices are used extensively by the United Nations for a wide variety of purposes. The Habitat Agenda, UNDESA, the Programme of Action resulting from the World Summit on Sustainable Development (WSSD), the Commission on Sustainable Development, the United Nations Educational, Scientific and Cultural Organization (UNESCO), the International Labour Organization (ILO), the World Health Organization (WHO) and the United Nations Department for Public Information are among the most frequent users of best practices to promote awareness-raising, support policy development, facilitate the sharing and exchange of expertise and experience, and as a tool for learning and capacity-building. These various demands for best practice value-added services have been integrated into a Best Practices and Policies knowledge management framework. Table 10.1 provides an overview of this system.

Awareness-Building

Awareness-building is an important part of any development process and an essential component for policy development. UN–HABITAT and its partners consider award and recognition systems as a highly effective means of awareness-building. In the case of international award systems such as the Dubai International Award for Best Practices, UNDP's Equator Initiative, the Stockholm Challenge, the Bremen Initiative, etc., outreach to decision-makers and to the general public can touch upon hundreds of millions of people with each cycle. In the case of national award and recognition systems, such as the Gawad Galing Pook Awards in the Philippines, the Impumelelo Award of South Africa, the Spanish National Committee for Habitat Awards and the Caixa Municipal Best Practices Award in Brazil, outreach typically can include most if not all relevant government agencies, local authorities and professional and civil society organizations. The awareness of what works and the practical value of good or best practices are particularly well suited for press and media reports and investigative journalism. Award and recognition systems provide the incentive for people, their communities and organizations to share their practices which otherwise would remain known only to a limited audience.

Table 10.1   Best Practices Knowledge Management Framework

Objectives/Activities	Target Audiences/Users	Instruments
Awareness-Building	• Informed public • Media • Media professionals • Decision-makers	• Dubai Award (DIABP) • ICLEI Local Initiatives[a] • Stockholm Challenge Award • UNDP Equator Initiative[b] • UNEP success stories[c] • UN Public Service Awards
Networking and Information Sharing	• Decision and policy-makers • Practicing professionals • Training and Leadership Development institutions	• Best practice databases • Publications/articles • Web pages, Newsletters • Listserv
Learning Tools and Capacity-Building	• Training and Leadership Development institutions • Local authority associations • Professional associations	• Best practice case studies • Best practice casebooks • Issue briefs and articles • Training materials
Peer Learning and Community-to-Community	• Local authority associates • Networks of NGOs/CBOs • International organizations • Multi- and bi-lateral assistance	• Transfer guides, methods and tools • Match supply/demand for expertise • Conferences and seminars • Advisory services
Policy Development	• Decision-makers at all levels • Policy advocacy groups • National governments • International and inter-governmental organizations	• Database on urban policies and enabling legislation • Policy trends and responses • Normative guidelines • State of the World's Cities Report

Source: UN-HABITAT, 2005
[a]International Council for Local Environmental Initiatives
[b]United Nations Development Programme
[c]United Nations Environment Programme

Information Exchange and Networking

The use of a standardized reporting format lends itself particularly well to establishing searchable and user-friendly databases. In the case of UN-HABITAT and UNDP, the database is both web-based and on CD-ROM. The use of Information and Communication Technologies (ICT) allows for full Boolean searches by theme, category, partners involved, scale of intervention, key words, region, etc. The incorporation of names and addresses of the proponents of the good or best practices further allows for networking. For UN-HABITAT, the development and maintenance of a fully searchable database has proven to be a very useful tool for comparative analysis and the analysis of emerging issues, trends, potential policy responses and lessons learned. In order to enhance the value-added dimension of the database, additional information pertaining to the socio-economic and political context of the practices is being implemented.

The temptation to design databases to serve all purposes is, however, not practical. For this reason, UN-HABITAT does not attempt to assign learning or other objectives to the database. Users of the database are informed of new additions, new developments and by-products through electronic and printed newsletters. Simple questions and answers facilities are provided through a listserv. There are currently four newsletters published by different partners, reaching out to over 50,000 institutions and organizations, a majority of which are government agencies and local authorities. A new best practices magazine is due to be published in collaboration with private-sector media in 2006, with an initial circulation of 300,000 in Chinese, English and Russian.

UN-HABITAT's Best Practices Database currently contains 2,200 practices from 140 countries in 24 thematic categories. Links to other databases provide users with access to over 3,000 practices from 160 countries.[4] Every two years, more than 400 new practices are included in the database as well as an average of 70 updates of previously submitted practices.[5] Practices that are not updated after six years are archived but remain retrievable, with the user being advised that the information is outdated and may be no longer reliable. The database is visited by an average of 200,000 users per month. The majority of users are professional and non-governmental organizations, followed by government agencies, educational institutions and individuals. Since 2000, UN-HABITAT has also developed a new product specifically targeting decision- and policy-makers. Known as Best Practice Briefs, this product consists of short summaries of selected practices in thematic areas of greatest demand. Since their inception, the Briefs have become very popular.

Learning and Capacity-Building

As mentioned above, the database cannot and should not serve all purposes. For this reason, UN-HABITAT and its partners developed a range of value-added products, including monographs, in-depth case studies, and casebooks. Best Practice Briefs are also systematically included in training and management development tools and materials. These products are designed for use by training and leadership development organizations targeting policy-makers and practitioners. The BLP is also involved in the organization of conferences, seminars and workshops on Learning from Best Practices. International conferences sponsored by UN-HABITAT typically involve 10 to 12 practices focusing on lessons learned from experience. Best Practice partners, in turn, organize in their respective areas of expertise an average of three or four conferences per annum while educational and training institutions incorporate best practices in their regular curricula.

Technical Cooperation and Best Practice Transfers

UN-HABITAT's mandate includes policy advocacy and technical assistance. The BLP focuses its activities on decentralized cooperation and peer-to-peer learning. It supports associations of local authorities and umbrella non-governmental organizations in the matching of supply with demand for expertise and experience. A set of guidelines on "Transferring Effective Practices" has been developed in collaboration with United Nations Development Programme (UNDP) and Regional Network for Local Authorities for Asia and the Pacific (CityNet). These guidelines have since been adapted by other partners for use in Spanish-speaking Latin America and the Caribbean and in French-speaking Africa.

In conceptual terms, the BLP defines transfers as "a structured learning process based on knowledge derived from real-world experience together with the human expertise capable of transforming that knowledge into social action." This concept starts with the identification and awareness of successful solutions, the matching of demand for learning with supply of expertise, and a step-by-step approach to help bring about desired change. The scope of change may cover policy reform, management and governance systems, technology, attitudes and behavior. In operational terms, a best practice transfer is a process whereby two or more parties engage in mutual exchange to learn from one another to improve processes, skills, knowledge, expertise or technology. Transfers can occur within a country or between countries. They include institutionalized transfers such as City-to-City Cooperation, or may take place spontaneously. Starting in 2006, UN-HABITAT and Dubai Municipality have decided that two of the twelve biennial best practice awards will be devoted to transfers as a further step to raise awareness of the role and contribution of peer-to-peer learning and decentralized cooperation in attaining international development targets and the Millennium Development Goals.

A best practice transfer is a value-added service. In many cases, value is greatly enhanced by the involvement of professional associations or capacity-building institutions. Their knowledge of and proximity to their respective communities place them in a good position to match best practices with the contextual conditions from which the demand emanates. The most common forms of transfer include: a) guided or structured study tours, often involving an intermediary such as a training or capacity-building institution; b) staff exchanges, primarily at the practitioner level; and c) city-to-city cooperation involving both the transfer of expertise and the implementation of demonstration projects which may involve financial support.

Policy Development

Policy change is the ultimate objective of the BLP. The scaling-up, transfer or replication of best practices depends to a large extent on an enabling policy environment whereby innovative approaches, methods and ideas can flourish and are not quashed by business-as-usual or resistance to change. The different types of approaches used to support policy change include:

- Presentation of evidence-based policy options derived from best practices to decision-makers at the highest level through, among other institutions, inter-governmental committees and commissions, the World Economic Forum, the World Social Forum and the World Urban Forum.

- Presentation of technical reports and guidelines targeting government officials, professional associations and non-governmental organizations through, among others, flagship publications such as UN-HABITAT's State of the World Cities Report and Global Report on Human Settlements.

- The documentation and dissemination of good urban policies and enabling legislation. This initiative, started in 2002, is designed to complement the Best Practices Database by providing matching sets of policies/laws and practices. The pilot phase, completed in 2004, involved 10 policies in local governance and decentralization, gender equality and social inclusion, crime prevention and social justice, local finance, primary health care, housing and water. The methodology includes a unified reporting format and a set of transparent criteria.[6] The pilot phase confirmed the validity of the approach, with seven out of ten countries involved having initiated changes to public policy. The methodology involves three key steps:

  o The unpacking of a law or policy in a format that is easily readable and accessible by all stakeholders and the general public. The unpacking, in most cases, involves an Institute of Public Administration or a government training institute and a peer-review panel consisting of three to four experts;

o A multi-stakeholder review of the law or policy to identify achievements and constraints in implementation; and

o Presentation of the combined results to decision-makers such as the Office of the President/Prime Minister, Parliamentarians, etc.

Impact of the BLP Knowledge Management Framework

The strength of the BLP Knowledge Management Framework lies in the involvement of a global network of partner institutions representing all major stakeholders in urban governance and development. UN-HABITAT's role is essentially that of a coordinator, ensuring the cross-fertilization of methods and concepts. This enables the BLP to compare lessons learned across a wide spectrum of themes, actors and socio-economic and political contexts. Partners, in turn, benefit from collective knowledge, expertise and experience.

The use of transparent criteria and a standardized reporting format has enabled the BLP to integrate new issues and themes while maintaining a set of generic questions that allow for the comparative analysis of practices covering different sectors involving a wide range of actors and scales of intervention. The most significant impact is most probably the adoption by several governments, institutions and organizations of the basic framework while adding criteria and questions to suit their particular needs. Examples at the international level include UNDP's Equator Initiative, UNEP's Success Stories initiative, the Commonwealth Secretariat and UNESCO's Social and Human Sciences (SHS) Programme. At the national level, the governments of Brazil, China, India and Spain have been using the framework since 1998. All four governments are applying the BLP system to national capacity-building and policy-development activities. In the case of Brazil, the Caixa Economica Federal has adopted the framework to support its municipal lending programme and to inform policy development at the national level.

Several non-governmental and community-based organizations have also adapted the system to their own needs. Examples include ENDA Tiers Monde and its extensive network in Africa, the Huairou Commission with its 400-plus grassroots women's groups in all regions of the world, the International Council for Caring Communities regarding issues of older persons and Youth for Habitat. All of these institutions and networks share their working methods, case studies, lessons learned and tools. This allows UN-HABITAT and its partners to continuously develop and refine generic terms of reference and guidelines that can be used by an increasing number and range of institutions and to achieve collective efficiency. Another tangible impact of the framework has been its ability to mobilize the media. The biennial award system provides the written press, radio and television with a source of positive news and raw material for investigative journalism. It is estimated that every two years the award system mobilizes media groups in over 100 countries to report on best practices.

Finally, best practices can be easily used to inform the political process. With the widespread adoption of democratically elected government, decision-making, especially at the local level, is increasingly shaped by perceptions and soft information. Best practices constitute an excellent source of information that can be used by decision-makers and by the general public. They are a source of inspiration for change and innovation based on tried and tested ideas. Peer learning and exchanges remain one of the most effective means of transferring lessons learned from good and best practices, as the perceived risk inherent to all forms of change can best be overcome by the testimony of a peer who has successfully implemented change.

Chapter 11

Transferring Effective Practices
Excerpts from a Manual
for South-South Cooperation[1]

Lakhbir Sing Chahl

This chapter examines the dynamics behind peer-to-peer transfer of innovations and highlights the key issues involved. It also examines the principal steps in the transfer process; the different types of peer-to-peer learning and exchanges that are possible; the stages of a transfer process; the key actors and supporting organizations; what cities and organizations need to know before entering into a transfer agreement; and it suggests an evaluation process to assess progress and measure the effectiveness of the transfer. Through examples of transfers, the chapter provides both information and worksheets that can be used in the transfer process. Finally, it proposes how to overcome obstacles and challenges, and how to select projects and partners for transferring best practices. Box 11.1 describes some of the key terms and concepts used in this chapter.

Peer-to-Peer Transfers

Multi-stakeholder partnerships are important to effective transfer and implementation of best practices since they include multi-lateral organizations, governmental agencies, NGOs, Community Based Organizations (CBOs) and the business sector. There is an increasing focus on peer-to-peer transfers because they promote technical cooperation; better match supply and demand for expertise and experience; and are not just donor to recipient.

CityNet and the City-to-City Transfer of Best Practices

CityNet, which is a Network of Local Authorities for the Management of Human Settlements in Asia and the Pacific, encourages peer-to-peer transfer

Box 11.1   Key Terms and Concepts

Peer-to-Peer Learning

- Exchange of knowledge, know-how, expertise and experience between people and organizations with similar roles and responsibilities, facing similar issues and problems.
- Decentralized cooperation that implies a demand-driven process in which one party is willing to learn and the other party is willing to share the lessons derived from its own experience.
- Examples: training, coaching, expert inputs and advisory services, site visits, study tours, staff exchanges and joint ventures.

Transfer

- Structured process of learning.
- Key components of a transfer can be identified as "knowledge derived from real-world experience together with the human expertise capable of transforming that knowledge into social action."
- The identification and awareness of solutions, the matching of demand for learning with supply of experience and expertise and a series of steps that need to be taken to help bring about the desired change.

Networking

- Capacity-building through information and communication technology.
- Useful tool in peer-to-peer learning and best practice transfers.
- An important means of accessing information, matching supply with demand for expertise and experience and of sharing lessons learned. It is not intended to replace the face-to-face dimension of peer-to-peer learning.

Source: CityNet, UNDP and UNCHS, 1998

by city-to-city cooperation, that is, best practice transfers at the local level. While previous transfers were characterized largely by one-way transfers from donors to recipients, the importance of peer-to-peer transfers is now increasingly recognized. Some of the most effective transfers have taken place between entities that are socially and economically similar. Being socially and economically similar, they also face similar problems—meaning they are able to form a common basis to develop cooperative solutions. Hence, with peer-to-peer transfers, there is a greater ability to match supply and demand for expertise and experience, as well as a greater opportunity for all the stakeholders to learn and improve.

CityNet has helped foster progress toward peer-to-peer transfer by connecting cities to each other and developing the concept of city-to-city cooperation. City-to-city cooperation focuses on a decentralized form of cooperation, by developing partnerships between stakeholders on the city and local levels. Transfer of best practices is supported through the fulfillment of the following activities by different organizations (Badshah, 1997, p. 9):

- Establishment of regional and national networks of urban practitioners;
- Documentation and dissemination of effective practices;
- Planning of international workshops;
- Initiation of dialogues between cities;
- Training activities;
- Organization of study tours;
- Cross-city consultation and technical assistance; and
- Initiation of transfers and adaptations of effective practices between and within cities.

City networks offer tremendous opportunities for the identification of common issues, problems and solutions as well as the sharing of knowledge, expertise and experience. Emphasis is placed on the establishment of collaborative mechanisms and networks for the ongoing transfer and exchange of information, results and ideas between urban practitioners.

Examples of Successful Transfers

In assessing the feasibility of a transfer, it is important to recognize the different types of transfers, which typically fall into three main categories:

- **Technical:** the transfer of skills and technology applications/processes;
- **Informational:** the transfer and exchange of ideas and solutions; and
- **Managerial:** a system or series of decision-making and resource allocation processes that can be transferred and adapted.

A programme developed by Yokohama, Japan to control flood waters is an example of the technical transfer of skills or technology applications. Not only has the project reduced the city's floodwater problems, but it has also led to a much better use of the river-front (see Box 11.2).

The transfer and exchange of management systems or approaches has fostered many relationships between local governments. A specific example is a transfer of a solid waste management system from Olongapo City in the Philippines to Tansen Municipality in Nepal (see Box 11.3). Olongapo City implemented an integrated garbage collection system that was coordinated by both the city government and local residents. The aim was to develop a set of values on cleanliness and responsibility that the residents would identify with and adopt as their own. This approach has been adapted for use in Tansen Municipality and is currently being transferred to Guntur in India.

Box 11.2   Bangkok Learns from Yokohama's Flood Control System

Bangkok is situated in the downstream flat deltoid plain of the Chao Phraya River, a scant 27-56 km from the river's mouth. The city's ground level is an average of 0.0-1.5 m above mean sea level. Bangkok suffers from frequent floods due to its low elevation and rapid urban construction that is turning the natural land into buildings and urban structures.

A technical transfer was initiated by dispatching experts from the Sewage Works Bureau of Yokohama to Bangkok in July 1997 to provide advice on flood–control strategies for Bangkok's flooding problem. Officials from the Bangkok Metropolitan Administration (BMA) became interested in this project after hearing about the innovative flood control methods developed by the city of Yokohama.

The project concept is simple, focusing on the development of reservoirs and "retention ponds" which store rainwater temporarily, especially in the early minutes of rain storms, to retard the outflow and thereby reduce peak discharge volume. The project concept is applied in more than a thousand places in Japan, but especially in the river basin around Yokohama.

Experts from Yokohama worked with officials from the BMA, showing them how to design retention ponds within the urban fabric of the city. This was similar to the design developed and applied in Yokohama and the Tsurumi River Basin area. Two engineers from the city of Yokohama went to Bangkok for a week to work with Thai planners at the Bangkok City Hall and establish the validity of this approach. The Thai engineers are now so confident of the approach that they are developing an application handbook and a computer programme with Chulalongkorn University in Bangkok to assist architects and engineers in applying this effective urban flood control system country-wide.

Source: CityNet, UNDP and UNCHS (1998)

Box 11.3   Solid Waste Management System in Tansen Municipality

Representatives from Nepal's Tansen Municipality, with financial support from CityNet, visited Olongapo, the Philippines, in 1997. The purpose of the visit was to study and observe the integrated Solid Waste Collection and Management Programme, which uses basic technology and focuses on health, sanitation and environmental pollution improvement. Moreover, the visit was intended to foster the possibility of transferring the successful experience in solid waste management for the betterment of Tansen Municipality.

The Pollution Programme works to eliminate garbage from the streets and to improve public education on sanitation, littering and garbage disposal. It plays a vital role in city schools in the information campaign on integrated solid waste collection, and there is a social pricing system to make the Olongapo "A Clean City," with voluntary group involvement.

As a follow-up activity, Tansen Municipality has decided to prepare a solid waste disposal master plan, replicating Olongapo's successful experience in managing solid waste. This plan includes the preparation of community awareness and cleanliness programmes as a pilot project to educate people on health, sanitation and the value of cleanliness. In order to implement this plan, Tansen Municipality has received assistance from Urban Development through Local Efforts Programme (UDLE). Tansen has already identified target areas for the implementation of the programme.

As a start, the Urban Hygiene and Environmental Education Programme (UHEEP) has been jointly conducted with UDLE and Tansen Municipality. Training is being provided to local NGOs on minimizing production of solid waste and its reuse. Further, one teacher from each school in the city is trained on school sanitation, reducing the volume of garbage produced, promoting environmental awareness and waste management. 10 days training on reducing waste disposal has been run in different parts of the city with the assistance of local NGOs and 400 people have been trained.

Source: CityNet, UNDP and UNCHS (1998)

The transfer of ideas or solutions involves a series of processes that participants may want to learn from and adapt locally. SEVANATHA Urban Resource Centre, in Sri Lanka, has adapted the savings and credit programmes of two Indian NGOs in low-income urban settlements with the aim of starting income-generating activities. The exchange of experiences of locally- and regionally-implemented best practices was seen as a vital factor for motivating local community groups in these settlements to see the value of locally-based credit and saving programmes. In this context, the achievements of Self Employed Women's Association (SEWA) Bank and Society for Promotion of Urban Resource Centres (SPARC) in organizing and empowering the poor urban communities were seen as programmes with the most value and benefit for the SEVANATHA team (see Box 11.4).

Box 11.4   Income–Generating Programmes for the Urban Poor

SEVANATHA, a local Urban Resource Centre in Sri Lanka, mobilized a study tour of two Indian savings and credit programmes that were initiated and implemented by local NGOs—SEWA Bank and SPARC. Five participants, who have been involved in urban low-income community development work, particularly in small group savings and credit programmes, were selected for the study visit.

SEWA Bank and SPARC both focus on empowering poor urban women to develop sustainable income-generating activities. SEWA focuses on women payment traders in Ahmedabad, organizing them into a cooperative through which they can access credit and save their earnings. Originally a small savings and credit programme, it has now grown into a larger banking institution. A unique aspect of SEWA's work has been that it has helped to provide an opportunity for women to sell their products in their own sales outlets, which cut exploitation by middlemen and allowed them to link directly into the mainstream market process. This has given rise to a number of training and other assistance programmes such as day-care, etc., to enable women to engage in their economic activities more effectively.

Box 11.4   *(Continued)*

SPARC undertakes effective community mobilization through a "mahila milan," or women's association, that has created a sense of hope and strength in poor women who live in pavement huts in Mumbai. The slum dwellers have been transformed into a resource group through community mobilization work that includes training, information, exchange of experiences, and savings and credit programmes.

After the study visit, SEVANATHA prepared a package that is displayed in its offices and also distributed to other provincial Urban Resource Centres (URCs) and local community organizations. Further, it has undertaken a concerted effort to inform the urban local authorities and other government organizations on the value of such programmes. Finally, a two-day workshop was held to review the progress of the community savings and credit programmes implemented by the URCs, utilizing the experiences of the study visits. One significant result of the transfer was change made by SEVANATHA in its lending policies based on lessons learned from SEWA Bank.

Source: CityNet, UNDP and UNCHS (1998)

Pre-Transfer Assessment

Several key questions should be answered before an agreement for a transfer is confirmed. Table 11.1 is intended to serve as a guideline for participants and hosts in assessing their level of preparedness for an exchange. The questions cover technical, socio-political, economic and cultural criteria. It should be reviewed and answered by participants interested in and/or involved in a transfer, since it helps in setting the overall framework within which a transfer can take place.

The questions are not exhaustive, but rather should be used as guidelines for participants and hosts in the evaluation phase prior to the transfer and adaptation of a best practice. Participants and hosts of a specific project should broaden the list by developing other questions suited to their particular case. By pursuing a detailed review prior to the transfer, participants and hosts can take a proactive rather than a reactive position.

Elements of a Transfer

The process begins by matching supply with demand by documenting and exchanging successful solutions through an intermediary that is knowledgeable about good and best practices. The four-step process and the proposed roles of the intermediary are detailed in the Table 11.2. The first step involves matching

Table 11.1   Key Questions When Considering a Transfer

Field	Question	Yes	No
Technical	Is the specific element of the best practice to be transferred clearly defined?		
	Is the quality and quantity of human resources sufficient to successfully implement the transfer?		
Social/Political	Does the transfer have the broad-based support of the community? (What is its role?)		
	Does the transfer have the support of key community leaders and local government officials? (What are their roles and responsibilities?)		
	Does the transfer have the support of the central government? (What is its role?)		
	Does the transfer require any changes in legislation, policy or institutional frameworks in order to take place?		
	If political change in any level of government is foreseen, will this change affect the long-term success of the transfer?		
	Have women's issues and gender considerations been incorporated into the transfer?		
Economic	Have resources been secured for the transfer?		
	Have resources been secured for follow-up and long-term sustainability of the transfer?		
	Are the funding and accounting mechanisms transparent?		
Environmental	Are there special social, economic or environmental considerations that could make the transfer difficult?		
	Are potential environmental impacts resulting from the transfer addressed?		
Cultural	If technology or management systems are involved in the transfer, are these appropriate to local conditions?		

Source: CityNet, UNDP and UNCHS, 1998

demand with supply, where the intermediary plays the role of a catalyst. The second step defines the scope of the transfer, with the intermediary acting as a broker between the two parties. The third step refers to the adaptation of the innovation to local conditions. Here the intermediary's role is that of a facilitator. The final step covers the actual implementation of the transfer and its evaluation. Here the intermediary is an evaluator. Awareness-building and media involvement are included throughout the four-step process, along with monitoring and evaluation.

Table 11.2 Four Principal Steps for Effective Transfers

Steps	Match Demand with Supply	Define Scope	Adapt	Implementation and Evaluation
Actions	Awareness of relevant best practices; and Agreement in principle to explore possibilities of exchange	Formation of transfer committees or task forces composed of key stakeholders and task managers on both sides; Transfer feasibility study (comparison of respective indicators, contexts and obstacles); Agreement and signature of MoU between stakeholders; and Documentation of lessons learned (supply side)	Adaptation of transfer to local context; Pilot demonstration project; and Documentation of lessons learned (demand side)	Full scale implementation; Assessment of results; and Evaluation report
Intermediary's Role	Catalyst	Broker	Facilitator	Evaluator
General Features		Awareness Building and Media Involvement Monitoring and Evaluation		

Source: CityNet, UNDP and UNCHS, 1998

Actors and Key Roles in a Transfer

Potential actors and their respective roles in a transfer may include:

- **Government:** National, state and local officials representing relevant agencies, departments or divisions;
- **City officials:** Elected and appointed officials, e.g., city councilors or mayor;
- **Non-governmental and community-based organizations:** Neighborhood associations, local interest coalitions, etc.;
- **Private sector:** Local businesses and industry, particularly those directly affected by the issues relating to the transfer;
- **Professional and civic organizations:** Professional associations that play a significant role in the community;
- **Media:** Local, national and international media should be included as much as possible in all planning, implementation and evaluation events to help raise awareness and political support and provide visibility;
- **Academic/research organizations:** Academic and research organizations can offer valuable insight and input into development projects and initiatives, including a mediation and/or monitoring and evaluation role;
- **Foundations:** Local, national and international foundations are increasingly interested in providing support to local development initiatives and projects and many of them also have inputs to provide on various aspects of project design and implementation; and
- **Multilateral and bilateral support programmes:** These represent a traditional source of funding support, but are increasingly involved in networking and facilitating access to information, technical and managerial know-how, and expertise and information.

The media should be included as an integral player in both the reporting of best practices and their transfers by raising awareness in the community of the transfer process; mobilizing political support; and encouraging greater transparency in the transfer process. Another important stakeholder is represented by NGOs, which can play a bridging role in brokering transfers between a local authority and community groups. Table 11.3 provides a picture of the main actors involved in a transfer and their roles in terms of political, financial, technical and management support, as well as what actors can best assist as facilitators/mediators. Box 11.5 illustrates the need to bring all parties within the local authority and the community to a clear understanding of new modes of working together. In the town of Kandy, Sri Lanka, a shared solution was found for two different groups that were both facing problems related to hous-

Table 11.3   Suggested Actors and Possible Functions of Key Roles

	Political Support	Financial Support	Technical Support	Admin./Mgt. Support	Facilitator/ Mediator
Government	X	X		X	
City Officials	X	X	X	X	
NGOs/Community-Based Organizations			X	X	X
Private Sector		X	X	X	
Professional Associations	X		X	X	X
Media	X			X	X
Academic/Research Organizations			X	X	X
Foundations		X		X	X
Multi- and Bi-lateral Support Programmes	X	X	X	X	X

Source: CityNet, UNDP and UNCHS, 1998

ing and infrastructure development. An intermediary agency aware of the predicaments of the two groups, facilitated collaboration between them as well as the implementation of a development programme that generated employment for the low-income groups, provided necessary housing and resulted in a higher-quality infrastructure.

Kandy's success was in partnering with a group of poor squatters of the Menikkumbura community and a similar group living on Buddhist temple land, through the facilitation of an intermediary. This led to a successful resolution of the problems of the respective groups. This experience is just one example of the various roles and participants that can be involved in an initiative.

Box 11.5   Low-Income Housing in the Town of Kandy, Sri Lanka

Main Actors

- Urban Local Authority of Kandy (ULA)
- SEVANATHA (NGO)
- National Housing Development Authority (NHDA)
- Buddhist temple squatters
- Community-based organization of the Menikkumbura community
- Housing and Community Development Committees of the Urban Local Authority (HCDC)

Problem

The extremely poor squatters of the Menikkumbura community were displaced from their shelters during the floods of the rainy season, but the ULA and some voluntary organizations had been unable to find suitable land where the squatters could relocate. At the same time, another poor community living on Buddhist temple land had asked the ULA to obtain permission from the temple for a low-income housing project on temple land. The ULA had no prior experience in undertaking community-based low-income housing projects. Though the people would be able to manage the cost of their house construction, they were lacking the resources for water supply and drainage. Once the temple had given permission, the ULA proposed bringing the Menikkumbura community into the low-income housing project with the temple community.

Process of Resolution

The ULA sought assistance from SEVANATHA, an NGO, which had experience in implementing community-based approaches. SEVANATHA agreed to advise the ULA and to conduct training workshops in the two communities to prepare them for the project. In this way, the NGO acted as a mediator between the Menikkumbura community, the temple community and the ULA. The project was implemented. The provision of infrastructure at low cost was realized through the use of the community construction contract (CCC) that enabled the municipality to hire community members to install drainage and water supply systems. This generated employment for low-income groups and resulted in a higher-quality, more appropriate infrastructure.

Facilitation of Collaboration

The HCDC is the institutional structure created to find solutions for low-income housing and infrastructure problems, set guidelines and facilitate implementation of development programmes. It facilitates links between all the actors. Chaired by the mayor, the HCDC is part of the ULA and its committee consists of elected members, governmental officials, NGO representatives and CBO representatives. It meets once each month.

Source: CityNet, UNDP and UNCHS, 1998

Key Indicators for the Effective Transfer of Practices

A transfer can be deemed successful even if it has encountered several obstacles during its development and implementation. The following process indicators provide a checklist for actors involved in the transfer process. They should be viewed as a tool for assessing an initiative's development and effectiveness:

- **Participation:** Does the transfer involve and/or promote participation of all possible stakeholders?
- **Transparency:** Is the transfer process open and accessible to all stakeholders?
- **Accountability:** Are mechanisms in place to ensure accountability for actions and responsibilities of all partners involved?

- **Inclusion:** Is the participation of all potential stakeholders considered in the transfer's design?

- **Financial feasibility:** Are resources and/or funding available to realize and sustain the initiative? Are funding alternatives identified?

- **Sustainability:** Does the initiative consider economic, environmental and social needs without trading off one at the great expense of the other, now or in the future?

Technical indicators should also be identified and adopted by transfer participants so that administrative and technical considerations can be assessed throughout the implementation phases. Table 11.4 summarizes key technical indicators for a transfer involving a local authority.

In addition to indicators, it is recommended that partners develop a mission statement and goals for their transfer. These should incorporate the use of process and technical indicators as well as what hosts and participants would like to achieve through the transfer. The mission statement and goals should be referred to frequently throughout the transfer process, both as a means of assessing progress and as a reminder of the original objectives and scope of the initiative. In summary, the key elements of a transfer should include the following:

- **Information dissemination and exchange:** Dissemination of innovative practices in order to promote initial matching of supply with demand for knowledge, expertise and experience;

- **Roles and responsibilities of actors/stakeholders:** Further matching of supply with demand in identifying and defining the social, economic and environmental issues to be addressed and the roles and responsibilities of hosts and participants;

- **"Matched" solution to problem:** Negotiation by two parties for a transfer commitment by recognizing that the host has been successful in implementing a process or solution from which the participant is willing to learn;

- **Education and adaptation:** Participants learn from hosts through site visits and surveys of the local application of a programme. Plans of the transfer are widely publicized so that potential stakeholders are aware of the proposed plan, and to encourage "ownership" by the community at large;

- **Implementation plan:** A plan and/or feasibility study for the adaptation and implementation of the transfer is developed;

- **Transfer:** Initially, a pilot demonstration should be undertaken to test the viability of the programme, followed by a full-scale transfer; and

- **Follow-up:** Monitoring and assessment of the effectiveness and impact of the transfer.

Table 11.4   Technical Indicators for the Effective Transfer
of Practices

Political

- Timing of elections
- Recent policies adopted or changed
- Number of years before next national and/or civic elections

---

Administrative and Managerial

- Indicators pertaining to roles and responsibilities and degree of autonomy
- Indicators pertaining to organic structure of the organization, number of employees per service, number of employees per thousand population
- Indicators pertaining to size of budget, percentage of own revenue, sources of grants, revenue per capita, etc.
- Indicators pertaining to performance, e.g., cost per unit of service delivered
- Indicators pertaining to proportion of professional staff
- Indicators pertaining to types of services delivered and by whom

---

Social and Economic

- Number of women involved
- Number of households below poverty line
- Literacy rate
- Infant mortality rate
- Crime rates
- Per capita income
- Household connection levels
- Median price of water

Environmental

- Per capita production of waste
- Percentage of waste recycled
- Per capita consumption of water, electricity, etc.

Cultural

- Religious composition of the society
- Ethnic make-up
- Other special considerations

Source: CityNet, UNDP and UNCHS, 1998

Overcoming Obstacles
and Challenges

There are several obstacles that can affect the transfer process and need to be overcome (see Table 11.5). They can be both internal and external to the transfer participants: political resistance, staff resistance, inappropriate rules and regulations, corruption, inter-departmental differences, little or no local participation.

Table 11.5   Overcoming Obstacles in the Transfer Process

Obstacles	Responses
Political Resistance to Change	Face-to-face meetings and discussions between elected officials can help overcome reluctance to engage in institutional change.
Staff Resistance to Change	Peer-to-peer learning and on-the-job training can help empower staff and allay fears that new ways of doing things may affect one's power base or cause major disruption in standard operating procedure.
Inappropriate Rules and Regulations	"Seeing is believing"—peer-to-peer learning and study tours can often be more convincing than textbook solutions, and help create the awareness and understanding of the need to modify outdated rules, regulations and norms.
Corruption	Best practices have, in many cases, forged a "win-win" situation, thus overcoming the traditional "win-lose" options that underlie corrupt practices. The involvement of multiple stakeholders and partners also contributes directly to more transparent and accountable processes.
Inability to Work Across Departmental or Divisional Boundaries	Study tours and staff exchanges involving a team of decision-makers and stakeholders can help forge a team spirit and break down fiefdoms. They can also provide an opportunity to re-examine the respective roles and responsibilities of different work units.
Little or No Local Involvement in Policy Formulation and Decision-making	Through best practice transfers, the effectiveness of partnerships with grassroots and community-based organizations can be effectively demonstrated.

Source: CityNet, UNDP and UNCHS, 1998

Building on New Opportunities

Beyond the practice actually being transferred, transfers also open the door for other kinds of positive changes, particularly within the following areas:

- **Policy reform:** The transfer of a best practice provides a unique opportunity for policy change and reform. The transfer process not only constitutes a legitimate reason to engage in broad-based consultations and dialogue with the host community, but also a chance to look at how others have introduced participatory planning and decision-making processes and passed new legislation, codes or by-laws;

- **Ensuring transparency and accountability:** A best practice transfer involving multiple stakeholders and actors in all stages of design and implementation can help introduce new levels of citizen involvement and help ensure transparency and accountability; and

- **Empowering/enabling local community and non-governmental organizations:** Best practice transfers also provide an opportunity to empower local communities by recognizing and acknowledging their potential and real contributions to bettering their own living environment.

The impact of partnerships is well illustrated by one transfer that involved many different participants. Three poor communities, Gol Tikri, Kaan 18-19 and Bhusa Lane, located in the municipality of Sukkur, Pakistan, were faced with a sewer problem that posed significant threats to their health and homes. Through the facilitation of a partnership between the three communities and several municipal agencies, the members of Gol Tikri, Kaan 18-19 and Bhusa Lane constructed a sewer system. Thus, the flooding and resulting health threats from contaminated water were solved for the communities' residents by the residents themselves. Box 11.6 highlights how the structure and organization of partnerships affected the efficacy of this project.

A key actor in this case was the non-governmental organization called the Orangi Pilot Project Programme (OPP) Research and Training Institute, which had faced a similar problem in Karachi, Pakistan (UNDP/TCDC, 1995, pp. 64–67). The OPP provided the training for the project director, social organizers, municipal counselors and community activists in the Sukkur sewer project. Without the OPP's training and advice, as well as its Orangi model, the Sukkur project would not have developed as it did (see Box 11.7).

Despite the successful completion of the project in Sukkur, it did face several obstacles during its development. The division of responsibilities between the actors is outlined in Table 11.6.

The Sukkur Municipal Corporation (SMC) did not have the capability to fulfill its designated responsibilities. There were many delays in external work

Box 11.6   Infrastructure and Sewage in Sukkur, Pakistan

Main Actors

- Urban Local Authority of Kandy (ULA)
- SEVANATHA (NGO)
- National Housing Development Authority (NHDA)
- Buddhist temple squatters
- Community-based organization of the Menikkumbura community
- Housing and Community Development Committees of the Urban Local Authority (HCDC)

Problem

The poor squatters of Gol Tikri, Kaan 18-19 and Bhusa Lane lived next to an abandoned stone quarry that was used to dispose of waste water, garbage and excreta. Shallow open drains or lanes carried effluent to the old quarry. It began filling and became a large, stagnant sewage pond covering 28 acres. Many lanes became waterlogged and houses near the pond suffered from overflow and flooding. The SMC and SKAA had little experience with infrastructure problems involving poor settlements. Two small pumps were installed by the SMC but they were ineffective.

Process of Resolution

The SKAA asked the OPP to help replicate their successful model to solve the problem. Residents agreed to do the internal work, such as installing latrines, local sewerage lines and collector drains, and the government agreed to do the external work, such as emptying the pond and building trunk sewers and a treatment plant. Social organizers were appointed from within the community to coordinate with households. OPP provided training for all of the actors in various aspects related to the internal and external work. The SMC recruited two social organizers from another government programme to coordinate external and internal construction.

There were many delays in the external work because the SMC lacked technical capacity, financial resources, accountability and managerial expertise. First, there were frequent changes of officials within the project. Also, the SMC failed to operate the pumping station to empty the pond regularly and efficiently. In addition, the SMC chose a contractor for the trunk sewer who had no experience, and plans and estimates for the project disappeared. The work was completed late and cost more than three times the initial estimates made by OPP. The residents mobilized, financed and successfully managed construction of the internal work by themselves. They learned technical and managerial skills and collectively pressured the government to fulfill its commitments.

Facilitation of Collaboration

OPP was the main catalyst that brought the actors together through training and advising. The social organizers recruited by SMC coordinated external and internal construction by interacting with all involved parties. Also, the project office was set up in the area and was open in the evening, providing residents with easier access to the project. It became a place for gathering and discussion.

Source: CityNet, UNDP and UNCHS, 1998

Box 11.7   The Orangi Pilot Project

This case study, a low-cost sewer and housing programme by low-income residents in the Orangi District, Karachi, Pakistan, represents a case in which a low-income community installed a sanitation system with the assistance of an NGO.

Main Actors

- Orangi Pilot Project Programme Research and Training Institute (OPP)
- Residents of Orangi
- Local community groups

Problem

Orangi is an unauthorized settlement within Karachi with approximately 800,000 inhabitants. Initially, there was no public provision for sanitation and most residents used bucket latrines that were emptied periodically into the unpaved lanes between houses. The cost of having local government install a sewage system would have been too high for the low-income residents.

Process of Resolution

A local NGO, the Orangi Pilot Project (OPP), initiated a self-help sanitation system that has been very successful. Meetings were held between staff of the NGO and residents to explain the benefits of such a system and to offer technical assistance. Lane leaders were elected who formally applied for technical help and organized the local project. Technicians from the OPP drew up plans for the local scheme and the sewers were installed with maintenance organized by local groups. As the project's feasibility became apparent, other stakeholders in Orangi showed interest in getting involved. To date, nearly 70,000 sanitary pour-flush latrines have been constructed.

Low-Cost Financing Strategy

A vital aspect of the project has been its low cost. Simplified designs and the use of standardized steel molds reduced the cost of sanitary latrines in manholes to less then one-quarter of contractors' rates. The cost of sewer lines was also greatly reduced by eliminating the profits of the contractor. The average cost of a small-bore sewer system is no more than US $66 per house. Today almost 75 percent of Orangi residences have sanitary latrines with an underground sanitation system.

Source: CityNet, UNDP and UNCHS, 1998

Table 11.6   Division of Responsibilities

Government: External Responsibilities	Community Residents: Internal Responsibilities
• Empty the pond	• Construct latrines
• Construct trunk sewers	• Lay local sewerage lines
• Provide treatment plant	• Construct collector drains

Source: CityNet, UNDP and UNCHS, 1998

because the SMC lacked the technical capacity, financial resources, accountability and managerial know-how (UNCHS and CityNet, 1997, p. 97). The obstacles posed by the SMC affected not only the technical aspects of the project, but also delayed its progress through poor organisation and hiring decisions for contractors integral to the project. Upon closer analysis, there is much to be learned from the obstacles the Sukkur project faced. The obstacles encountered and lesson learned in Sukkur, Pakistan are shown in Table 11.7.

Table 11.7   Obstacles and Lesson Learned

Obstacles Encountered	Lesson Learned
Political changes and low expertise levels of government officials in given subjects	
Government initially made technology choices that were difficult to implement; initial plans were inconsistent with needs of the low-income groups; historical hostility between state agencies and low-income groups; lack of training for officials in partnership building.	It is essential to assess realistically the relationships between all actors involved in the project and to ensure that the planning process involves all stakeholders, beneficiaries in particular.
Underestimation of project costs and failure to address long-term funding for financial sustainability	
The funding structure, both short-term and long-term, should be determined prior to the project's initiation. Alternative funding sources and strategies should be identified in the event that costs exceed initial estimates, or primary funding sources fail to follow through on commitments.	A monitoring and evaluation system is essential so that progress on the project or initiative can be assessed at each phase. Changes in funding levels should be reflected in project revision and re-design, if necessary, again involving all stakeholders.
Lack of clear leadership roles and responsibilities	
In the Sukkur project, a general lack of respect for the different lead actors had an impact on the project because relations between the residents and government officials became increasingly strained as certain responsibilities of the government were either completed at a low level of quality or not at all.	The role of an intermediary (third party) during the project's negotiation and implementation phases can help defuse conflicts and friction, and help define the respective roles and responsibilities of each actor involved.
Lack of transparency in project design (objectives) and implementation	
It is essential to a project's long-term and short-term success that the public is allowed to participate in the project's development and that the process is transparent.	In the Sukkur project, a project office was set up in the area. The office was open during evening hours so residents could access it to ask questions, gather and discuss progress.

Source: CityNet, UNDP and UNCHS, 1998

Considerations for the Selection of Partners and Projects

Although successful transfers take place every day involving different countries, regions and actors, there are several considerations that can help enhance the effectiveness and efficiency of a transfer process. These considerations include:

- A common or shared set of problems and issues;
- Similarities in social, economic and demographic contexts;
- Local support for such partnerships and co-operative exchanges;
- A mutual commitment to share and to learn;
- Documented evidence of a proven solution in the form of a good or best practice; and
- An understanding of the similarities and differences in administrative and political contexts and procedures.

Many best practices involve smaller NGOs/CBOs and municipalities which may have limited capacities to engage in transfers. An important indicator of whether such a host is capable of engaging in a transfer is to ask whether the initial practice has been scaled-up locally and whether it has actively engaged in training and/or advocacy.

Negotiating a Partnership Agreement for a Transfer

It is important to be aware of the different types of peer-to-peer learning and exchanges that are possible, as well as their implications for both participant and host. Some of these types are briefly listed below.

Study tours: These are relatively common and easy to organize. They necessitate a formal exchange of letters regarding the object and purpose of the visit by the participant and a setting of dates and number of people involved. Advantages include ease of organization and a low level of expectations for both parties. The effectiveness of a study tour can be greatly enhanced by prior exchange and sharing of information on key indicators, by focusing on specific issues for learning and exchange and by well-matched counterparts.

Study tour with action planning: A more elaborate transfer process which involves formal and prior exchange of information regarding the intent of the partner to learn from the host within the framework of an ongoing or about-to-be implemented action plan. This will require the hosts to reflect on their lessons learned and to share their knowledge and know-how on various aspects of design, implementation, decision-making and impact assessment. The main advantage is a more detailed mutual understanding of the needs, contexts and priorities of the host and participant situations. This process demands much more preparation on behalf of both parties and a serious commitment to mutual learning and exchange. Expectations for both parties should be clearly stipulated in terms of reference for the study tour and any follow-up activities.

Staff exchange: Similar to above and recommended as a follow-up to a study tour whereby staff, usually from the participants' side, stays with the host for the purpose of on-site, on-the-job learning and coaching. It can also involve the host sending staff to the participant for follow-up cooperation during critical phases of implementation. This form of exchange can be very effective. In terms of preparation, at a minimum, terms of reference should be agreed to. In cases of prolonged exchanges, other administrative arrangements should be clearly settled.

Technical cooperation agreement: An agreement which may encompass all of the above plus the use of or secondment of technical staff and/or experts from the host to the participant. Such an agreement usually involves some costs, such as travel and accommodation, and may also include contractual arrangements. Clear terms of reference should be used to ensure that all aspects of the co-operation agreement are fully discussed, agreed to and approved by both parties.

Twinning arrangements: They imply a long-term commitment on behalf of both parties to systematically engage in peer-to-peer learning, exchanges and study tours. Twinning arrangements usually involve sharing and exchange at all levels, including the political, social-cultural and technical dimensions.

A checklist for an effective partnership agreement would include:

- Develop clear and achievable mission and goals;
- Identify type of partnership agreement;
- Develop estimated timeline;
- Secure required resources;
- Set clear expectations; and
- Provide necessary staffing and training.

Lessons Learned

The following are some of the practical lessons drawn from actual transfers. Box 11.8 summarizes the general lessons observed from effective and innovative transfers.

- Visits provide hosts with an opportunity for learning, capacity-building and evaluation. Hosts can learn from visiting teams, and also benefit from reviewing and further improving their ongoing good and best practices;

> **Box 11.8   General Lessons Observed from Effective and Innovative Transfers**
>
> - Innovation champions play a critical role in the transfer process
> - Successful implementation of transfers requires partnerships—a participatory, integrated and flexible approach
> - Transfer provides a non-crisis incentive for cross-cultural collaboration
> - Transfer is not only a product, but also a process
> - Extraneous factors can derail a transfer
> - Open-ended learning works best
> - Failures teach as much as success
> - It is important to celebrate the replicator
>
> *Source:* CityNet, UNDP and UNCHS, 1998

- Transfers should focus on the process that made innovations possible and not just on technology or know-how. Staff exchanges and visits should be conceived as an action-planning exercise to help participants share experiences on the processes involved and to assess opportunities and constraints for adaptation or transfer;
- Visiting and host teams should be matched and should include various actors: decision-makers, community leaders, technical and managerial staff, as well as other relevant stakeholders. In addition to focusing on the current good or best practice, actors should identify other aspects of current work of potential interest to participants such as other projects, management and information systems, etc.;
- Learning can take place at individual, organizational and institutional levels, and therefore there are different types of transfers that can take place: NGO-NGO, NGO-city, city-city or institutional programmes. The transfer of process skills, such as participatory planning, conflict resolution, mediation, community mobilization and participation are as important as technical skills and know-how;
- Assessing the cost-effectiveness of initiatives is an important aspect of the learning and transfer process; and
- There is a need to understand the local administrative/political and social/economic context in order to fully assess the opportunities and constraints to a successful transfer. The costs involved in peer-to-peer learning and exchanges, particularly within a given region, are often lower and more cost-effective than using experts or consultants or sending staff to supply-driven training courses.

Monitoring, Evaluation and Feedback

The sustainability of a transfer and the implementation of an innovative practice rely upon the follow-through process and an honest evaluation of both the innovation and the transfer. Prior to the transfer, a clear monitoring plan should be devised to provide a framework by which progress can be assessed, impacts measured in accordance with initial objectives or anticipated results, and the implementation process analysed for lessons learned.

Assessments of the process, successes and failures should be scheduled both on a short-term and long-term basis, with all key players represented. Feedback meetings should be public and widely advertised so that all stakeholders have an opportunity to get involved in the ongoing evaluation and follow-up processes.

A key aspect of monitoring is to identify the obstacles faced, keeping track of how they were overcome. This will provide others with valuable information on how to avoid some of the obstacles and also how to overcome them when encountered. It is important to remember that every project runs into obstacles at some point in the implementation process, and in the euphoria of success, these obstacles are often forgotten.

The effective transfer of a practice is not simply replication but rather an innovative adaptation using lessons derived from successes as well as failures. Developing a solution applicable to a community's specific problem is itself a good practice and should be evaluated and documented for the benefit of others. Table 11.8 outlines a strategic process for programme evaluation.

Table 11.8   Strategic Process for Programme Evaluation

Step	Process
Impact Evaluation	Gather key participants together as a group to evaluate the results of the transfer.
Constructive Critique	Develop a list of criteria from the previous stages of the transfer process that best represents the critical factors of the project.
Survey	Using the criteria developed by the participants, develop a survey-feedback instrument to be distributed to and completed by community stakeholders, e.g., residents, NGOs, businesses, government.
Document	Collect, compile and document survey results.
Identify	Identify key success and problem areas.
Long-term	Schedule ongoing evaluation processes to highlight successes and discuss remedies/alternatives for problems.

Source: You, 1998 in CityNet, UNDP and UNCHS, 1998

In the short term, evaluation results should be documented and discussed to determine whether modifications are necessary to the initial plan. Should modifications be deemed necessary, the same processes used in developing the initial plan can be repeated, focusing on the areas identified for change.

In the medium to long term, the transfer process, including its impact and its process, should be documented and disseminated widely to enrich the body of best practice knowledge. This expertise and experience can be used by other people, communities and organizations, thus continually enhancing the potential for matching supply with demand for South-South and decentralized forms of cooperation.

Without sharing, innovations and best practices will remain islands of excellence in a sea of "business as usual." Yet, it is also important to know that transfer and peer-to-peer learning are not a panacea, but a process requiring time, commitment and an open participatory system that allows for different opinions and voices to be heard. Although the benefits to the demand-side may seem obvious, hosts stand to benefit as well, through developing their capacity as a learning organization, or one that continually grows in knowledge of its own strengths, weaknesses, and challenges.

Chapter 12

Replication Strategies and Transferability of Best Practices and Innovations

The Gawad Galing Pook Awards in the Philippines

Austere Panadero

This chapter examines replication strategies for local governance as applied and experienced by the Gawad Galing Pook Foundation in the Philippines. It describes elements needed to transfer or replicate an exemplary practice, critical factors in the replication process, and the main characteristics of those who replicate exemplary practices. We begin with a brief introduction to the Gawad Galing Pook Foundation and its Awards programme for innovation and excellence in government.

The Shift of Powers to Local Governments

The Local Government Code (LGC), enacted in the Philippines in 1992, radically transformed the country's politico-administrative system. The Code is considered revolutionary in the Philippines because it devolved certain powers and functions to provinces, cities, municipalities and *barangays* (villages, the smallest political unit) that were hitherto controlled by the central government. Local government was made responsible for the delivery of basic services such as health, agriculture, social services, as well as aspects of environmental management and infrastructure. In addition, the Code increased financial commitments to local governments, established the foundation for cooperation between civil society and local governments, and encouraged entrepreneurship in local government.

As a result of the Code, Local Government Units (LGUs) are compelled and expected to consider local demands when making policy and implementing programmes and projects. The responsibility for accessing and mobilizing resources is also an opportunity to unlock the LGUs' entrepreneurial energies in order to increase their revenues and improve local services. The Local Government Code created the policy infrastructure for good governance at the local level, but it is up to the LGUs to deliver on these expectations. Local officials had little preparation, and in some cases insufficient resources, to properly respond to these changes and challenges. Yet some LGUs found creative ways to better serve their constituents, in part by looking to themselves, their communities and their peers for new ideas and approaches. The Gawad Galing Pook Awards were created to recognize these successes.

Recognizing Excellence in Local Governance

The Gantimpalang Panglingkod Pook, or Gawad Galing Pook, was launched in 1993 to recognize innovation and excellence in local governance. Its mandates include: recognizing innovation and excellence in local governance; inspiring replication of these practices; and advocating citizen awareness of and participation in innovative local governance programmes. The Gawad Galing Pook Awards include the following categories:

- **Outstanding Local Governance Programme and Trailblazing Programme:** The award for Outstanding Local Governance Programme is given yearly to the ten top-ranking local governance programmes according to the Galing Pook Foundation's selection criteria. The Trailblazing Programme Award is given to the next ten finalists from the same screening process;

- **Award for Continuing Excellence (ACE):** Every five years, an ACE is given to past winners of the Outstanding Local Governance Programme Award that have made the most significant progress since receiving the original award; and

- **Special Citations:** These are awarded to programmes judged to have accomplished the most significant achievements in specific areas of local governance development, such as child-rights-responsiveness and gender-responsiveness.

Candidates for the Gawad Galing Pook Awards pass through a rigorous multi-level screening process. Major selection criteria include whether the programme has a positive impact on economic, socio-cultural, environmental and gender-equity issues; whether it promotes citizen empowerment; it is transferable and sustainable; it is efficient; and it makes creative use of local powers provided by the LGC and related legislation. Specific standards are associated with each of these major selection criteria. This comprehensive screening process is spearheaded by a National Selection Committee (NSC) and supported by a Regional Selection Committee (RSC). The screeners are distinguished individuals from government, NGOs, academia, the business sector and media who bring diversity of views, gender, geographical location and technical expertise.

To date, the Gawad Galing Pook Awards have recognized 195 innovative and excellent programmes in local governance. Municipalities have received the most awards, followed by city-level programmes. This is quite understandable considering the large number of applications received from municipalities. Environmental and healthcare categories have garnered the most Gawad Galing Pook awards. The environmental programmes range from river rehabilitation to forest protection, while the healthcare programmes focused on providing more innovative, efficient and affordable services to constituents.

What Prompts Innovation?

Some of the circumstances that led to innovations recognized by the Gawad Galing Pook Awards are described below.

"Triggering crises": Innovations may occur in response to a crisis, such as environmental degradation, floods, etc. When pushed against the wall and confronted with a crisis, various stakeholders in society, whether governmental or civil, become creative and innovative. A Bantay Dagat ("protecting the sea") programme was launched in Puerto Princesa, a city in Palawan province, in response to the threat of rapid depletion of its fisheries.

Dynamic leadership and active civil society: Political leaders usually take the initiative in addressing felt or articulated needs. They do so in response to practical or political expediency. The point is that aggressive leadership and a committed government prompted and sustained most of the innovations awarded by Gawad Galing Pook. Pressure from members of civil society led to the initiation of fewer programmes.

Inadequate financial resources: Limitations on financial resources can prompt local authorities to think of ways to generate revenues in addition to the conventional means of taxation and allotments from the national government. Various local financial initiatives have received awards in the last ten years.

Demand for specific basic services: Local governments may become creative in response to a pressing basic need that simply must be addressed, such as healthcare and housing.

National policies and programmes: While the national government may provide the policy framework for, say, addressing certain basic needs (housing, healthcare, infrastructure development, etc.), local governments may build upon the framework and adapt it to local conditions. The national government's policy on solid waste management, for example, has led some LGUs to develop their own strategies for implementing this policy locally.

Gawad Galing Pook Replication Experiences

Gawad Galing Pook believes that the value of harvesting best and innovative practices is greater when shared with other LGUs, prompting them to explore their potential, respond to local needs, maximize their resources—and realize good governance. This is why the Foundation works to provide venues and create opportunities in the form of learning and replication circles that aid policy discussion, model-building and cross-fertilization of lessons among LGUs.

Gawad Galing Pook's replication strategies range from exchanges of information and ideas to the actual replication of a particular exemplary practice. Galing Pook defines replication as a structured learning process that facilitates sharing and the development of advocacy strategies across programmes and organizations in order to build the capacities of individuals, groups and institutions to improve their situations. Its replication strategies are characterized by collaboration and partnership, as they involve making a conscious decision to learn and work together.

Three of the Foundation's replication strategies are analysed throughout this chapter: information transfer, nationally driven transfers, and peer-to-peer coaching. In the next sections we describe these replication strategies; the last two strategies—nationally driven transfer and peer-to-peer coaching—are implemented primarily by partner institutions of Gawad Galing Pook.

Information Transfer

Information transfer, or the exchange of ideas and solutions, is a key method of transfer or replication used by Gawad Galing Pook. It involves the unpacking of technologies that make best practices possible and dissecting which combination of features, e.g., framework, systems and tools, would apply to a similar but also unique situation in another community. Information transfer also involves enhancing the "learning transferability" of the best practices recognized by the Gawad Galing Pook.

The Replication Strategies

Gawad Galing Pook has instituted several mechanisms to promote and implement information transfer. These include:

Development of knowledge products: Creating a best practices compendium. Gawad Galing Pook documents its awarded practices as inputs to the replication process. It has published a compendium of exemplary LGU practices in a multi-volume series titled Kaban-Galing: A Case Bank of Exemplary Programmes in Local Governance). The series is organized by the following development themes: good local governance; environmental governance; local economic transformation; poverty reduction; urban governance; child-friendly governance; and peace and development.

The documentation highlights the tools, methodologies and strategies that are useful to replication efforts. It contains, but is not limited to, the following: the name of the approach, its proponent/initiator, and sources of funding; its objectives and key processes; any tools developed and their features; what participatory structures and processes were strengthened; what partnership arrangements were developed; the output and outcome of the intervention(s); gains and impact generated; factors that contributed to the results; enabling and limiting factors; plans and components for sustaining the innovation; and prospects for replication and mainstreaming. Each volume begins with a replication guide based on the lessons and insights generated by analysing the different cases under each development theme.

Learning circles: Workshops for sharing knowledge. Galing Pook also uses learning circles—conference workshops that bring together past award winners and selected LGU officials—as a more interactive way to transfer information. The Galing Pook winners featured in these meetings serve as resources for peer-to-peer learning. This sharing and dialogue between and among LGU winners and international counterparts provides new perspectives and strategies to local leaders on how to address development and governance concerns in their local entities. The latest learning circle events conducted by Galing Pook concerned solid waste management, coastal resource management and the strengthening of local school boards.

LOGOSHARE: Local governance knowledge-sharing network. LOGOSHARE is the latest strategy being developed by Galing Pook to facilitate information exchange and transfer, undertaken in partnership with the Center for Conscious Living Foundation. It is an information communication technology (ICT) that will use the power of information technology and the internet to promote and encourage replication of best practices in local governance.

Nationally Driven Transfers

Nationally driven replication or transfer involves cooperation between the Philippines' Department of Interior and the Department of Interior and Local

Government (DILG). Specifically, the two departments develop a particular mechanism or practice into a national programme and undertake a nationwide effort to encourage LGUs to adopt it. This replication scheme has been applied in the government's Anti-Red Tape Programme, whereby local government units are encouraged to set up a one-stop-shop processing system for business permits, and in the Bayanihan Savings Replication Project (BSRP). The BSRP is described in more detail in the following section.

An Example of a Nationally Driven Transfer

The BSRP developed out of the Bayanihan Banking Programme (BBP), a Galing Pook awardee in 2002. The BBP, located in Pasay City in Metro Manila, is an adaptation of the Grameen Bank, a micro-finance model developed by Dr. Mohammad Yunus of Bangladesh. Essentially, the programme aims to empower the poor by enabling them to save and gain access to credit. Under the BBP, small groups of 26-30 beneficiaries set up their own financial center with its own system and policy on savings and loans. Financial centers create their own emergency fund using savings pledged during weekly meetings. Members cannot borrow if they do not save, as their savings record serves as their credit record. In addition to credit lines, members have access to accident insurance. A unique feature of the BBP is its emphasis on values and spiritual development. To cultivate better relationships and a culture of trust among members, its capability-building interventions include a values-formation programme and the integration of spiritual exercises such as prayers and bible reading into their meetings. In barely two years, the Pasay City BBP has formed 251 financial centers with a total of 10,000 members who have generated savings of P3.7 million.

The Replication Process

Having seen the success of BBP in Pasay City, the DILG adopted the programme for replication; the department saw value in the way BBP fosters savings among its members and strengthens their values by participating in an activity that enhances their relationship with their communities. The programme was found to be a very relevant way for LGUs to participate in the national government's anti-poverty programme, as it strengthens LGUs' capacities to be effective entrepreneurs and development managers and provides them with opportunities to forge stronger links between various NGOs, people's organizations (Pos) and community-based organizations. It is in this context that the Bayanihan Savings Replication Project (BSRP) was launched.

The BSRP is an attempt to replicate the success of the Bayanihan Banking Programme implemented in the cities of Pasay and Pasig. The word "savings" is used instead of "banking" to emphasize that this is essentially a community-based savings programme. The replication process has two objectives: a) to build on the demonstrated success of Pasay and Pasig in creating enterprising, dynamic and self-reliant communities; and b) to institutionalize a mechanism to strengthen LGU capacities as well as links among NGOs, POs and community-based organizations, and to develop community self-reliance.

The following specific steps were undertaken to replicate the BBP nationwide:

- Sponsor a national conference on the Bayanihan Savings Replication Project attended by key stakeholders.

- Build a strategic alliance among the key stakeholders and forge a memorandum of agreement for delivering training and technical assistance to implement the BSRP.

- Create a national project structure to oversee the implementation of the entire replication process.

- Issue DILG memoranda pertaining to the implementation of BSRP. For example, one memoranda (MC 2003-03), which was addressed to all regional directors and heads of local government sector bureaus and operating units, offered guidance on implementing BSRP within their respective offices/departments.

- Train DILG city/municipal government operations officers on BSRP.

- Implement BSRP at the local level.

- Establish other support mechanisms, such as the Bayanihan School of Entrepreneurship and Management (BSEM), to develop leadership capacities among local authorities and initiate behavioral change.

As of May 16, 2005, a total of 622 LGUs nationwide had implemented the BSRP in their respective local entities, generating total savings of approximately PHP52 million (almost USD1 million) from 4,309 Bayanihan Centers with 108,302 members.

Peer-to-Peer Coaching: KAAKBAY

KAAKBAY is a Filipino term meaning "arm-in-arm." The term is used to introduce peer-to-peer coaching and learning as a capacity-development methodology to replicate exemplary practices in local governance. KAAKBAY was developed and implemented by DILG, the League of Cities in the Philippines (LCP), the League of Municipalities of the Philippines (LMP) and the Philippines-Canada Local Government Support Programme (LGSP). Its pilot programme identified six exemplary practices (EPs) in the Philippines and brought together 30 LGUs—10 that successfully pioneered the practices and 20 to replicate them—in a one-year replication programme. Four of these exemplary practices are Galing Pook awardees.

KAAKBAY's Replication Process

In general, the KAAKBAY project selects two or three LGUs to replicate a specific exemplary practice. Cities and municipalities taking part in the project visit the LGU that implemented the best practice and take part in a peer-to-peer learning workshop to determine how they will replicate it. During this visit, they learn about the key steps for implementing the practice; the success factors and difficulties in implementing it; who the key stakeholders are and how they contributed; what to avoid; how long the practice takes to implement; and the main benefits of implementing it. The visiting officials also determine how they will work together as a cluster of LGUs to replicate the practice. Finally, they develop a work plan for implementing the exemplary practice in their municipality or city within one year. KAAKBAY provides technical assistance and monitors the LGUs' progress to help them to achieve the targeted results within this timeframe. The KAAKBAY replication programme consists of these five tasks/steps as illustrated below.

Task 1: Determining the modalities of the programme. In this preparatory stage, the necessary structures, procedures and resources are determined and mobilized to manage an effective transfer of learning. This includes deciding on the partnership agreements and management structure; formulating objectives, policies, principles and framework/criteria; leveling off roles and functions involved in the programme; developing mechanisms and systems to manage and coordinate the key stakeholders, monitor and evaluate the programme, and provide support to hosting and replicating LGUs; and identifying and leveraging needed and available resources. Task 1 activities principally involve the key organizing institutions of the overall programme, i.e., DILG, LCP, LMP and LGSP. These organizations formulate and execute memoranda of agreement in order to clarify each other's roles, responsibilities and contributions to the programme.

Task 2: Identifying exemplary practices to be offered for replication. While there is an available list of exemplary practices (EPs), careful study and selection is undertaken to ensure the success of the replication programme, including developing the framework and criteria for identifying EPs; searching for initial documentation and identification of EPs; packaging the identified EPs for dissemination to prospective replicators; building relationships and arrangements with host LGUs; and setting up mechanisms to continue the search for relevant EPs. The EP identification process emphasizes initiatives that address poverty alleviation and resource mobilization. These issues, considered to be among the major priorities of the national government and the felt needs of local communities, are being actively pursued by all of KAAKBAY's institutional partners. Beyond poverty alleviation and resource mobilization, LGU exemplary practices considered for replication include as many of the following characteristics as possible:

- *LGU-initiated:* The exemplary practice was initiated by an LGU at the city or municipal level. The initiative is sustainable and not dependent for its success, implementation or resources on any other programme, project or agency;

- *Creative use of Local Governance Code powers:* The exemplary practice demonstrates the creative use of governmental and/or corporate powers provided to LGUs by the Local Government Code of 1991;

- *Simple and implementable in one year:* The initiative is easily replicable and can progress to the application stage in a relatively short time;

- *Proven and effective solutions to common or similar problems:* The exemplary practice has proven over a reasonable period to be an effective response to the identified needs of its target beneficiaries. It has also made a significant contribution to the improvement of the beneficiaries' social and material conditions;

- *Demonstrated level of sustainability:* This means that the project has been in place for a considerable time; it survived the arrival of a new administration; it has become a permanent programme or structure in the LGU; the community as well as executive and legislative bodies are involved in and support it; and related legislation is in place in the LGU;

- *Least possible cost and effort to replicate:* The exemplary practice does not require huge amounts of resources or funding to replicate and is easy to implement. It's a "common sense idea" as opposed to a capital-intensive project. Also, the exemplary practice is able to mobilize and maximize the use of indigenous resources;

- *Potential for multiplier effect or further replication:* The processes and approaches of the exemplary practice have the potential to address other needs or deliver services beyond those originally targeted or intended. This means that the initiative has relatively high potential for success. The success of the practice in a few LGUs may incite other LGUs to adopt it; and

- *Documented exemplary practice:* Considering all other features equal, preference will be given to initiatives with existing documentation on the EP's benefits, key milestones, success and hindering factors, results, key stakeholders, processes and mechanisms.

Task 3: Selecting local governments to replicate the exemplary practices. The KAAKBAY programme carefully selects the LGUs that will replicate the exemplary practices. The selection process includes: developing the criteria for selecting the replicating LGUs; establishing modes and media for disseminating information about the programme and the EPs proposed for replication; screening applications and finalizing the selection; and building relationships and arrangements with replicating LGUs. LGUs selected to replicate the identified EPs are called "recipient LGUs." The KAAKBAY pilot programme created small groups or clusters of recipient LGUs which may or may not have been geographically contiguous with each other. This pilot project involved some 16 to 20 LGUs, either as host or recipient. Of this number, 75% were municipalities and 25% were cities. To be chosen, candidate LGUs had to demonstrate the initiative, commitment and resources to replicate EPs. Specifically, recipient LGUs should:

- *Express a need for assistance:* LGUs which demonstrate greater need for assistance are prioritized in the selection;

- *Demonstrate the will to replicate a specific practice:* The recipient LGU should have the daring, desire and interest to pursue the exemplary practice proposed to it;

- *Willing to take part in an institutional cooperation process with other LGUs:* Participating LGUs are asked to enter into a formal collaborative agreement with other LGUs to pursue the replication process. The support of each LGU's local chief executive and their local legislative councils or Sanggunians is required;

- *Ready to implement the exemplary practice:* Recipient LGUs should have, among other elements, the political support, basic capacity and required equipment to implement the EP. In addition, they should be ready to start the replication process as soon as possible so that initiatives are completed or are well under way before the local elections;

- *Provide the resources required for the replication process:* While LGSP provides a small project support fund to the KAAKBAY project, recipient LGUs are expected to provide the majority of resources and other in-kind contributions required for the replication process;

- *Assign a strong local government operations officer (LGOO) in the LGU:* The LGOO, with support from a local resource partner (LRP), is expected to coach the LGU through the replication process;

- *Minimum prerequisites already in place:* The recipient LGU should have available for utilization and deployment the necessary facilities, human resources and equipment to replicate the specific exemplary practice; and

- *Be a team player:* The recipient LGU should be willing to abide by and commit to the roles and responsibilities within the KAAKBAY replication cluster.

Task 4: Managing and supporting the actual replication process among LGUs. After completing the preparatory steps, in Task 4, the LGUs go through the replication process itself. The processes involved in Task 4 are subdivided into the pre-replication phase and the replication phase. These activities are illustrated in Figure 12.1.

The pre-replication phase consists of a) preparing for replication and b) building relationships between host and replicator LGUs. First, to ensure their readiness to undertake the process and increase their chances for success, LGUs must build capacity for hosting or replicating a local government practice. Host LGUs that are sharing their exemplary practice with others will need to do more work at the start of the process, while replicating LGUs take on greater responsibility during the actual replication process. The second part of the pre-replication phase involves initial communication and coordination between LGUs through email, telephone, fax or letter. Initial communication includes introducing the host and replicating teams to each other, arranging for the peer-to-peer learning workshop and clarifying questions and expectations. The

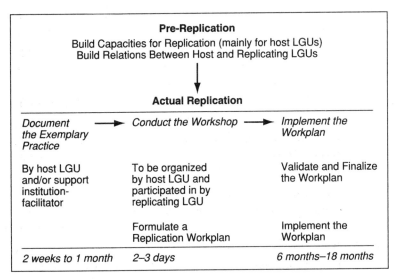

Figure 12.1 Replication Overview
Source: Panadero, 2005

replication itself consists of three steps: a) documenting the exemplary practice (done by the host LGU); b) conducting a peer-to-peer learning workshop (for host and replicating LGUs); and c) formulating and implementing the replication work plan (done by the replicating LGU). Below, we provide more details on the tools that the KAAKBAY replication programme has designed and developed to help these three steps run smoothly.

As noted above, documenting the exemplary practices is the responsibility of the host LGU. It aims to make available essential information about the EP, presented in a way that facilitates its use by the replicating LGU in developing its work plan and implementing its replication project. KAAKBAY developed the "Guideline for Documenting the Exemplary Practice" to facilitate this step. Using this tool produces the following information about the EP: the host LGU's objectives in implementing the practice; conditions in the LGU prior to implementing the practice (its rationale for trying the EP); key steps in implementing the practice; resources used in implementing it; the results or impact on the LGU/community of implementing the practice; analysis, including lessons learned and insights gained in implementing the practice; samples of the specific forms, plans, tools, etc., used by the host LGU in implementing its project. From the perspective of replication, the most crucial part of the guideline is probably the key implementation steps, as they constitute the actual implementation process of the initial project and will be adapted and modified by the replicating LGU. Hence, the host LGUs are encouraged to be objective and thoughtful in documenting these steps, with the goal of making the process as simple and cost-effective as possible. Accomplishing this goal typically requires ongoing interaction between the individuals who implemented the original project.

After documenting the exemplary practice, the host LGU needs to plan, prepare for and conduct the peer-to-peer learning workshop. This workshop should allow the host LGU to share its EP with replicating LGUs to help them better appreciate the practice and to formulate a first draft of their replication work plan with inputs from the host LGUs. The peer-to-peer learning workshop may be the first opportunity for host and replicating LGUs to meet and get to know each other. It should therefore be structured in a way that affords the greatest opportunity to build a solid foundation and take-off point for the replication process. KAAKBAY has developed a generic workshop design and facilitator's guide to help the host LGUs with this step (see Table 12.1).

The key activity in Part 3 of the workshop is formulating and implementing the replication work plan, whereby the replicating LGUs, with the help of host LGUs, identify the specific steps and actions they will undertake to replicate the exemplary practice. Here, KAAKBAY has developed a work plan template. This tool serves as a guide for the replicating LGU in identifying its objectives for replication; who should be involved; key replication steps and

Table 12.1   Workshop Design

Introduction

- Opening ceremony
- Introduce participants and set expectations
- Overview of the workshop and the exemplary practice
- Fellowship activity

Appreciation of the exemplary practice

Seeing is Believing	• Comprehensive presentation of the exemplary practice
	• See the practice in operation (visit)
	• Participants' reflection on the exemplary practice
Analyzing the exemplary practice	• Rationale and purpose of the exemplary practice
	• Key implementation steps and related resources

Implementing the exemplary practice in the replicating LGU

- Managing the project in your LGU
- Formulating the work plan
- Working as partners—memorandum of agreement
- Next steps

Source: Panadero, 2005

activities; required resources; and potential problems, constraints and issues and ways of resolving them. This template includes the following key components: context for replication; objectives and expected results; implementation plan/ key implementation steps; coordination mechanisms between host and replicating LGUs for monitoring and evaluation; and budget.

Task 5: Monitoring and evaluating the programme. The work plan becomes the basis for monitoring and evaluating the replication process once it's under way. This final step of the process is the responsibility of the replicating LGU. In the KAAKBAY replication programme, there are four key concerns to monitor and evaluate at the LGU level. These are: understanding and using the three replication tools; effectiveness and appropriateness of the implementation steps outlined in the work plan; the LGU's ability to implement the replication process; and the results achieved and lessons learned.

Learning and Insights

This section presents conclusions drawn from the experiences of the Gawad Galing Pook in replicating and transferring exemplary or best practices. The following includes elements that make a practice transferable/replicable:

- **Simple process and tools:** An emphasis on simple processes and methodologies to facilitate tangible results is a key element in making a practice transferable. In most cases, exemplary practices must be generic enough for replicating LGUs to modify and adapt them to their own situation. Practices that are too context-specific, require too many preconditions, or are subject to a lot of external factors may be difficult to replicate;

- **Quick wins:** Based on the lessons of the KAAKBAY experience, exemplary practices that take no more than one year to replicate are preferred. This is particularly relevant to the LGUs, where elections are held every three years. In addition, practices that take longer than a year to replicate may be more difficult to manage: LGUs may lose momentum or enthusiasm for the process and monitoring may become less effective;

- **Cost-effectiveness:** One of the principles of replication is that it should require the least effort and least amount of resources. Thus, selected exemplary practices should have proven their cost-effectiveness by achieving their objectives vis-à-vis available resources;

- **Addresses an expressed/felt need:** The presence of a concrete need or issue that is addressed by the exemplary practice makes it more replicable; and

- **Validity of the exemplary practice:** "Seeing is believing." Hence, a practice becomes more replicable and transferable if the LGUs see evidence of its validity and/or effectiveness and understand the key reasons for its success. It is useful to compare the practice to other existing models as this builds credibility and confidence among the replicating LGUs in identifying the most appropriate exemplary practice for their own situation.

Critical Factors Needed for Any Replication Process

Even more than the exemplary practice itself, the factors affecting the replication process must be given careful attention to make the intervention work. Our discussion of the relevant factors in Gawad Galing Pook experiences reflects the following framework:

Host LGU (source of exemplary practice)	Learning Processes	Recipient LGU (learns from Host LGU's exemplary practice)

Each of these elements requires preparation for a replication project to succeed; more details are provided below. The Host LGU (source of the exemplary practice) must do the following:

Document the exemplary practice. The exemplary practice that is being promoted must be documented in a way that will facilitate learning and sharing with other organizations/LGUs.

Have enterprising and innovative people to spearhead the transfer of learning. The Host LGU needs people with the ability to contribute/articulate their experience.

Willingness and commitment. The Host LGU must see the value of the replication processes to its own development in order to generate the necessary commitment to it. In the KAAKBAY pilot programme, some motivating factors identified by Host LGUs included: enhancement of reputation and prestige, potential income, and professional development of staff.

The Recipient LGU (replicator of the exemplary practice) must exhibit the following:

Presence of expressed need. Replication must be an expressed demand of local governments. Recipient LGUs should clearly and strongly identify the need to replicate a particular practice; further, they must see this practice as a solution to a problem or situation they are seeking to resolve. When local governments have a real and recognized need to replicate a particular project, the Recipient LGUs are more likely to show sustained commitment and active participation and, consequently, are more likely to succeed. Poorly selected Recipient LGUs can lead to early dropouts or lackluster participation.

Political will and commitment of the stakeholder or replicator. As noted above, LGUs' commitment to the replication process is crucial. This was a recurring lesson throughout the KAAKBAY programme. The lack of sustained support from the mayor or chief executive and the local legislative body can spell failure for a replication project. An indication of real commitment is the willingness to provide resources to support the programme and its personnel. Equally important is openness to change and new ideas. Recipient LGUs must be willing to provide counterparts and share resources, such as budget and human resources, that may be needed in the replication process.

Need for champions and advocates. In addition to the resources described above, there must be a champion or sponsor of the replication process within the LGU. This becomes very important during the implementation phase, when resistance among the affected people is expected to occur. Ideally, the local chief executive plays the role of the sponsor. Having a champion or advocate also facilitates the mobilization of additional resources if necessary.

Creation of a multi-sectoral implementation structure and team. The Recipient LGU must identify a core project team to oversee and monitor the replication process. This need was seen both in KAAKBAY and the replication of the Bayanihan centers. Support of other stakeholders in the process is also important, as this strengthens the sustainability of the replication process; these stakeholders could include society at large, business, church, NGOs and citizen's organizations.

Issuance of policy instruments. Experience shows that the right policy environment is among the imperatives for innovation and creativity. It is therefore necessary for a replication process to be supported by policy directives, such as an executive order, ordinance, etc., to make the effort more binding and lasting.

The following factors are crucial to the replication process:

Availability of institutions and people to facilitate learning. Replication is a learning process that can be maximized only if necessary elements and opportunities are provided, such as a learning facilitator. This facilitator could come from the exchanging LGUs or a third party, such as an outside institution.

Tools and guidelines. Host and Recipient LGUs develop or use tools that can be employed by both LGUs to facilitate learning and the exchange of ideas.

Adaptation rather than adoption. Tools and processes to be used in a replication process must encourage adaptation, not adoption, of the exemplary practice. Further, the replication must involve not only the transfer of the solutions or models but also the transfer of the processes.

Integration of monitoring and evaluation into programme implementation. Because a replication programme is an innovation, monitoring and recording one's own experience as well as the experience of replicating LGUs helps an organization build its capacity for undertaking similar programmes in the future. It also contributes to the larger goal of disseminating good governance practices and building effective programmes for replicating these practices.

Cultural considerations. Local cultures are characterized by considerable diversity of political and institutional arrangements, cultural conditions, social and economic conditions, local capacities and so on. Thus, tools and processes are more effective when adapted to the local context. In fact, the opportunity to use the Recipient LGU's existing or indigenous practices in the replication process will facilitate its implementation.

Celebrate small successes. It is important to celebrate incremental successes in a replication process to encourage the replicators, sustain their commitment and encourage leadership participation in the programme.

Managing a replication programme involves the following elements:

Systematic and strategic dissemination of exemplary practices. Information transfer strategies remain crucial in laying the groundwork for actual replication processes. A systematic and faster way of disseminating (and accessing) information about exemplary practices to a larger number of local governments and other stakeholders also serves as channel and mechanism for coordinating and brokering the replication process. Note, however, that information must be packaged and presented in a specific way for a specific target audience. For example, experience shows that local chief executives prefer to learn about exemplary practices through visuals and short success stories rather than case studies.

Formulate relevant, appropriate and viable frameworks and criteria to identify practices for replication. This approach helps ensure that identified practices may be realistically replicated by other LGUs. Poor criteria for identification may result in exemplary practices that are not suitable for replication. Practices should be categorized by the degree of complexity in replicating them (their toll on the time, resources, capacities of the LGU). Exemplary practices that prove more difficult than expected can place greater burdens on the replicating LGU and may ultimately result in the LGU abandoning the project.

Use or develop a replication process that is adapted to the LGU's situation. In the KAAKBAY pilot programme, the three interconnected tools prescribed (documentation, peer-to-peer workshops, and a work plan) were developed based on knowledge of Philippine LGUs and their capacity development needs. Before KAAKBAY, study tours were common practice but rarely structured to maximize replication; often, local government officials would return to their respective towns without knowing how to apply what they learned. The KAAKBAY tools address these gaps and are generic enough to be adapted to many different contexts. Thorough study of the tools, their purposes and contents, and how they relate to one another, are important to maximize their use.

Consider timing when implementing the programme. Timing might not be everything, but it is critical. It is best to start a programme or replication process right after an election. This improves prospects for the replication being completed and institutionalized, and minimizes the chances that it will be disrupted by changes in local government leadership.

Scaling-up of replication programme requires national machinery. Large-scale replication of exemplary practices is greatly facilitated by support provided by national machinery such as the DILG.

Concluding Remarks: The Way Forward

The following are some of the challenges faced by Gawad Galing Pook in its continuing efforts to promote and inspire replication of innovative and excellent practices in local governance:

Promoting best practices vis-à-vis determining LGUs' needs. Being an award-giving institution, there is a tendency for Gawad Galing Pook to initiate the identification of replicable practices and exert a great deal of effort in packaging and promoting the practices of the awardees. The challenge is to ensure that such practices are the ones needed by the recipient LGUs. To address this concern, LGUs are being surveyed to ascertain their need and demand for specific programmes. Once a demand is identified, it will be matched against the roster of Galing Pook-awarded best practices. Other exemplary practices will continue to be promoted and marketed, but in the form of benchmarking to be used as standards for local government performance. As a result, the promotion of such practices will be used not only to address a particular need, but to inspire and challenge other local governments to do things differently and better as they work toward the general goal of good governance.

Aspiring to be better. Knowledge-sharing among the Gawad Galing Pook winners encourages them to achieve even more and to set benchmarks for certain programmes or services at the local level. The Foundation aims to develop and organize a critical mass of local leaders who can mentor and inspire their peers in situations beyond workshops and conferences.

Creative documentation and dissemination of information on best practices. Identifying and utilizing the proper and cost-effective medium to promote best or exemplary practices remains a challenge. Hence, Gawad Galing Pook is maximizing the use of technology such as the internet, ICT and media to promote the best practices. It is also in the process of exploring the use of social marketing strategies to effect behavioral changes among the LGUs. In addition to the documentation of best or exemplary practices, the Foundation is putting resources into developing tools, training modules and other learning kits and materials (such as videos, CDs, etc.) to facilitate LGUs' replication interventions and processes.

Transcending political barriers. Gawad Galing Pook operates in a political milieu where leadership changes every three years. To address this circumstance, the Foundation is very keen on the timing of its replication interventions at the local level. Moreover, it will continue to strengthen its partnership with the DILG and LGU leagues in order to have the necessary political support to implement advocacy and replication programmes at the local level.

Partnership with other institutions in field replication. To augment its limited funds, particularly for implementing on-field replication programmes, Gawad Galing Pook continues to seek partnerships through consultations and consensus-building among key stakeholders at the national and local levels. Leveraging and complementing resources and strategies with those of other institutions, particularly Official Development Assistance, may be necessary to have a greater impact and avoid duplication of work. Local partnerships with academic and other institutions will be continued in order to support the learning processes of the LGUs, particularly for the replication phase. During replication procedures, these partner academic and local-resource institutions can be tapped as learning facilitators in the documentation of best practices at the local level. The Foundation also seeks to influence the corporate sector and international institutions to take a close look at local governments in the Philippines as effective agents of change and reform.

Provision of support mechanisms. LGUs often face resource limitations in documenting their best practices or supporting their learning processes during replications. In view of this, the Gawad Galing Pook is establishing the Replication Programme (RePro), a fund and technical assistance facility jointly administered with the DILG; RePro can be accessed by LGUs interested in replicating Galing Pook's exemplary programmes. Through RePro, the Foundation provides seed funds to jumpstart replication initiatives. In addition, it provides technical assistance in programme design, monitoring and evaluation, case study documentation and mass media popularization, while LGU adaptors and their partners provide on-site resources. This is a cost-sharing facility wherein the LGU proponent shoulders counterpart expenses to pursue the replication initiative.

Endnotes

Chapter 1

1. The Chapter incorporates key lessons learned and findings that emerged from the International Experts Meeting on "Approaches and Methodologies for the Assessment and Transfer of Best Practices in Governance and Public Administration" organized by UNDESA.

2. See Gowher Rizvi, "Bringing Back Social Justice to the Discourse on Reinventing Government" paper prepared for the Sixth Global Forum on Reinventing Government held in Korea in May 2005.

3. The term "best practice" will be used here with the understanding that it has many limitations and that "successful practices" is, as underlined by the United Nations Committee of Experts on Public Administration in its 2005 Final Report, a much more pertinent term.

4. See *http://www.unpan.org/dpepa_psaward.asp.*

5. For more information, see *http://www.impumelelo.org.za.*

6. This section has been adapted from a chapter prepared by Vilhelm Klareskov for a forthcoming UNDESA publication on *Innovations in Governance and Public Administration in the Mediterranean Region.*

7. For further information on this case, see: *http://www.innovations.harvard.edu/.*

8. See "Citizen Participation on Pro-poor Budgeting," DPADM, UNDESA, 2005.

9. DPADM is developing adaptations of the Citizens' Report Cards in cooperation with a number of developing countries' audit institutions. It is also devising programmes to build capacity of developing countries' audit institutions to engage civil society in auditing the performance related to service delivery. Technical cooperation activities have been launched to build capacities to empower local authorities to better address local needs, improved use of budgetary resources allocated to the poor, data analysis

of regional and district disparities, and empowering local stakeholders to enhance their participation in the preparation, evaluation and revision of the Poverty Reduction Strategy Papers (PRSPs).

10. For further information, see *http://www.unpan.org/dpepa_worldpareport.asp.*

11. "Broadband refers to telecommunications in which band of frequencies is available to transmit information. As a result more information can be transmitted in a given amount of time" (UN World Public Sector Report 2003, page 4).

12. The government's portal address is: *http://open-government.mn.*

13. The mentioned study on Mexican Awards for Public Service confirms the above.

14. See Joseph Galimberti in Chapter 7.

15. For more information on this specific case, see: *https://www.arashi.com/pipermail/ccpg/2004q1/001294.html.*

16. For more information on the GII, visit: *http://www.innovationkorea.gii.*

17. See the UN-HABITAT best practices web-site at: *http://www.bestpractices.org.*

Chapter 2

1. See Glor, Eleanor D. (2001). "Key Factors Influencing Innovation in Government," in Innovation Journal, vol. 6, issue 2, February–June 2001, *http://www.innovation.cc/peer-reviewed/key-factor-gor.pdf.*

Chapter 3

1. A more complete version of this proposal may be examined in Barzelay and Cortázar (2004). An earlier version of this methodological proposal is found in Barzelay, Gaetani, Cortázar and Cejudo (2002).

2. This definition is directly inspired by Bardach's concepts of management practices in general (1998, p. 36).

3. Kingdon (1995) reflects on the way social situations that are deemed unsatisfactory are elevated to the category of public problems that warrant action through public policy. By contrast, Barzelay (1998) analyses the problems faced within a public organization that are related to unsatisfactory performance of the organization's functions.

4. See Mayntz (2003) regarding the centrality of the task of causal reconstruction to understanding the social mechanisms that, among other things, can explain management practices.

5. However, the study of a practice that did not yield good results may prove interesting in order to understand the conditions that yielded this result, thus avoiding similar outcomes. For that reason, one must learn not only from successful experiences or practices, but also from situations that resulted in failure (Oyen, 2002, p. 26).

6. This definition is consistent with Metcalfe and Richards's definition of management as "taking responsibility for the performance of a system" (1993, p. 37).

7. It is important to bear in mind that the same group of events may be narrated according to different plots or, in other words, different plots can explain the same experience. The choice of one plot or another has to do with which can better explain the process being studied, as well as the theoretical concerns guiding the research.

8. Although the text may suggest a sequence among the six types of interaction presented in Figure 3.4, it is clear that the mutual influences and interactions do not follow a linear time sequence.

9. Overall, while the external factor has been influential in assuring transfer of the two governance institutions considered in this chapter in terms of diffusion, their influence in ensuring the institutions' effective functioning has been very limited. This is due partly to factors within individual countries beyond the control of the external actors (some of them are addressed later) and partly to contradictions and inconsistencies in the governance agenda of the majority of the external actors. Regarding the latter point, when there is conflict between promoting good governance and the pursuit of commercial interests (for example, competitions over procurements), external actors most often put the tenets of good governance on the back burner.

Chapter 5

1. The discussion of the Ombudsman institution in this paper draws on Adamolekun and Osunkunle (1982).

2. The problem of corruption in the private sector is also widespread across all continents but is excluded from consideration in this chapter, which is focused on the public sector.

3. As of 1 July 1997, Hong Kong became the Hong Kong Special Administrative Region (SAR) of China.

4. It is important to stress that given the complex nature of the problem of corruption and its presence in all modern states, tackling it through a dedicated agency is only one option; the reliance on existing justice systems in

Italy and France to tackle the problem from the early 1990s to the present is another option. Many developing and transition countries combine the ICAC-inspired dedicated institution with reliance on the justice system.

5. The communiqués of the conferences are featured on Transparency International's website *(www.ti.org)*.

6. In the Nigerian case, there is one ombudsman, called Public Complaints Commissioner, at the central government level and one each at the level of the component 36 states of the federation.

7. See Adamolekun and Osunkunle (1982) on the Nigerian experience in the early years of the Ombudsman institution. Evidence provided in the annual reports of the institution from 2000 through 2003 confirms the continued relevance of the use of local languages in the work of ombudsmen. See Government of Nigeria (2000–2003).

8. In a more recent study Ayeni (1994) focuses on new operational issues.

Chapter 6

1. Translation by the author (original in Portuguese).

2. Fundo de Manutenção e Desenvolvimento do Ensino Fundamental e de Valorização do Magistério (in Portuguese).

Chapter 7

1. Survey is available at *www.unpan.org, www.ipac.ca* or *www.iapc.ca*.

Chapter 8

1. There are three: *Asociación de Municipios de México* (AMMAC), the *Asociación de Autoridades Locales de México* (AALMAC) and the *Federación Nacional de Municipios de México* (FEAMM). These associations are integrated into the Mexican Municipality National Conference (CONAMM), which constitutes itself as negotiator with state governments and the federal government. See Paz Cuevas (2005).

2. With the addition of 451 programs presented at the Award in the 2005 competition, the total number is 2,211.

Chapter 10

1. The other key instrument is the use of urban indicators.

2. Documented best practices are the intellectual property of the submitting parties within the public domain.

3. Submissions from least developed and developing countries benefit from feedback on their submissions. Submissions that do not qualify are provided with explanations.

4. Including UNDPs database on best practices in biodiversity and ICLEIs database on local initiatives.

5. The validation and selection process typically eliminates approximately 30% of submissions.

6. The criteria are presented in the form of a checklist designed specifically for assessing the relevance and pertinence of a law or policy to the Millennium Development Goals.

Chapter 11

1. This chapter is based on a 1998 joint publication by CityNet, UNDP and UNCHS: "Guidelines for Transferring Effective Practices: A Practical Manual for South-South Cooperation." Available from *http://www. blpnet. org/learning/transfers/transfer.pdf.*

References

Chapter 2

Albury, D. (2005). "Fostering Innovation in Public Services," in *Public Money and Management*, vol. 25, no. 1, January 2005, pp. 51–56.

Bessant, J. (2005). "Enabling Continuous and Discontinuous Innovation: Learning from the Private Sector," in *Public Money and Management*, vol. 25, no. 1, January 2005, pp. 35–42.

Bhatta, S. (2003). " 'Don't Just Do Something, Stand There!': Revisiting the Issue of Risks in Innovation in the Public Sector," in *Innovation Journal*, vol. 8, issue 2, April–May 2003, *http://www.innovation.cc/peer-reviewed/bhatta-risks.pdf*.

Borins, S. (2000). "Loose Cannons and Rule Breakers, or Enterprising Leaders? Some Evidence About Innovative Public Managers," in *Public Administration Review*, vol. 60, no. 6, Nov./Dec. 2000, pp. 498–50.

Borins, S. (2001). The Challenge of Innovating in Government, New Ways of Managing Series, PricewaterhouseCoopers Endowment for the Business of Government, website: *endowment.pwcglobal.com*.

Centre for Public Service Innovation (2004). Case Study—Client-Centred Innovation: Fitting Technology to Service Delivery at the South African Revenue Services.

Centre for Public Service Innovation (2004). Case Study—Embedding Continuous Improvement: Creating a Culture of Innovation at the South African Post Office.

Denhardt, J.V. and Denhardt, R.B. (2001). Creating a Culture of Innovation: 10 Lessons from America's Best Run City, New Ways of Managing Series, PricewaterhouseCoopers Endowment for the Business of Government, website: *endowment.pwcglobal.com*.

Donahue John D. (2005). Dynamics of Diffusion: Conceptions of American Federalism and Public-Sector Innovation, unpublished, available from author at Harvard University.

Farah, M.F.S. (2005). "Dissemination of Innovative Cases: Learning from Sub-National Awards Programs in Brazil," paper prepared for the Ad-hoc Experts Meeting on Approaches and Methodologies for the Assessment and Transfer of Best Practices in Government and Public Administration, Tunis, Tunisia, June 13–14, 2005.

Galimberti, J. (2005). "Best Practices and Innovations in Government: Perspectives, Challenges, and Potential," paper prepared for the Ad-hoc Experts Meeting on Approaches and Methodologies for the Assessment and Transfer of Best Practices in Government and Public Administration, Tunis, Tunisia, June 13–14, 2005.

Glor, Eleanor D. (2001a). "Innovation Patterns," in *Innovation Journal*, vol. 6, issue 3, July–November 2001, *http://www.innovation.cc/volumes-issues/patterns_eleanor.pdf.*

Glor, Eleanor D. (2001b). "Key Factors Influencing Innovation in Government," in *Innovation Journal*, vol. 6, issue 2, February–June 2001, *http://www.innovation.cc/peer-reviewed/key-factor-gov.pdf.*

Hannah, S.B. (1995). "The Correlates of Innovation: Lessons from Best Practice," in *Public Productivity & Management Review*, vol. 19, December 1995.

Hartley, J. (2005). "Innovation in Governance and Public Services: Past and Present," in *Public Money & Management*, vol. 25, no. 1, January 2005, pp. 27–34.

Kamarck, E.C. (2003). Government Innovation Around the World, Ash Institute for Democratic Governance and Innovation, November 2003.

Moore, M.H. (1995). *Creating Public Value: Strategic Management in Government*, Harvard University Press, Cambridge.

Moore, M.H. (2005). "Break-Through Innovations and Continuous Improvement: Two Different Models of Innovative Processes in the Public Sector," in *Public Money & Management*, vol. 25, no. 1, January 2005, pp. 43–50.

Rashman, L. and Radnor, Z. (2005). "Learning to Improve: Approaches to Improving Local Government Services," in *Public Money & Management*, vol. 25, no. 1, January 2005, pp. 19–26.

Roste, R. (2004). "Studies of Innovation in the Public Sector: A Literature Review," Publin working paper, version 2, *www.step.no/publin/reports/d8-litterature-survey-march2004.pdf.*

Sachs, J.D. (2005). The End of Poverty—Economic Possibilities for Our Time, Penguin Press, New York.

UNDESA (2005). Aide-Memoire: Ad-Hoc Experts Meeting on Approaches and Methodologies for the Assessment and Transfer of Best Practices in Governance and Public Administration, Tunis, Tunisia, June 13–14, 2005.

Yapp, C. (2005). "Innovation, Futures Thinking and Leadership," in *Public Money & Management*, vol. 25, no. 1, January 2005, pp. 57–60.

You, N. and Kitio V. (2005). "Best Practices Knowledge Management Framework: An Overview," paper prepared for the Ad-hoc Experts Meeting on Approaches and Methodologies for the Assessment and Transfer of Best Practices in Government and Public Administration, Tunis, Tunisia, June 13–14, 2005.

Walters, J. (2001). Understanding Innovation: What Inspires It? What Makes It Successful?, New Ways of Managing Series, PricewaterhouseCoopers Endowment for the Business of Government, website: *endowment. pwcglobal.com.*

White, G. (2003). "Developing Institutional Mechanisms to Catalyse Innovation," paper presented to the 9th International Winelands Conference, September 2003.

Chapter 3

Abbott, Andrew (2001). *Time Matters: On Theory and Method,* The University of Chicago Press.

Bardach, Eugene (1998). *Getting Agencies to Work Together: The Practices and Theory of Managerial Craftsmanship,* The Brookings Institution, Washington.

_____ (2000). *A Practical Guide for Policy Analysis: The Eightfold Path to More Effective Problem Solving,* Chatham House, New York.

_____ (2004). "Presidential Address—The Extrapolation Problem: How Can We Learn from the Experience of Others," *Journal of Policy Analysis and Management,* vol. 23, no. 2. pp. 205–220.

Barzelay, Michael (1998). Atravesando la Burocracia: Una Nueva Perspectiva de la Administración Pública, Fondo de Cultura Económica, Mexico.

_____ (2001). The New Public Management: Improving Research and Policy Dialogue, University of California Press, California.

Barzelay, Michael and Cortázar, J.C. (2004). *Una guía práctica para la elaboración de estudios de caso sobre buenas prácticas en gerencia social,* Social Development Institute, Inter-American Development Bank, Washington, DC.

Barzelay, Michael; Gaetani, F.; Cortázar, J. C.; and Cejudo, G. (2002). "Research on Public Management Policy Change in the Latin America Region: A Conceptual Framework and Methodological Guide," in *International Public Management Review*, vol. 4, Issue 1, 2003, pp. 20–41.

Barzelay, Michael and Gallego, Raquel (2005). From "New Institutionalism" to "Institutional Processualism": Advancing Knowledge about Public Management Policy Change (on press).

Kingdon, John W. (1995). *Agendas, Alternatives and Public Policies*, Second Edition, Longman, New York.

Metcalfe, Les and Richards, Sue (1993). *Improving Public Management*, European Institute of Public Administration/SAGE Publications, London.

Mayntz, Renate (2003). "Mechanisms in the Analysis of Social Macro-Phenomena," in *Philosophy of the Social Sciences*, vol. 34, no. 2, June, pp. 237–259.

Moore, Mark H. (1998). Gestión Estratégica y Creación de Valor en el Sector Público, Piados, Buenos Aires.

Oyen, Else (2002). Best Practices in Poverty Reduction: An Analytical Framework, CROP, London.

Pettigrew, Andrew M. (1997). "What Is Processual Analysis?," in *Scandinavian Journal of Management*, vol. 13, no. 4, pp. 337–348.

Polkinghorne, Donald E. (1988). *Narrative Knowing and the Human Sciences*, State University of New York.

Ragin, Charles (1987). *The Comparative Method: Moving Beyond Qualitative and Quantitative Strategies*, University of California Press.

Rose, Richard (1993). *Lesson-Drawing in Public Policy: A Guide to Learning Across Time and Space*, Chatham House, New Jersey.

Stake, Robert E. (1995). *The Art of Case Study Research*, SAGE Publications, Thousand Oaks, CA.

Yin, Robert K. (1994). *Case Study Research: Design and Methods*, Second Edition, SAGE Publications, Thousand Oaks, CA.

Chapter 4

Adamolekun, L. (ed.) (1999). *Public Administration in Africa: Main Issues and Selected Country Studies*, Westview Press, Boulder, CO.

Bardach, E. (2000). Practical Guide for Policy Analysis: The Eightfold Path to More Effective Problem Solving. Chatham House, New York.

Barzelay, M. and Campbell, C. (2003). *Preparing for the Future: Strategic Planning in the U.S. Air Force,* Brookings Institution, Washington, DC.

Beatty, E. (2003). "Approaches to Technology Transfer in History and the Case of Nineteenth Century Mexico," in *Comparative Technology Transfer and Society,* vol. 1, no. 2, pp. 167–197.

Blair, H. (2000). "Participation and Accountability at the Periphery: Democratic Local Governance in Six Countries," in *World Development,* vol. 28, no. 1, pp. 21–39.

Borins, S. (1998). "Lessons from the New Public Management in Common-wealth Nations," in *International Public Management Journal,* vol. 1, no. 1, pp. 37–58.

Brinkerhoff, D. and Coston, J. (1999). "International Development in a Globalized World," in *Public Administration Review,* vol. 59, no. 4, pp. 346–361.

Brudney, J., O'Toole, Jr., L., and Rainey, H. (2000). *Advancing Public Management: New Developments in Theory, Methods, and Practice,* Georgetown University Press, Washington. DC.

Dale, R. (2003). "The Logical Framework: An Easy Escape, a Straightjacket, or a Useful Planning Tool," in *Development in Practice,* vol. 13, no. 1, pp. 57–70.

Dilulio, J., Garvey, G., and Kettl, D. (1993). *Improving Government Performance: An Owner's Manual,* Brookings Institution, Washington, DC.

Fredland, R. (2000). "Technology Transfer to the Public Sector in Developing States: Three Phases," in *Journal of Technology Transfer,* vol. 25, pp. 265–275.

Goldspink, C. and C. Kay (2003). "Organizations as Self-Organizing and Self-Sustaining Systems: A Complex and Autopoietic Systems Perspective," *International Journal of General Systems,* vol. 32, no. 5, pp. 459–474.

Heady, F. (1998). "Comparative and International Public Administration: Building Intellectual Bridges," in *Public Administration Review,* vol. 58, no. 1, pp. 32–40.

———— (1996). *Public Administration in Comparative Perspective.* 5th Ed., Marcel Dekker, New York.

Hirschman, D. (1999). "Development Management Versus Third World Bureaucracies: A Brief History of Conflicting Interests," in *Development and Change,* vol. 30, no. 2, pp. 287–306.

Hoogvelt, A. (2001). *Globalization and the Postcolonial World: The New Political Economy of Development,* 2nd Ed., Johns Hopkins University Press, Baltimore, MD.

Jones, L. and Kettl, D. (2003). "Assessing Public Management Reform in an International Context," in *International Public Management Review*, vol. 4, no. 1, pp. 1–16.

Julnes, P., and Holzer, M. (2001). "Promoting the Utilization of Performance Measures in Public Organizations: An Empirical Study of Factors Affecting Adoption and Implementation," in *Public Administration Review*, vol. 61, no. 6, pp. 693–708.

Kabeer, N. (1999). "Resources, Agency, Achievements: Reflections on Measures of Women's Empowerment," in *Development and Change*, vol. 30, no. 3, pp. 435–464.

Kettl, D. (1997). "The Global Revolution in Public Management: Driving Themes, Missing Links," in *Journal of Policy Analysis and Management*, vol. 16, no. 3, pp. 446–462.

———— (2002). *The Transformation of Governance*, Johns Hopkins University Press, Baltimore, MD.

Klingner, D., Nalbandian, J., and Romzek, B. (2002). "Politics, Administration, and Markets: Conflicting Expectations and Accountability," in *American Review of Public Administration*, vol. 32, no. 2, pp. 117–144.

Klingner, D., and Washington, C. (2000). "Through the Looking Glass: Realizing the Advantages of an International and Comparative Approach for Teaching Public Administration," in *Journal of Public Affairs Education*, vol. 6, no. 1, pp. 35–43.

Knott, J., and Wildavsky, A. (1980). "If Dissemination Is the Solution, What Is the Problem?" in *Knowledge: Creation, Diffusion, Utilization*, vol. 1, no. 4, pp. 537–578.

Landry, R., Lamari, M. and Amara, N. (2001). "Utilization of Social Science Research Knowledge in Canada," in *Research Policy*, vol. 30, no. 2, pp. 333–349.

Landry, R., M. Lamari, and N. Amara (2003). "The Extent and Determinants of the Utilization of University Research in Government Agencies," in *Public Administration Review*, vol. 63, no. 2, pp. 192–205.

Lester, J., and J. Stewart (1996). *Public Policy: An Evolutionary Approach*, West Publishing Co., St. Paul, MN.

Lindblom, C. (1959/1997). "The Science of 'Muddling Through'," in Shafritz, J. and Hyde, A. (eds.) (1997). *Classics of Public Administration*, 4th ed., Harcourt Brace, Fort Worth, TX.

Mavhunga, C. (2003). "Firearms Diffusion, Exotic and Indigenous Knowledge Systems in the Lowveld Frontier, South Eastern Zimbabwe, 1870–1920," in *Comparative Technology Transfer and Society*, vol. 1, no. 2, pp. 201–231.

Narayan, D. (1999). "Can Anyone Hear Us? Voices from 47 Countries," in *Voices of the Poor,* vol. 1, World Bank Poverty Group, PREM, The World Bank, Washington, DC.

Peters, B. G. (1988). *Comparing Public Bureaucracies: Problems of Theory and Method,* The University of Alabama Press, Tuscaloosa.

Pollitt, C., and Bouchaert, G. (2000). *Public Management Reform: A Comparative Analysis,* Oxford University Press, Oxford.

Rich, R. (1997). "Measuring Knowledge Utilization Process and Outcomes," in *International Journal of Knowledge Transfer and Utilization,* vol. 1, no. 1, pp. 6–30.

Riggs, F. (1968). "Administration and a Changing World Environment," in *Public Administration Review,* vol. 28, no. 4, pp. 348–361.

———— (1980). "The Ecology and Context of Public Administration: A Comparative Perspective," in *Public Administration Review,* vol. 40, no. 2, pp. 107–115.

———— (1991). "Public Administration: A Comparativist Framework," in *Public Administration Review,* vol. 51, no. 6, pp. 473–477.

Roberts, N. (2000). "Wicked Problems and Network Approaches to Resolution." *International Public Management Review,* 1 (1): pp. 1–19.

Rostow, W. (1971). *The Stages of Economic Growth: A Non-Communist Manifesto,* Cambridge University Press, New York.

Rutgers, M. (1998). "Paradigm Lost: Crisis as Identity in the Study of Public Administration," in *International Review of Administrative Sciences,* vol. 64, no. 4, pp. 553–564.

Sabet, G., and Klingner, D. (1993). "Exploring the Impact of Professionalism on Administrative Innovation" in *Journal of Public Administration Research and Theory,* vol. 3, no. 2, pp. 252–266.

Schrage, M. (2004). "Making Good Ideas Matter" in *Technology Review,* vol. 107, no. 10, p. 18.

Seely, B. (2003). "Historical Patterns in the Scholarship of Technology Transfer," in *Comparative Technology Transfer and Society,* vol. 1, no. 1, pp. 7–48.

United Nations Development Programme (UNDP) (1998). "Latin America: Poverty Up Close," in *Choices,* 6, pp. 16–18.

Van Wart, M., and Cayer, N. (1990). "Comparative Public Administration: Defunct, Dispersed, or Redefined?" in *Public Administration Review,* vol. 50, no. 2, pp. 238–248.

Webber, D. (1987). "Legislators' Use of Policy Information" in *American Behavioral Scientist,* vol. 30, pp. 612–631.

Webber, D. (1992). "The Distribution and Use of Policy Knowledge in the Policy Process" in *Knowledge and Policy*, vol. 4, no. 4, pp. 6–35.

Williams, G., Véron, R., Corbridge, S., and Srivastava, M. (2003). "Participation and Power: Poor People's Engagement with India's Employment Assurance Scheme" in *Development and Change*, vol. 34, no. 1, pp. 163–192.

World Bank (2002). *World Development Report 2002: Building Institutions for Markets*, Oxford University Press and The World Bank, New York.

Chapter 5

Adamolekun, L. and E. Osunkunle (1982). *Nigeria's Ombudsman System*. Ibadan: Heinemann Educational Books.

Adamolekun, L. (1984). "The Nigerian Ombudsman Experience" in *International Review of Administrative Sciences*, vol. 50, no. 3, pp. 227–229.

Government of Nigeria (2000–2003). Public Complaints Commission. *25th, 26th, and 27th Annual Reports*.

Burbridge, C. (1974). "Problems of Transferring the Ombudsman's Plan" in *International Review of Administrative Sciences*, vol. 40, no. 2, pp. 103–108.

Ayeni, V. (1994). "The Ombudsman's Statistics: On Data-Gathering and Management in the Enforcement of Public Accountability in Africa" in *International Review of Administrative Sciences*, vol. 60, no. 1, pp. 55–70.

Chapter 6

Cooke, Bill (2004). "O Gerenciamento do (Terceiro) Mundo," in *RAE—Revista de Administração de Empresas*, vol. 44, no. 33, July/September, pp. 62–75.

Farah, Marta Ferreira Santos (2001). "Inflections and Directions in Social Policy—the Role of Sub-National Governments in Brazil," paper delivered at XXIII International Congress of Latin American Studies Association—LASA, Washington.

Farah, Marta Ferreira Santos (2004). Apresentação a artigo de Bill Cooke: O Gerenciamento do (Terceiro) Mundo, in *RAE—Revista de Administração de Empresas*, vol. 44, no.33, July/September, pp. 57–61.

Ikenberry, G. John. (1990). "The International Spread of Privatization Policies: Inducements, Learning, and 'Policy Bandwagoning'," in Suleian, E. and Waterbury, J. (eds.) *The Political Economy of Public Sector Reform and Privatization*, Westview, Boulder, CO.

Latour, Bruno (2000). *Ciência em ação*, Editora Unesp, São Paulo, Brasil.

Melo, Marcus André (2004). "Escolha institucional e a difusão dos paradigmas de política: o Brasil e a segunda onda de reformas previdenciárias," in *Dados,* vol. 47, no. 1, Rio de Janeiro.

Myers, Stephanie; Smith, Hayden; and Martine, Lawrence (2004). *Conducting Best Practices Research in Public Affairs,* working paper for Center for Community Partnerships, College of Health & Public Affairs, University of Central Florida.

Rogers, Everett (1962). *The Diffusion of Innovation,* Free Press, New York.

Schumpeter, Joseph Alois (1982). Teoria do desenvolvimento econômico: uma investigação sobre lucros, capital, crédito, juro e o ciclo econômico, Abril Cultural, São Paulo.

Spink, Peter (2000). "The Right Approach to Local Public Management: Experiences from Brazil," in *Revista de Administração de Empresas,* vol. 40, no. 3, pp. 45–65.

Sugiyama, Natasha Borges (2004). "Political incentives, ideology and social networks: the diffusion of social policy in Brazil," paper delivered at LASA 2004—Latin American Studies Association Meeting, Las Vegas, Nevada, October 7–9, 2004.

UNDESA (2005). Aide-memoire: Ad Hoc Expert Meeting on Approaches and Methodologies for the Assessment and Transfer of Best Practices in Governance and Public Administration, Tunis, Tunisia, June 13–14, 2005.

Walker, Jack L. (1969). "The Diffusion of Innovations among the American States," in *American Political Science Review,* vol. 63, no. 3, pp. 880–899.

Wampler, Brian (2004). "The Diffusion of Participatory Budgeting in Brazil," paper delivered to LASA 2004—Latin American Studies Association Meeting, Las Vegas, Nevada, October 7–9, 2004 (draft version).

Weyland, Kurt (2004). "Learning from Foreign Models in Latin American Policy Reform: An Introduction," in Weyland, Kurt (ed.) (2004). *Learning from Foreign Models in Latin American Policy Reform,* Woodrow Wilson Center Press, Washington, DC.

Chapter 7

Bernier, Luc (2001). "Developing the Public Service of Tomorrow: Imaginative Government" in *Public Sector Management,* vol. 12, no. 2.

Bernier, L., K. Brownsey and M. Howlett (2005). *"Executive Styles In Canada: Cabinet Structures and Leadership Practices in Canadian Government."* IPAC Series on Public Management and Governance. Toronto: University of Toronto Press.

Dutil, Patrice (2004). "Pulling Against Gravity: The Winners of the 2004 Award for Innovative Management" in *Public Sector Management*, vol. 15, no. 1.

Evans, Gordon (2005). "Exporting Governance: Lithuania Adapts a Canadian Policy Management Model" in *Canadian Public Administration*, vol. 48, no. 1 (Spring 2005).

Fortier-Balogh, Marie and Dan Lemaire (2002)." China: Public Policy Options Project (PPOP)" in *Public Sector Management*, vol. 13, no. 1.

Kernaghan, K., Marson, B. and Borins, S. (2000). *The New Public Organization*. Toronto: Institute of Public Administration of Canada.

Linquist, Everett (1997). "1997 IPAC Award for Innovative Management Breakthroughs: Connecting Citizens and Government" in *Public Sector Management*, vol. 8, no. 2.

Chapter 8

Cabrero Mendoza, Enrique (1995). La nueva gestión municipal en México: análisis de experiencias innovadoras en gobiernos locales. México, D.F., CIDE-Miguel A. Porrúa.

Guillén López, Tonatiuh (1996). Gobiernos municipales en México: entre la modernización y la tradición política. México, D.F., COLEF-Miguel A. Porrúa.

Guillén López, Tonatiuh and Pablo Rojo, coords. (2005). *Gobernar con calidad y para el desarrollo. Experiencias de innovación en los municipios mexicanos.* México, D.F., CIDE and the Ford Foundation.

Paz Cuevas, Cuauhtémoc (2005). Las asociaciones municipales: nuevos actores reconstruyendo el federalismo en México. México, D.F., IGLOM.

Chapter 9

Andersen, S. and Eliassen, K. (1993). "The EC as a New Political System," in Andersen, S. and Eliassen, K., *Making Policy in Europe: The Europeification of National Policy-Making*, SAGE Publications, London, pp. 3–18.

Bennett, Colin J. (1991). "What Is Policy Convergence and What Causes It?" in *British Journal of Political Science*, 21, pp. 215–233.

Bomberg, E. and Peterson, J. (2000). "Policy Transfer and Europeanization: Passing the Heineken Test?, in *Queen's Papers on Europeanization*, no. 2/2000.

Bulmer, Simon and Padgett, Stephen (2004). "Policy Transfer in the European Union: An Institutionalist Perspective," in *British Journal of Political Science*, no. 35, pp. 103–126.

Conde Martínez, Carlos (2004). "Le Renforcement des Capacités Administratives au Maroc à travers la Formation: le Défi du Partenariat Euro-Méditerranéen," in *Revue Marocaine d'Administration Locale et Dévelopement*, no. 54.

Dolowitz, David P. and Marsh, David (2000). "Learning from Abroad: The Role of Policy Transfer in Contemporary Policy-Making," in *Governance: An International Journal of Policy and Administration*, vol. 13, no. 1, January (pp. 5–24).

Ghesquiere, Henri (1998). "Impact of European Union Association Agreements on Mediterranean Countries," in IMF Working Paper (WP/98/116).

Halligan, John (1995). "The Diffusion of Civil Service Reform," in Bekke, H., Perry, J., and Toonen, T. (eds.), *Civil Service Systems in Comparative Perspective*, Indiana University Press, Bloomington and Indianapolis, IN, pp. 288–317.

Joffé, G. (1999). "The Euro-Mediterranean Partnership Initiative: Problems and Prospects," in *The Journal of North African Studies*, pp. 247–266.

Keohane, R.O. and Hoffmann, S. (1991). "Institutional Change in Europe in the 1980s," in Keohane R.O. and Hoffmann, S. (eds.), *The New European Community: Decision-Making and Institutional Change*, Westview, Boulder, CO, pp. 1–40.

Lerner, Daniel (1964). *The Passing of Traditional Society: Modernizing the Middle East*, The Free Press, New York.

Muller, Pierre (1997). "L'Européisation des Politiques Publiques," in *Politiques et Management Public*, vol. 15, no. 1, March, pp. 3–11.

Radaelli, Claudio (2000a). "Policy Transfer in the European Union: Institutional Isomorphism as a Source of Legitimacy?" in *Governance: An International Journal of Policy and Administration*, vol. 13, no. 1, January, pp. 25–43.

Radaelli, Claudio (2000b). "Whither Europeanization? Concept Stretching and Substantive Change" in European Integration Online Papers (EIOP) vol. 4, no. 8; *http://eiop.org.at/eiop*.

Sbragia, A. (1993). "Asymmetrical Integration in the European Community: The Single European Act and Institutional Development," in Smith, D. and Ray, J.L., *The 1992 Project and the Future of Integration in Europe*, M.E. Sharpe, New York, pp. 92–109.

Verheijen, T. and Connaughton, B. (eds), Higher Education Programmes in Public Administration: Ready for the Challenge of Europeanisation?, Centre for European Studies, Limerick.

Chapter 10

UNCHS (1996). Best Practices Initiative. A/CONF.165/8, Istanbul, Turkey.

Chapter 11

Badshah, Akhtar (1997). One-Day Workshop to Initiate Capacities and Needs Matching Exercise Among Mayors. 31 July, United Nations, New York.

CityNet, UNDP & UNCHS (1998). *Guidelines for Transferring Effective Practices: A Practical Manual for South-South Cooperation*, Thailand, *http://www.blpnet.org/learning/transfers/transfer.pdf.*

UNCHS and CityNet (1997). Partnership for Local Action: a Sourcebook on Participatory Approaches to Shelter and Human Settlements Improvement for Local Government Officials, Bangkok, Mitnara Printing.

UNDP/TCDC (1995). Monograph on the Inter-regional Exchange and Transfer of Effective Practices on Urban Management, New York.

You, Nicholas (1998). Learning from Best Practices, Conclusions of the Seminar on Learning from Best Practices, 4 October, Best Practices and Local Leadership Programme, Dubai.

Chapter 12

(2000). *Improving Local Governance: A Scrapbook of Awards Programs,* Ford Foundation, New York.

(2001). *Kaban Galing.* Gawad Galing Pook Case Studies, Instrumedia Marketing Corporation, Quezon City.

(2003). *National Orientation-Launching of the Bayanihan Savings Replication Project,* Terminal Report, Bureau of Local Government Development.

(2004). Memorandum on the Status of BSRP, Bureau of Local Government Development.

(2004). *Replication of Best Practices in Local Governance,* Accomplishment Report.

Brillantes, Jr., Alex B. (2003). *Innovation in Local Governance in the Philippines.* Innovations and Excellence. Center for Local and Regional Governance, Quezon City.

CityNet, UNDP & UNCHS (1998). Guidelines for Transferring Effective Practices: A Practical Manual for South–South Cooperation, Thailand, *http://www.blpnet.org/learning/transfers/transfer.pdf.*

Galing Pook Foundation (2000). Gawad Galing Pook Awards Management Guidelines.

Galing Pook Foundation (2002). Gawad Galing Pook Awards Ceremony Program.

Galing Pook Foundation (2004). *Chairperson's Report,* Accomplishment Report presented during annual membership meeting.

Galing Pook Foundation (2004). Gawad Galing Pook Awards Ceremony Program.

KAAKBAY (2004). *Learning from Peers for Good Governance,* Philippines–Canada Local Government Support Program (LGSP), Manila, *www.lgsp.org.ph/pdf/Replication.pdf.*

Laux, A. and Kolinska, R. (2004). *Mother Centers International Network for Empowerment (MINE),* Case Study presented in World Urban Forum, Barcelona, September 2004.

Navarro, Rico. "Government Launches Savings Project; P1 Billion Funds Seen," in *National News Bulletin, Manila Bulletin,* March 1, 2003.

Organisation for Co-operation and Development (2001). *Best Practices in Local Development,* Paris, OECD Publishing, *http://europa.eu.int/comm/regional_policy/innovation/innovating/pacts/pdf/leed_en.pdf.*

About the Contributors

Ladipo Adamolekun is currently a Professor of Management at the Federal University of Technology, Akure, Nigeria. From 1987 to 2004, he was a Management Specialist at the World Bank and worked on public sector governance and management issues. Prior to joining the World Bank, he was a university teacher in Nigeria for eighteen years, the last eight as a Professor of Public Administration. He served as Head, Department of Public Administration and Dean, Faculty of Administration. Professor Adamolekun holds a B.A. (French), and M.Phil. (Public Administration) degrees from universities in Nigeria and a D.Phil. (Politics) from the University of Oxford, England. He is the author or co-author of over twenty books and monographs and numerous articles and contributions to books on politics and public administration in Africa.

Adriana Alberti is Chief Technical Adviser of the Programme for Innovation in Public Administration in the Mediterranean Region (North Africa, Middle East and Western Balkans) at the United Nations Division for Public Administration and Development Management, Department of Economic and Social Affairs. She received a Ph.D. in Social and Political Sciences from the European University Institute in Florence, Italy and has worked for over fifteen years on governance issues including at the United Nations, University of Bologna and Princeton University. She was also Professor of Comparative Politics and European Union at Syracuse University and Dickinson College. She recently took part in the Executive Education Programme on "Innovations in Governance" held at the Kennedy School of Government at Harvard University. She has published a number of articles and her books include the United Nations World Public Sector Report on Globalization and the State, as well as "Citizens, Businesses and Governments: Dialogue and Partnerships for Development and Democracy."

Guido Bertucci is Director of the Division for Public Administration and Development Management, Department of Economic and Social Affairs, United

Nations. He has served the United Nations in a number of capacities for over twenty-five years, including in the areas of governance and public administration, human resources, financial management and administration. In March 2005, he received an Honorary Doctoral Degree in Public Administration from the Universidad Inca Garcilazo de la Vega, Lima, Peru. He graduated with a degree in Political Science from the Catholic University of Milan, Italy and holds a post-graduate degree in Administrative Sciences from the same university. From 1971 to 1974, he was Associate Professor of Comparative Constitutionalism at the Catholic University of Milan. From 1992 to 1993, he was an Associate Professor of Public Administration at New York University, Robert F. Wagner School of Public Service.

Juan Carlos Cortázar is Specialist in Modernization of State in the State and Civil Society Programs Division at the Inter American Development Bank (IADB). He has professional experience in public management, social programmes design, training programmes for public servants, and human resource management in addition to experience as public sector senior official and consultant in social policy issues and in tax administration. He has also served as an international consultant on public sector reform. He is a reader in sociology and public management at the *Pontificia Univesidad Católica del Perú*. He received a Master in Management and Public Policies from *Universidad de Chile* and holds a Ph.D. in Management-Public Sector from the London School of Economics and Political Science in London (UK).

Carlos Conde Martínez is Associate Professor of Political Science at the University of Granada, Spain. He has previously taught at Complutense University and Almería University, both in Spain. His teaching activities have focused on public administration and public policy issues, including a large number of national and international training activities for civil servants. He had visiting positions at the Minda de Gunzburg Center for European Studies at Harvard University (1995–96), the Centre d'Etude de la Vie Politique Française in Paris (1997) and the Institut d'Etudes Politiques de Bordeaux in France (2005–2006). He has published several works on the territorial distribution of power in Europe and the Europeanization of national public administration systems. Since 1997 he has been an active member of the Steering Committee of the European Public Administration Network (EPAN).

Marta Ferreira Santos Farah is professor at the Graduate Programme on Public Administration and Government at Fundação Getulio Vargas, in São Paulo, Brazil, which she has directed for five years. She is since 2004 the Academic Associated Dean for the Undergraduate Programmes at FGV (Escola de Administração de Empresas de São Paulo), which includes a programme in Business Administration and a programme on Public Administration. Since

1996, she is the co-director of the Public Management and Citizenship Programme in Brazil—an award programme on Brazilian Innovations in Government. She received a Ph.D. in Sociology from the University of São Paulo and her areas of interest are innovation in public policies and public administration; social policies, local government and gender.

Joseph Galimberti is Executive Director of the Institute of Public Administration of Canada (IPAC). As chief executive officer, he is responsible for the general management of IPAC's affairs and the quality of its products and services. These include regional programs conducted in its seventeen chapters; research, publications, awards, conferences, workshops and colloquia as well as its extensive international activities. He conceived the IPAC Award for Innovative Management, inaugurated in 1990, which attracts an average of 100 submissions per year. He also instituted IPAC's international development programs involving more than twenty countries covering areas such as centre of government, public sector reform, decentralization and climate control. He received a MA in Economics from the University of Toronto and is the author of more than a dozen articles and papers in public policy and management.

Tonatiuh Guillén López is researcher at *El Colegio de la Frontera Norte* (Tijuana, Mexico), where he has been Director of the Department of Public Administration Studies and Director of the academic journal *Frontera Norte*. His research focuses on regional policy, modernization of local governments, federalism and decentralization. He is member of the National System of Investigators and President of the Network of Researchers in Mexican Local Governments (IGLOM) and Executive Coordinator of the Government and Local Management Award (2005). He holds a Ph.D. in Social Sciences with Specialty in Sociology and has been author and coordinator of 12 books and more than 40 chapters in books and articles in academic journals.

Vincent Kitio, a Best Practices Officer within the Best Practices & Local Leadership Programme of UN-HABITAT, is architect and holds a Ph.D. on Appropriate Energy Technologies for Developing Countries, from the University "La Sapienza" of Rome. He is the focal point for the United Nations Human Settlements Programme, of the Dubai International Award for Best Practices to Improve the Living Environment.

Donald Klingner is a Professor in the Graduate School of Public Affairs (GSPA), University of Colorado. He is co-author of Public Personnel Management (5th edition 2003), also published in Spanish and Chinese as well as an international consultant on public management capacity building. He is a Fulbright Senior Scholar in Central America (1994); and ASPA International Coordinator and past chair, Section on Personnel and Labor Relations and

Section on International and Comparative Administration. He co-edits *Comparative Technology Transfer and Society*, published by The Johns Hopkins University Press. Prior to joining GSPA, he was a faculty member at IUPUI (1974–1980) and Florida International University (1980–2001). He worked for the US government's central personnel agency (1968–1973) before earning a Ph.D. in Public Administration from the University of Southern California (1974). Web site: *http://web.uccs.edu/klingner/index.html.*

Austere Panadero is the Managing Trustee of the Galing Pook Foundation based in the Philippines. He conceptualizes and promotes the Foundation's programs and projects; establishes partnerships and networks with local and international institutions involved in promoting best practices in governance; and acts as national screener of nominations for Galing Pook Awards on Excellence and Innovations. He is also Assistant Secretary for Administration and Human Resources Development of the Department of Interior and Local Government and holds the position of Coordinator of Official Development Assistance. Furthermore, he is Senior Action Officer for the Localization of the Millennium Development Goals; DILG Programme Manager, Decentralization and Local Governance Programme of the GOP-UNDP and is Officer-in-Charge of the Office of Project Development Services. He is member of various national and international committees working on governance related issues, including Vice-Chairperson of the Literacy Coordination Council; Vice-Chairperson of the Philippine National Aids Council; and Member of the Presidential Committee on Educational reform.

Imraan Patel is responsible for research and knowledge management at the Centre for Public Service Innovation (CPSI) in South Africa. Employed by the CPSI since April 2002, he had managed a series of research projects aimed at identifying innovation possibilities for the South African public service. He led a major project that focuses on replicating service delivery innovations through knowledge products and learning. Knowledge products included case studies as well as sectoral reviews called "Innovation Insights." His theoretical understanding of innovation is complemented by involvement in applying innovation in the public service including the improvement of one-stop centres in South Africa and facilitating service delivery improvement through e-government. He is also involved in a number of training and capacity building initiatives focusing on innovation management and trends in public service innovation (see *www.cpsi.co.za*).

Lakhbir Sing Chahl is the Secretary General of CityNet (the Regional Network for Local Authorities for the Management of Human Settlement for Asia and the Pacific) since 1990. He has served as Municipal Secretary of the

Municipal Council of Penang Island, Malaysia as well as appointed official in various capacities in the Local Government sector in the State of Penang, Malaysia. He has also served as an expert and member of a number of UN Committees and other multi-national organizations. As a commentator he has experience with a wide variety of local government themes, heritage conservation, local government laws, subsidiary legislation and public administration. He is a Barrister at Law, London, United Kingdom and an Advocate and Solicitor of the High Court in Malaysia.

Nicholas You is Special Advisor for Strategic Planning of UN-HABITAT. An architect and economist by training, he joined UN-Habitat in 1982 where he helped establish municipal training and leadership development programmes worldwide, with a particular focus on public-private partnerships, financial management and environmental planning and management. In 1994 he joined the Secretariat for the Habitat II Conference which resulted in the Habitat Agenda—the global plan of action for sustainable human settlement development. As a follow-up to the Conference, he established the Best Practices and Local Leadership Programme, a global network of advocacy and capacity-building institutions dedicated to the transfer of lessons learned from best practices in improving the living environment. He is the author of 4 books and numerous articles on urban management and sustainable development and from 2000 to 2004 a visiting professor at the University Federico II in Naples.

كيفيـة الحصـول على منشـورات الأمـم المتحـدة

يمكـن الحصول على منشـورات الأمم المتحـدة من المكتبات ودور التوزيع في جميع أنحـاء العالـم . استعلـم عنها من المكتبة
التي تتعامـل معها أو اكتـب إلى : الأمـم المتحـدة ، قسـم البيع في نيويـورك أو في جنيـف .

如何购取联合国出版物

联合国出版物在全世界各地的书店和经售处均有发售。请向书店询问或写信到纽约或日内瓦的
联合国销售组。

HOW TO OBTAIN UNITED NATIONS PUBLICATIONS

United Nations publications may be obtained from bookstores and distributors throughout the
world. Consult your bookstore or write to: United Nations, Sales Section, New York or Geneva.

COMMENT SE PROCURER LES PUBLICATIONS DES NATIONS UNIES

Les publications des Nations Unies sont en vente dans les librairies et les agences dépositaires
du monde entier. Informez-vous auprès de votre libraire ou adressez-vous à : Nations Unies,
Section des ventes, New York ou Genève.

КАК ПОЛУЧИТЬ ИЗДАНИЯ ОРГАНИЗАЦИИ ОБЪЕДИНЕННЫХ НАЦИЙ

Издания Организации Объединенных Наций можно купить в книжных магазинах
и агентствах во всех районах мира. Наводите справки об изданиях в вашем книжном
магазине или пишите по адресу: Организация Объединенных Наций, Секция по
продаже изданий, Нью-Йорк или Женева.

COMO CONSEGUIR PUBLICACIONES DE LAS NACIONES UNIDAS

Las publicaciones de las Naciones Unidas están en venta en librerías y casas distribuidoras en
todas partes del mundo. Consulte a su librero o diríjase a: Naciones Unidas, Sección de Ventas,
Nueva York o Ginebra.

Litho in United Nations, New York
05-63961—June 2006—2,320
ISBN 92-1-123158-2

United Nations publications
Sales No. E.06.ll.H.1
ST/ESA/PAD/SER.E/72